Garden
Paths

Gordon Hayward

GARDEN PATHS

Inspiring Designs and Practical Projects

Gordon Hayward

CAMDEN HOUSE PUBLISHING

A division of Telemedia Communications (USA) Inc.

FRONTISPIECE. **In the East Landscape Garden of Daison-In Daitokuji, a Buddhist temple complex north of Kyoto.** *The scale of these rocks, with their symbolic snowy, mountainous peaks, suggests a scale much larger than actually exists. This is a bridge for the imagination.*

Library of Congress Cataloging-in-Publication Data

Hayward, Gordon.
    Garden paths: inspiring designs and practical projects/Gordon Hayward. — 1st ed.
        p.   cm.
    Includes bibliographical references and index.
    ISBN 0-944475-40-X (h/c): $29.95. — ISBN 0-944475-39-6 (pbk.): $19.95
    1. Garden walks — Design and construction. I. Title.
TH4970.H37 1993
717 — dc20   92-42932
                                                        CIP

Cover and Interior Design by: Jill Shaffer
Illustrations by: Elayne Sears

Cover Photographs by (starting at top left and moving clockwise):
David Schilling; Cynthia Woodyard; David Schilling; Cynthia Woodyard;
Saxon Holt; Richard Brown.

Camden House Publishing
Ferry Road
Charlotte, Vermont 05445
First Edition

Trade distribution by
Firefly Books Ltd.
250 Sparks Avenue
Willowdale, Ontario
Canada M2H 2S4

Printed and bound in Canada by
D.W. Friesen & Sons
Altona, Manitoba

To John Barstow

Acknowledgments

THANK YOU Helen Pratt and John Barstow for all your encouragement and sound advice throughout this three-year project. Thanks too to the people at Camden House who have been wonderful to work with, and special thanks to Howard White for his faith in my idea and to Julie Stillman, my editor. Thank you Tom Cooper for your interest over the years in my writing and in this project. Thanks to Elayne Sears, for her remarkable skill and good will; to Patrick Chassé, who helped in more ways than I can list, and to all the photographers who were so patient: Richard Brown, Saxon Holt, Sandra Ivany, Peter Jones, Jerry and Joanne Pavia, Jane Reed, David Schilling, Michael Selig, Erika Shank, Alan Ward, Martin Webster and Cynthia Woodyard.

Thank you for sharing your time and your thoughts about design: Ryan Gainey, Willem Wirtz and Cy Roossine, Jeff Blakely, John and Craig Eberhardt, Ron Lutsko, Joe Eck and Wayne Winterrowd, Grace Hall and Mrs. Thomas Church, Harland Hand and Jonathan Plant, the late James Rose, Dan Kiley, David Engel, James Wheat, Steve Martino, Linda Grotzinger and Peter Curé, Bill Shank, Robert Dash, Margy Kerr Richenburg, Thomas and Martina Reinhardt, Maryssa LaRose, Madame Mary Mallet, Constance Kargere and Princess Greta Sturdza, Christopher Lloyd, Rosemary Verey and Penelope Hobhouse. And thank you to Ethne Clarke who helped me better understand Hidcote.

Thank you to my wife Mary, Peter Knapp, Monica Schultz and Deborah Krasner for your help with research. And many thanks to Gary Koller of the Arnold Arboretum for help with plant identification. And thanks to the many owners of the gardens represented in this book, with special thanks to Nick and Joan Thorndike, William and Ginger Epstein, Tim and Raewyn McMains, Cyndy and Gerry Prozzo, Barry and Elsa Waxman, Mrs. Alfred Stepan and Fred Watson, Mr. Larry Hyer, Margo and John Ratliff, Mr. and Mrs. Robert Ligon and to Dick and Alice Thall for reading the early drafts.

Thank you Hans and Quita Vitzthum, Neilson Brown, Marilyn Schwartz, Dory Small and Alice Christie for your hospitality.

Finally, thank you to Mary and Nathaniel for your endless patience and good will. Without your love this book would not have been possible. ❧

CONTENTS

INTRODUCTION

THE IDEA FOR THIS BOOK grew out of my work as a garden designer. Time and again I found myself turning to paths for help in starting a design. They organize space, break design problems down into related parts, and help my clients understand a design process that results in a garden they can use and enjoy. After countless designs for clients, after years of developing our own gardens here in southern Vermont, I still approach the garden design problem the same way. First, I establish where the major elements of the garden—terraces or patios, a grape arbor, perennial beds, the vegetable garden, large trees—will go in relation to the house or existing outbuildings. Then I turn to paths as a way of linking the house to existing as well as planned elements of the garden. Finally, I turn to plants to help me define the nature of each area. It is this process, this sequence, and particularly the role of the path within it, that I want to share in the hope that it will enable you to more confidently design your own landscape, for it is an approach to garden design I know works for me and for others.

The goal of this book, then, is to give you the confidence and the knowledge to begin designing your own garden. While it cannot provide you with all the plant information you need, it will give you a place to start your own plant choices within a framework. Confidence will build on confidence, and you'll be surprised how successful you really can be at designing your own garden once you let the path lead you.

Of course, I did not invent this idea of the path's importance in good garden design. When I spoke to garden designers working throughout America and England, and when I turned to the writings of great garden designers from the past century, I found support for my notion that the path is central to the early stages of garden design. In 1962, Russell Page, the late and eminent English garden designer, wrote in *The Education of a Gardener*,

> Paths are all-important. Before I begin to elaborate my composition, I like to establish . . . the lines of communication between house and garden . . . . Paths indicate the structure of a garden plan, and the stronger and simpler the lines they follow the better. They help define the organic shape of your garden; an indecisive arrangement of paths will make an amorphous and weak garden, a basic error which even the most skillful planting will never be able to put right.

Lanning Roper, a distinguished landscape designer who moved from America to England to live and work, wrote in 1957, "No matter what the size of your garden or what the design, there are inevitably paths or terraces,

> *It was when I figured out the itinerary of my garden that it finally began to gel, to feel like a garden.*
>
> MICHAEL POLLAN
> *Second Nature*

and often both. The design of the whole garden will depend to a large extent on these features."

And Fletcher Steele, an influential American garden designer, places paths at the very heart of the landscape. In 1924 he wrote, "Beds and decoration are but to enhance the path. . . . Paths play an important part in giving character to the garden."

THE ROLE OF THE PATH IN DESIGN

It is one thing to be assured by great garden designers past and present that paths make a big difference, but quite another to be given guidelines on how to use paths in your own property to make a good garden. The way you lay out the paths through your garden will determine how you and your visitors experience it. As you pass from one garden space to the next along the path, the meaning and feeling of each, through contrast, becomes clearer. When I asked Rosemary Verey, an English gardener and writer, for her understanding of the role of paths in garden design, she underscored this idea:

> Their layout and material will determine the garden style. Paths, allées and walks also dictate the way you wish people to move around your garden. They are the skeleton of the garden. They frame beds into manageable sizes and divide the garden into different areas, leading you on from one section to the next, through gates, under archways, round corners and along vistas.

Often the word "path" conjures an image like that of W. Eugene Smith's 1946 photograph, "The Walk to Paradise Garden," the last in the photographic essay, *The Family of Man*. The photo shows the backs of his two very young children, hand in hand, walking from a shaded woodland path into a sunny idyllic garden. Or we imagine a nineteenth-century Helen Ellingham painting depicting an English woman sweeping a simple way between two borders to the front door of her rustic thatched cottage. These certainly are paths, but in this book, I expand the definition to include any combination of footpaths, walkways, footbridges, boardwalks or stepping-stone paths, whether curving, straight or meandering, narrow or wide. Pathways may be made of cut stone, fieldstone, lawn, brick, concrete, wood, gravel, trodden earth or the naturally occurring woodland floor. Steps, too, are paths in that they also focus our movement, inviting us to enter new garden spaces.

Redefined, the garden path not only leads you from one area of the garden to the next, but also provides you with a sequential design process. The concept of the path can help you divide spaces into specific forms and shapes, dividing the design problem in such a way that you can think of parts of your design, and then use the path, and later, plants, to create a whole garden. Here is an example.

In a sense, the entire design for the 1½-acre garden my wife Mary and I are developing around our 200-year-old farmhouse in southern Vermont started from one gently curving 20-foot-long lawn path. We had created a spring garden under wild plums, and across an amorphous patch of lawn, a rectangular herb garden answering the rectangular shapes of an old wooden garden shed. But the two did not relate in any way. Out of the amorphous lawn, we cut a curving 5-foot-wide path, extending the herb garden toward the spring garden in the process. Instantly the two garden areas were drawn into a relationship with one another. The path simultaneously established logical edges for the herb garden and spring gardens. And as we followed the line of the path around the other side of the herb garden, it helped us draw the nearby rock garden into a relationship with the herb garden too. And so it went. The effect of making that first path eventually rippled the length and width of our property, and continues to do so, nine years later. Without realizing it at the time, we were following a precept of Russell Page's: all the lines in a garden—whether initially established by streams, driveways, the edges of beds, the driplines of overhead trees, or, in our case, a single path—should relate to one another. The application of that idea when gathered around paths that lead articulately throughout a garden results in a coherent design that has what Capability Brown, an influential garden designer in 18th-century England, called an itinerary.

But Harland Hand, an artist who gardens in Berkeley, California, pointed out to me that the concept of the path goes even deeper than design:

> For a garden to be more than color or form or variety—for it to inspire and move you—it must contain three elements that fulfill ancient, primitive human needs: shelter, trails and lookouts, not garden rooms, paths and views. These words are removed from the natural world. They do not speak directly to the feelings you might have when, having hiked all day along a high, exposed ridge trail, you come, as dusk falls, upon a ravine where a knot of trees offers shelter for the night. When you find such a place you feel good and warm and safe. Trails produce mixed emotions, a sense of expectation and a sense of direction. A lookout brings a sense of power and exhilaration. This is how primitive people saw nature and how modern people experience nature and even gardens, whether they know it or not.

Throughout the history of civilization, paths have been important in determining the shapes and spaces of gardens. The nature of path, and thus garden design, also reflects the cultural and religious attitudes of the society in question. For instance, the earliest Egyptian frescoes show formal, geometric walled gardens with straight paths, the lines of which were imposed, in part, by the irrigation channels and the protective walls. Early Persian gardens, similarly walled against an unforgiving, largely featureless landscape, also had straight paths which, far better than natural curves and meanderings, bespoke humanity's control over nature.

The notion of straight paths through symmetrical gardens, perhaps brought back from the Middle East and northern Africa to Europe during the crusades, inspired generations of garden designers who especially, in France, lined up their paths and thus their gardens. For centuries, paths were straight. The usual medieval European garden was a walled square with four paths leading to a central fountain symbolizing the waters of life. The Renaissance gardens of Italy and Holland and the great European gardens of the eighteenth century all had straight paths.

There was one ancient exception to this rule: in China, where the attempt to recreate the natural world in the garden has been the guiding principle for at least 2,500 years, the early designers, surrounded by a verdant and varied landscape and influenced by Taoist nature worship, created paths that meandered through gardens, along streams, around ponds and up hillsides. Around 600 A.D., this style of gardening reached Japan by way of Korea.

It did not reach Europe—and even then in a very different form—until the eighteenth century in England, where the landscape school replaced straight paths with ones that meandered through parklands or pleasure grounds. Design since then has been shifting between the formal and informal, the architectural and natural.

So, path design, and thus garden design, clearly reflects cultural characteristics. As Charles Moore writes in *The Poetics of Gardens,*

> The paths of Islam are straight and narrow, leading directly into the heart of paradise. Those of Versailles are equally single-minded but climax in the bed chamber of the Sun King. The goose-foot patterns of seventeenth- and eighteenth-century French hunting parks tell of the headlong flight of the stag, while English parks may be patterned on the winding tracks of the devious fox. Rococo gardens cut paths into the curlicued rhythms of courtly frivolity, and Japanese gardens have, for centuries, deployed precarious stepping-stones with such artful irregularity that the placement of each geta-constrained foot must become a conscious, exquisitely shaped act.

The garden path also has psychological overtones; the meandering walk to the Japanese tea house is subtly designed to help visitors slough off the cares of the day so that they arrive mentally prepared for the tea ceremony. This emotional aspect can also be highly personal. Shortly after the premature death of his wife, Henry Hoare, the designer of the famous Stourhead Garden in Wiltshire, England, created a path that was meant as a therapeutic journey. The path travels around a lake, and the buildings, statuary, views and plantings along it were arranged symbolically to suggest the return of Aeneas from Troy. The path was intended to gradually confront Hoare with the darkness in a grotto that symbolized his tragedy, only to have that darkness relieved at the sunlit conclusion of the walk in the Temple of Apollo.

While the psychological effect upon visitors to Stourhead depends on what they see along the gravel path, in other gardens the paving materials themselves, and the way they are laid out, can create various feelings. A pine needle path through a Maine coastal woodland garden is calming, while the broad, straight and long gravel path that leads from the formal garden to the Doric temple at Blickling Hall (once owned by Anne Boleyn's father) in England implies all the feelings associated with power and grandeur. At the same time, materials can add movement, a new level of interest, beauty and even craftsmanship to your garden. Surface materials and patterns, especially in the hands of Japanese or Chinese garden designers, can be artful yet remain functional.

Carefully conceived and properly laid out, paths are practical too; they provide year-round access throughout the garden for you and your maintenance equipment. Furthermore, paths reduce maintenance in a garden by helping control surface drainage, weeds, lawn, mud, heat and dust.

The path, then, is far more than a means of getting from here to there on dry, solid ground. It is a way to organize your thinking about garden design; it is a way to organize space and clarify the meaning of your whole garden; it is a means, by which you can, in the words of Harland Hand, "choreograph your visitors' movements," and thus their feelings.

The well-designed path is irresistible. It invites, even pulls people into the garden. Put a curve in a path that disappears around a corner and visitors will yearn to know what is around that corner. Then let that path lead to other thoughtfully designed paths throughout your property and your garden will become coherent while simultaneously offering intrigue, surprise, movement, variety and ever-changing perspectives.

A path determines the sequence by which you move up, down or through a garden, and the many vantage points from which you see it. To look at a garden in terms of its paths, then, is to look at the garden as a whole, for it is the path that links all parts and thus helps create a sense of place.

IN PART I OF THE BOOK, I look closely at four model gardens that exemplify how paths can create unity and a sense of expectation. The models include a small urban garden, both small and large suburban gardens and an estate garden.

In Part II, I look at fine gardens throughout the world in terms of their paths. It is organized from the most formal gardening style, often near the house, to increasingly informal gardens further away. For example, I begin with a chapter on cut stone, the most formal material, frequently used right near the house. I end with a chapter on informal paths of gravel, pine needles and trodden earth. These are often associated with woodland, fields or the edges of a meadow.

In Part III, I describe how you can create paths of these materials so that they will last a long time and do their job well. Included is a plant list to give you ideas for what Harland Hand calls "crevice gardening"; that is, plants that are appropriate for gaps between paving stones or steps.

Finally, in the appendices, I provide sources for: garden structures and gates; benches and furniture; garden ornaments, statuary and planters; lighting; fine tools; associations and manufacturers. There is also a list of indigenous paving materials available across the country and finally a list of public gardens worldwide that use paths in interesting ways. ❧

PART I

Model Gardens

Chapter One

PATHS TO FOLLOW:
Four Inspirations for Garden Design

THE PATH IS WHERE MANY DESIGNERS begin to look for answers to such common questions as: How can I connect our house to our garden? How will I move from one garden space to the next, and how will those spaces differ so I can introduce variety, suspense and excitement into my garden? How can I link existing elements of my garden with ones I want to add? What materials should I use for our paths, and how will they help create the feeling I want in each garden space? Where should I add which plants?

By first looking closely at the use of paths in four models—three in the United States; (a 1988 urban design, a 1989 and a 1928 suburban garden) and one in England, (a single path through an extensive 1907 garden)—you can learn how to use trees, shrubs, perennials and annuals, paving materials, gates, benches, potted plants and any number of elements that go into the making of a garden. Though diverse in style, content and tradition, each example has a great deal to teach about design principles and methods. The total will give you a useful introduction to garden design, no matter where you garden or on what scale.

AN URBAN GARDEN

Urban lots lack space. They are typically narrow, flat rectangles without privacy from above, and are shaded by tall buildings or a neighbor's trees. What space is available is typically featureless, boring and even uninviting. On the other hand, such spaces are small enough to be unthreatening and manageable; their scale may be much like that of a living room. The challenge for the designer is to make the small space come alive: to give it intrigue, movement, a feeling of greater size and vitality; to draw people outdoors into a space that feels like a world apart from the harshness of the city. (And the way paths help accomplish these goals in an urban lot can also be used in the creation of satisfying, small enclosed gardens in any larger suburban or rural landscape.)

Paths helped landscape designer Maryssa LaRose overcome the limitations of an 18-by-32-foot site in Manhattan, where wooden decking and a footbridge set at different levels and unexpected angles simultaneously organize and animate the space so that it looks larger than it really is (Figure 1.1). In creating the decking, LaRose also provided dry footing, and created surfaces for chairs, tables, potted plants and garden ornaments or sculptures. She then used the sight and sound of a small waterfall, koi fish in a pool and naturalized plantings to create a low-maintenance garden that is lively and refreshing year-round.

> *No single element in the design of a garden is as important as where you put your paths.*
>
> HUGH JOHNSON
> *The Principles of Gardening*

FACING PAGE: **An Atlanta, Georgia garden.**

The entire design started from three requirements: first, a firm surface when one steps out of the house; second, a sitting area near the house; and third, a graceful transition from the house into the garden. When you walk out of the back door, you step onto a 7-foot redwood deck that runs across the 18-foot width of the garden and connects at both ends with an 8-foot-high redwood fence that provides screening around the perimeter of the garden. LaRose notes that the deck is wide enough to be functional for small parties, yet narrow enough to read as a path. In front of you is a small pool roughly

LaRose Garden

in the center of the space. From an extension of the deck to your left, to the fence on your right, a wooden bridge suspended on a concealed steel beam runs at a most unexpected angle over the pool. LaRose told me, she used diagonal lines and oblique angles for the paths in this garden:

> They add movement and animation, whereas lines that are parallel or perpendicular to the perimeter would be static and formal. And as you see in the pictures, when I change the purpose of the wood, I change the direction of the planks, thus adding further animation, creating a feeling of greater space, and at the same time moving people in the right direction.

> Because the bridge and back deck are set at oblique angles, there are several asymmetrically shaped spaces between them and the fence for garden ornaments set within the plants. Had the plank decking and bridge been aligned with the fence, the adjacent planting spaces would have been predictable and static.

The Suitability of Wood

While any number of other materials could have been used instead of wooden decking—cobble, brick, concrete pavers or a mix of any number of these materials—and the bridge could have been made of large flat stones, redwood provided a long-lasting, readily available, easily workable material for all three architectural elements: fence, decking and bridge. No other material could have offered such unity and simplicity for a setting that includes trees, shrubs, perennials, annuals and vines as well as stones and a pool. It's

FIGURE 1.1: LaRose Garden. *As small as the garden is, it offers an itinerary. Water, fish, a variety of greens punctuated by the dark red impatiens make this garden planted with restraint feel a world apart.*

FIGURE 1.2: LaRose Garden. *Suspending the bridge above the water with hidden steel I beams enabled LaRose to construct this bridge out of finely proportioned materials set in carefully considered ways. The footbridge, then, is not only a means of access but also a beautiful element of the garden.*

a little like using the same color paints for several rooms in your home; use too many colors and your home can look busy and unsettled.

The broad wooden decking in the back also solved a problem that no other material could have solved so easily. Early excavation for the pool turned up granite bedrock. Jackhammering was the only solution, but what to do with the rock? LaRose turned a potentially expensive removal problem into a subtle design solution; she used the rubble to create a second grade level at the back of the garden. Decking was then built over the debris to hide it. By using the excess rock in this way, she created a second level at the back of the garden that made the space feel larger, created a new vantage point from which to look down on the rest of the garden, and, as LaRose told me, "we caught a little more sun for my clients."

Animating a Small Space

Near the end of the bridge (Figure 1.2), by a waterfall, you can step off to your left onto the first of three stone steps that will take you up to a rectangular deck also set at an oblique angle relative to the fence. This deck is, in many ways, the destination of all the paths in the garden. From here, you can return to the house down a second set of stone steps from the left-hand side of the upper deck to the extension of the lower one. These two sets of steps not only provide access and mark the transition between grade levels and garden spaces but also introduce a second path material, stone. They add variety to the garden, reinforce the natural feel of it and provide a visual link to the three low stone retaining walls that run across the garden between the pool and the back deck. Steps also provide a good context for ground covers—LaRose used ivy—as well as for garden ornaments that also help mark the transition from one garden space to another. Furthermore, she pointed out that the base of steps can be seen as an entrance to a new garden space, and can be planted to emphasize that role. By dividing the space, LaRose made the area feel bigger. It's like the room in a house that when furnished feels much larger than when empty.

While this particular design required the costly skills of a jackhammer operator, a pool contractor and a fine carpenter, simpler design solutions could have meant an easier and less costly installation: a Japanese stroll garden with many more plants and hidden spaces, a formal garden with a central path that links three smaller rooms created by brick walls or hedges through which gates pass; a woodland garden with an earth path that meanders through dense wild plantings to a rustic bench. Part II of this book will offer countless sources of inspiration for designing such a small space.

Plants

To reinforce the division between the pool and the upper deck, to further mark the grade change and to increase the sense of space in such a small area, LaRose planted a Japanese maple (*Acer palmatum*) near a flowering, glossy-leaved abelia (*Abelia grandiflora*). These are underplanted with Christmas ferns (*Polystichum acrostichoides*), impatiens and sweet woodruff (*Asperula odorata*) among others. When you are on the upper back deck, two trees—in the back left corner, a star magnolia (*Magnolia stellata*); in the right corner, a pink flowering dogwood (*Cornus florida Rubra*)—provide shade and a degree of privacy from the neighbor's upper-story windows. Around the perimeter of the upper deck, and acting as underplantings for the two trees, are several evergreen and deciduous shrubs as well as herbaceous plants all set out in a naturalized way that softens the edges of the decking. Foliage from low evergreen shrubs such as the hemlock *Tsuga canadensis* 'Gardeners,' the lily-of-the-valley bush (*Pieris japonica*), and *Leucothoe fontanesiana* provides year-round interest, whereas the herbaceous plants, including hostas, astilbes and day lilies provide seasonal foliage, texture and color.

To take advantage of the vertical space, LaRose cloaked the outer fence with *Wisteria floribunda* 'Texas Purple' and English ivy (*Hedera helix*) and then repeated the use of ivy around the two sets of stone steps.

The two decks on two different levels with the bridge linking them offer not only a variety of ways to move around the space, but also create logical places for potted plants, tables, chairs, a bench or even a broad canvas umbrella on the back deck to provide further privacy and intimacy. Because the decking provides so much space for sitting near as well as at a distance from the lower level of the dwelling, the garden has become two outdoor rooms and thus a natural extension of the house.

A SMALL SUBURBAN GARDEN

The space around a suburban house is typically more generous than that available to the city-dweller, but it, too, is generally flat. The house is normally in the middle of the site, which consists of four areas: the semi-public front lawn that extends out to the sidewalk; two narrow spaces on either side of the house where you rarely walk; and a back "yard," as we call it, where you do most of your gardening, lawn mowing and outdoor living. There is no privacy in the front or side yards, and often little in the back.

There are many similar garden design problems in the city and the suburbs: how to gain privacy, reduce traffic noise and create a garden that is personal, satisfying and a world apart. But there are also problems specific to the suburbs: how to create an entry garden that invites guests to the correct front

FIGURE 1.3: **Plant Garden.** *Gardens completely surround this California home of an avid gardener. Skillful planting along with paths of brick, slate and fieldstone knit the parts together to help create a coherent whole.*

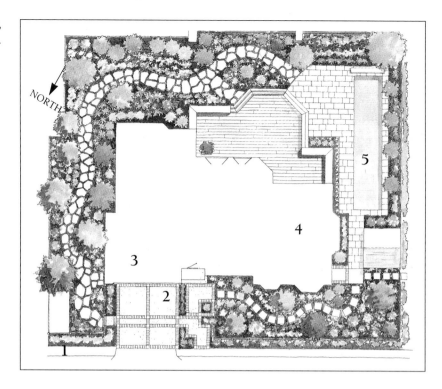

Plant Garden: (1) street, (2) driveway, (3) garage, (4) house, (5) pool.

door; how to make an interesting, private, intimate garden between the front of the house and the street; how to design the frequently narrow space between your home and the neighbors' on either side so that you and your guests feel drawn into the spaces; how to create different moods in garden spaces so close to one another, and how to make graceful transitions between them; how to link the front, side and back gardens to the house and to one another so as to create a coherent sense of place.

In 1989, California landscape architect Jonathan Plant created a small suburban garden for a client, an enthusiastic gardener living in the Palo Alto area near Stanford University (Figure 1.3). The house with garage sits in the center of a 90-by-100-foot corner suburban lot with only 16 feet of garden space at the front and back, and 20 feet on either side. At the front, Plant designed and installed a cottage garden with brick steps, and along one side, a woodland stroll garden with stepping-stones. At the back is a continuation of the woodland garden that comes up to a raised redwood deck. A slate patio wraps around the other side of the house to form coping and a path around a lap pool. The design provides everything the client wanted within this very limited space: no lawn anywhere, privacy, space to entertain and a variety of richly planted gardens all tied together with walkways.

In this case, the paths do not determine the shapes of adjacent beds; the proportions and directions of the paths are largely determined by the house and the available space. Here, paths provide access and invite people to explore the plants and the gardens. In turn, the materials reinforce the mood and suggest the pace of movement through the individual garden spaces.

Path and Plant Coherence

Having parked your car in the driveway, you step out onto concrete paving embedded with panels of brick that inspired the brick "step pads" that run through the cottage garden at the front of the house. The first of these is behind a pair of pink Canadian redbuds (*Cercis canadensis* 'Rubye Atkinson'). Plant told me he did not want to break up the already small area by running a continuous brick path through the narrow space. Because there are separate pads, the drifts of *Campanula muralis* on either side can flow across the path and between the pads. Furthermore, the gaps provide more plantable space in this 16-by-55-foot area for such perennials as *Diascia fetcamiensis*, *Coreopsis verticillata* 'Moonbeam,' *Aquilegia* hybrids, *Verbena bonariensis* and *Aster frikartii*. To help lend a logic to the curves in the path, Plant situated a flowering dogwood *Cornus florida* 'Cloud Nine' by the first curve and an offset pair of evergreen pears (*Pyrus kawakamii*) on either side of the next one. Then the path arrives at a gate at the beginning of a slate walk that leads along the lap pool to the back patio.

Plant told me that he chose slate as a paving material around the pool and entertaining area because it picks up some of the colors of the house, helps tone down and blend the dark pool into the garden setting and also adds a greater degree of formality than would be offered by river rocks or brick. He also widened the coping between the pool and fence to enable people to walk all around the pool, for pleasure and maintenance. Between the fence and the coping, Plant put in four Blue potato bushes (*Solanum rantonnetii* 'Grandiflorum'); along the base of the fence he set out the low shrub *Hebe* 'Patty's Purple' behind open soil for annuals that would provide seasonal color. To cover the fence, he planted Boston ivy (*Parthenocissus tricuspidata*). Plants of

FIGURE **1.4: Plant Garden.** *The stepping-stone path can be integrated into the garden by planting ground-hugging perennials between the gaps and along the edges of the walkway.*

great interest and variety are everywhere in this small, yet remarkable garden.

Once you pass the pool, you arrive at a slate patio that leads up to a redwood deck or onto a washed river stone path. The path that takes you through the woodland garden then runs across the back of the house, along the other side and back to the driveway. A Japanese maple (*Acer japonicum* 'Vitifolium') marks the transition from slate to river rock and, in conjunction with the edge of the deck, forms a kind of entrance to this area. Because the woodland area is slightly larger than the other parts of the garden, Plant was able to use larger, more massive stepping-stones so that in strolling you could concentrate on looking at the garden rather than at your feet. Also, the use of the river rocks allowed the garden to creep in among the individual steps, thus fusing path to garden (Figure 1.4).

As you walk through this shady area, you pass under the massive canopy of two huge oak trees; the redwood deck surrounds one of the trunks. You also walk under a Japanese Snowbell tree (*Styrax japonica*), a Japanese Stewartia tree (*Stewartia pseudocamellia*), *Cornus florida rubra*, *Pyrus kawakamii* and finally, three redwood trees (*Sequoia sempervirens* 'Santa Cruz') before passing through a gate and onto the driveway again. The entire length of the path is set into a ground cover of rupturewort (*Herniaria glabra*) that gives way, further into the adjacent gardens, to broad sweeps of *Lamium* 'White Nancy' and *Ajuga reptans*. The shoulders of the garden are provided by such shade-tolerant shrubs as *Viburnum davidii*, *Rhododendron* 'Fragrantissimum', *Pittosporum tobira*, *Azalea* 'Gumpo White' and *Ribes sanguineum* 'Spring Showers.' Perennial color comes from such shade-tolerant plants as *Astilbe* 'Deutschland,' *Trillium grandiflorum*, *Brunnera macrophylla* and *Digitalis purpurea*. The plant list for this garden numbers 92, excluding trees.

The key, of course, to this whole concept as a model for your own garden is that you have to be willing to "secede from the national lawn," in Michael Pollan's words. Once you make that step, and play with the shapes, materials and plants that could go into a rich and varied set of gardens such as this, there will be no end to the pleasure and privacy your own place will offer.

A LARGE SUBURBAN GARDEN

The larger suburban lot offers more scope for the designer than the city garden does, and thus a different set of questions arises. How do you create a garden measured in acres rather than square feet that holds together and takes advantage of the whole property, yet does not present overwhelming maintenance problems? How can you give form, shape and coherence to so much space? How can you define the differences between and similarities among the garden areas so their individual meanings are clear? How do you solve the problems of slopes and access through so much land? The Epstein garden offers many answers to these questions.

The bones of this elegant garden were laid out in 1932, shortly after the original owners completed construction of a white-painted brick house. The property, under a canopy of mature open oak woodland, has about 200 feet of frontage on the street and extends about 350 feet up a steady south-facing slope. The home is about 150 feet up the slope near the east side.

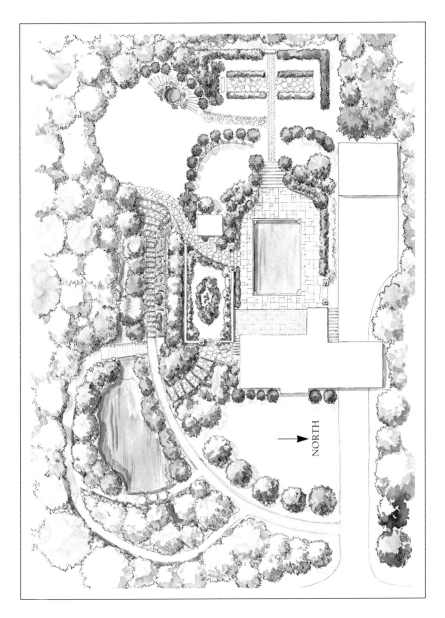

NORTH

In 1968, the present owners, Mr. and Mrs. William Epstein, purchased the property, named the gardens Bride's Bower and set about rescuing the gardens from ivy and other symptoms of neglect that had taken hold since the original owners had passed away. In 1983, the Epsteins sought help from Atlanta landscape designer Ryan Gainey. The work he did in their walled secret garden, named the Pegasus Garden because of the Wheeler Williams sculpture at its center, was his first as a professional designer.

Linking Garden Spaces

The landscape is divided into five major areas linked by paths: one, the swimming pool garden; two, the sunken and walled Pegasus garden just below it; three, the herb garden; four, the nearby fountain garden; and five, the stroll garden around the pond, including a broad azalea border at the bottom of the lawn that sweeps down from the house. The gardens and paths closest to the house are the most formal; the further you get from the house, the less formal the gardens and their paths become, until you are in natural

woodland at the outer perimeters of the property. This same pattern of decreasing formality helped determine plant choice: Boxwood hedges and clipped hydrangeas are planted around the pool, and the Pegasus garden is a carefully pruned azalea garden with fine perennial borders, yet beyond these two areas, tall rhododendrons and naturally occurring vegetation predominate.

The bones of the overall garden are its paths, steps, walkways and adjacent retaining walls. These feel natural and right because the designers clearly took their cues from the lay of the land and the need for level areas within a sloping property, which is greatest near the house. Such level ground makes the house feel stable and settled, and extends the livable space of the house into the garden. Steps and paths can emanate from these level spaces adjacent to the house to give structure and accessibility to your whole property.

Starting from the House

You step out of a sitting room on the north side of the Epstein's house onto a brick patio. The choice of material was clearly suggested by the painted brick house, yet the unpainted patio signals a different use for the same material. In a way, one could say that the entire garden path system emanates from this brick patio, for when you stand on it, you have two main choices, either of which will send you on your way into the whole garden.

Here is the first choice, which will lead you to three other choices. In front of you, and one step up, is a 5-foot-wide bluestone walkway that takes you around a rectangular swimming pool and also acts as no-maintenance edging for adjacent shrub and perennial beds (Figure 1.5). Because the band of flat, blue-gray stone is narrow enough to read as a path, you don't feel overwhelmed by the amount of bluestone around the relatively small pool.

If you step up onto this bluestone walkway, you find that you can follow any of three paths. Along the east side is a 6-foot-high boxwood hedge that screens the driveway and garage from the pool area. Access from the pool to the garage is through a wrought iron gate set between brick pillars about 3 feet apart. On the west side of the pool is another pair of brick pillars, with a 3-foot-wide bluestone step between them that signals the entrance to a new but subordinate garden space (Figure 1.6). On the other side of the brick pillars, the paving material changes to a carpet of fieldstone laid in concrete that leads past the garden house on the same level, to the topmost of a 30-step stone staircase that takes you down through azaleas and rhododendrons to a gravel path along one side of a pond (Figure 1.7). At the north end of the pool is the third and dominant path. It leads up a flight of 8-to-10-foot-wide fieldstone steps set into a 3-to-4-foot-high retaining wall of similar dark gray stone. That set of 11 steps leads across a lawn either into an enclosed herb garden with 2-foot-wide brick paths or to the left along a 2-foot-wide gravel path to a secluded sitting area from which you could look out over the garden from rustic Adirondack chairs.

FIGURE 1.6: Epstein Garden. *The path from the pool to the garden house: gateways can become transition points between changing moods in the garden.*

FIGURE 1.7: **Epstein Garden.** *An important juncture of several paths. Each has its own mood, but the element that holds all together is the simplicity of the planting—pachysandra, oakleaf hydrangea, windmill palm (Trachlea sperma) and liriope.*

FIGURE 1.8: **Epstein Garden.** *The entrance through the brick wall provides a setting for two lead pineapples whose color and material link them with the sculpture of Pegasus. Inside the gravel path/edging is a garden of azaleas edged with liriope.*

Here is the second choice from the brick patio off the sitting room. You could turn left and, under the shade of hemlocks and oaks, walk down a set of bluestone steps to fieldstone stepping-stones where you would have to make a choice. Turn right and you walk between a pair of low pillars of the same material as the stepping-stones into the walled Pegasus Garden (Figure 1.8). If you do that, you can walk around the garden on a narrow, scallop-edged gravel pathway. You could also turn left and walk down stepping-stone steps with a rhododendron handrail (Figure 1.9) that would deliver you to the same 5-foot-wide gravel walkway to which the stone staircase leads. The pond would be directly in front of you; turn right and the gravel path would lead you to the bottom steps of the stone staircase; turn left and you would follow the gravel path between the edge of the pond and an azalea garden to the driveway and street. Partway along that gravel path, you could turn right and take a narrow subordinate stepping-stone path across the dam of the pond and around its side on an unobtrusive oak-leaf-covered path. It leads across a wooden bridge back to the beginning of the gravel walk and the bottom step of the stone staircase.

Paving Materials for Mood and Coherence

The proportions, direction and material of each of these paths were clearly suggested by their purpose and the degree of formality or informality implied by their surroundings. The bluestone around the pool, for example, is a generous width, is flat, smooth and a comfortable texture for bare feet, and its formality so close to the house is appropriate. There is a graceful transition from bluestone to fieldstone walls and steps because the same stone is used for the retaining walls at the north end of the pool and for the steps up to the herb garden. Once you are in the smaller space of the herb garden, you are on carefully laid brick paths. Intimacy is suggested by the use of the warmer and more finely designed surface and you are reminded of the patio near the sitting room.

Here's another example. The path along the east side of the pond and out to the driveway is visually strong, a 5-foot-wide, strictly-edged ribbon of honey-colored gravel that serves many purposes. First, because it is broadly curved and partly obscured by the azaleas, and is so wide and so lightly colored in a shady garden, it is irresistible. You feel swept up by it and are thus drawn along to three secondary paths. Second, it is such a strong band of color through this woodland garden that it gives form and shape to the entire area through which it passes; in a way, the whole lower garden and pond relate visually to this firm central statement. Third, the gravel introduces sound when you walk on it. And finally, the broad gravel path encourages a faster pace to get you from the driveway into the garden. Once within it, you slow down to step onto one of three connecting subordinate paths: stepping-stones across the dam; narrow fieldstone steps up to the Pegasus Garden; across a narrow bridge and onto an oak-leaf-covered, trodden earth path into woodland, around the pond and over the dam back to the gravel path.

Where such a variety of path materials and widths might have broken coherence in a smaller garden, the variety in this larger garden helps define the different moods and shapes of the various areas while linking them. Further coherence grows from the fact that the choices of paving materials are, in many cases, suggested by the material of adjacent features: the brick house and pillars, the fieldstone retaining walls, the oak leaves on the woodland floor. Where paving materials were not suggested by existing features—the bluestone pool coping and the broad gravel path—the materials were chosen for their color, purpose, texture and mood.

The paths and steps, then, in concert with adjacent retaining walls, play many roles in this garden: They provide the structure, the bones of the garden; they link separate areas; they make the entire two acres comfortably accessible, and their materials and proportions underscore the mood of the individual garden areas. The various destinations—the sitting area above the fountain garden, the pond, the swimming pool, the bench in the herb garden—add further logic to the placement and direction of the paths. And because there is no external feature—no extraordinary view, for instance—the garden is an inward-looking one, a peaceful, self-contained haven of great variety, coherence and elegance.

AN ESTATE GARDEN

While you probably don't have a 10-acre garden, or even want one, the brilliance of the gardens and the paths through the Hidcote Manor Garden near Chipping Campden in Gloucestershire, England, can nevertheless help you answer many garden design questions. Where do I start? What clues do the existing features offer to help me proceed? How do I relate the house to the landscape? How do I make transitions from one garden space to another? How can I integrate existing or planned architectural elements, such as outbuildings, gates, steps, hedges or gazebos? How can I create drama in my garden? Where do I

FIGURE 1.9: Epstein Garden. *While the white-painted bridge and its unpainted surface add a note of formality to the woodland, the rhododendron handrail and stepping-stones through a field of English ivy (Hedera helix) are informal.*

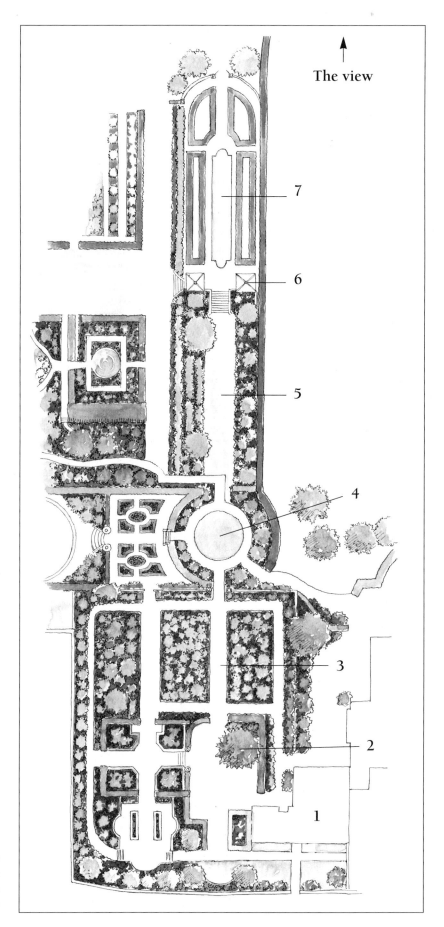

The view

7

6

5

4

3

2

1

Hidcote Manor: (1) Manor House,
(2) Cedar of Lebanon, (3) Old Garden,
(4) Circle garden, (5) Red Borders,
(6) gazebos, and (7) Stilt Garden.

FIGURE 1.10: Hidcote. *A large or even small garden can have a main axis, such as this one at Hidcote Manor that leads in a straight line from a back patio or terrace to even the furthest reaches of the property. Here, the lawn path sets off such plants as the pink-blooming beauty bush* (Kolkwitzia amabilis), *the large grass* Calamagrostis acutifolia *and the purple-pink* Rosa rubrifolia *near the grand cedar of Lebanon* (Cedrus lebani).

put potted plants? And on another level altogether, how can I apply what I see at estate gardens to my own considerably more modest situation?

The fact that this once private garden (now under the care of seven National Trust gardeners) is so large need not overwhelm. Admittedly, I was overwhelmed the first time I visited it, but because my wife was born and raised in the village across the fields, we have visited her family and the garden many times over the years and have come to feel comfortable in it and have learned many lessons from it.

Lawrence Johnston, the designer, began his work in 1907, shortly after his American-born mother, Gertrude Winthrop, purchased the village of Hidcote Bartrim, a 300-acre property that still includes the manor house, seven cottages and adjacent farmland. When Mrs. Winthrop bought the property, there was no garden, only rose beds, a few stone and brick walls, a field and a mature cedar of Lebanon by the house. It was that tree and a distant vantage point some 300 feet away that suggested the structure of the garden.

In the autumn of 1907, Johnston began to lay out the garden in a way that reflected his knowledge of the then influential garden designer Thomas H. Mawson, who argued that a garden could be like a house. It could have a central corridor—the main garden path—and rooms reached by perpendicular subordinate paths. Furthermore, the closer the garden areas were to the house, the more formal they should be; the further away, the more natural.

Johnston began designing his garden from the house, a crucial first step. He wanted to be able to walk from the sitting room down stone steps and onto a lawn under the only existing feature of the garden, the old cedar of

FIGURE 1.11: **Hidcote.** *The Old Garden is reminiscent of a cottage garden, with salvias, hardy geraniums, dianthus, iris, roses and flowering shrubs all bundled together in beds on either side of a straight lawn path.*

Lebanon. Standing under that tree in 1907, he could look west and see the distant Malvern Hills in Warwickshire, clearly the best view from the flat plateau. That view would become the destination for the primary path, the main axis, the main corridor of his garden. Perhaps your own garden has such a view that would lend logic to such an important axial path. (Unfortunately, today the lawn under the cedar of Lebanon is closed to the public, so the entire length of this important axial path and its relationship to the house is not wholly apparent to the visitor.)

Once Johnston had conceived of the roughly 300-foot-long main path on that east-west axis, he could develop ideas for subordinate paths, perpendicular to the main axis. These secondary paths would lead into and through hedged garden rooms, into increasingly informal gardens and eventually to woodland and wild gardens, particularly to the south. The placement and boundaries for the secondary and possibly tertiary garden rooms along this main axis were in all likelihood suggested by existing brick or stone walls.

The germ of this design, then, came from a large tree, nearby derelict walls, the best view, and the idea that the structure of a garden should relate to the structure of the house, which can be seen as the center, the heart, the focus of the garden. Another way to look at it is the way Lawrence Halprin, a California landscape architect, did in a design notebook he kept in 1966. In his notebook, which had nothing specifically to do with Hidcote, but everything to do with what he called a "form for a path problem," he drew a simplified human spine with ribs and wrote near it, "This could be a way to ORDER the paths—all cross the main artery path."

FIGURE 1.12: **Hidcote.** *This is the point of transition from the Old Garden to the Circle. A circular brick walk garden passes through the entrance to which is marked by grand wrought iron gates and a potted pelargonium.*

Designing from the Back Door

The main path at Hidcote starts in the first garden room at the back of the house under the cedar of Lebanon. The floor is lawn, the wainscoting is low yew hedging, the ceiling the cedar boughs. From that room, the path leads through four distinctly different garden spaces, each with a mood and structure that contrasts with adjacent ones (Figure 1.10). The first, third and fifth are architectural, with trees, shrubs and green foliage predominant. The sec-

ond and fourth are dominated by pairs of mixed shrub and perennial borders on either side of rectangular lawn paths. The borders in the second, the Old Garden, are reminiscent of a gentle cottage garden with soft blues and pinks. The borders in the fourth, the Red Borders, are scarlets and purples that demand one's attention.

Linking Garden Spaces

There are several ways that Johnston made transitions between these areas, transitions that make the differences between the gardens more apparent. When you stroll from the first garden area to the next, you walk in shade down stone steps and onto a narrow lawn path that takes you out from under the boughs of the huge evergreen into full sun between the richly planted borders of the Old Garden (Figure 1.11). You will remain in full sun until the end of the fifth garden space. To mark the entrance into the third garden, which like the first is predominantly green, Johnston set a pair of intricate wrought iron gates in a gap in the brick walls (Figure 1.12). Between the base of these gates, he installed a panel of cut stone, probably to mark the transition between the two garden spaces and also to provide a suitable site for large terra-cotta pots of geraniums, whose bright reds contrast with the

FIGURE 1.13: Hidcote. *The entrance to the Red Borders is marked by two sections of purple beech hedge (Fagus sylvatica 'Purpurea'). This hedge forms the theme of dark red repeated in the nearby beds by such red-foliage plants as the purple-leaved filbert (Corylus avellana 'Purpurea') and potted cordylines. For contrast, there is the dark green of mugho pines and the lighter green of the grass at the edge of the left bed,* Miscanthus sinensis gracillimus.

FIGURE 1.14: **Hidcote.** *The view from the Red Borders toward the manor house shows how a single color can become a theme for a garden. Reds are intensified by the green of the lawn path and the hedges, grasses and pines within the beds. The color red comes from the flowers of canna lilies, dahlias, Lychnis chalcedonica, Lobelia cardinalis, fuschias and roses, the berries of plants such as baneberry (Actaea rubra), the foliage of such plants as Acer platanoides 'Crimson King,' the pissard plum (Prunus cerasifera 'Atropurpurea'), red-leaved barberry (Berberis thunbergii 'Atropurpurea'), and purple-leaved sage and sedums.*

black ironwork, while the pots' color complements the similar brick walls and path. To further mark the transition into this third garden space, Johnston changed the path surface from lawn to brick, and the path shape from rectangular to circular. In all likelihood, he shifted to brick because it was the material of the nearby walls. The circular path within this third garden gave Johnston several opportunities. First, it enabled him to link the broad main path to two smaller paths that led into adjacent gardens: one gravel path curves north through a tall hedge into the Great Theater lawn; the other, straight and also of brick, leads south into a series of three gardens, all of which employ the circle as a theme. Second, it enabled him to create a bit of drama. By following the circular brick path, you momentarily lose sight of the dramatic main axis and follow a planting of Rouen lilacs (*Syringa chinensis*) backed by a tall, curved hedge. Once you arrive at the other side of the circle, the length of the main path is again revealed. It's another moment of surprise and drama reminiscent of the feeling of stepping out of the house and looking down the length of the main corridor.

The brick path then leads through a break in a hedge into the fourth gar-

FIGURE 1.15: **Hidcote.** *The change of level at the top of the steps provides a new vantage point for viewing the Red Borders.*

den, the Red Borders (Figure 1.13). To help make the transition, Johnston planted purple-leaved beeches within a yew hedge to echo the dominant color of the borders in the adjacent hedge. The Red Borders is clearly the most intense in its demands on the stroller on this main path, so the soft green lawn path in the center is the perfect choice, given that the green heightens the red but also soothes the eye (Figure 1.14). A patterned stone or brick path next to such complex planting would have confused the image.

The transition to the fifth garden is marked by strong architectural elements: broad steps whose treads are stone, the risers brick. On either side at the top of the steps are gazebos made of the same brick and Cotswold stone as the house and nearby walls (Figure 1.15). By introducing architecture similar to that of the house well out in the garden, Johnston visually linked garden to house. The two gazebos also frame the view into the sixth garden area, the Stilt Garden.

You step off the top step between the gazebos, walk across a panel of cut stone between the two and onto a gravel path made from the same Cotswold stone as the slates on the gazebo roofs. The gravel path splits to surround a central panel of lawn between two rectangular hornbeam hedges (Figure 1.16). You follow that path in under the raised hedges or walk on the lawn between the hedges to arrive at a wrought iron gateway in a brick wall.

There by the gate, you find yourself under the shade of mature Holm oaks looking out at vast English oaks and beeches in the fields. These trees echo the great cedar of Lebanon where you started the journey. But there is a difference. You are now on a rough gravel path looking out over sheep grazing in a pasture punctuated by these trees, beyond which you can see the distant Malvern Hills in Worcestershire and the checkerboard of farms, fields, and villages between you and the distant hills. The highly refined garden is linked to the surrounding area by the views through the gateway as well as by the gravel path that led you to the edge of the fields.

But turn around just outside that final wrought iron gate and look back along the main path. You will see that only four materials were used to create the paths: lawn, brick, stone and gravel—not too many elements, but enough for variety and to set one garden area off from the next. You will also see where the designer chose to set potted plants, if the places used today reflect his sensibilities: at the sides of steps, at the base of pillars holding gates, on cut stone panels in passageways which double as the transition material between lawn and brick.

WHAT IS THE DESTINATION of this path? Is it the gateway with its view into the Malverns? Is it the gazebo with its shelter from a shower, or the views it frames of the Long Walk? Is it the paths that lead off from it to any number of other garden spaces? I suspect that Johnston's destination was different every time he walked his path. ✍

FIGURE 1.16: Hidcote. *The final leg of the journey down the main axis at Hidcote. The lawn path between raised clipped hornbeams (Carpinus betulus) hedges of the Stilt Garden, in combination with the grand Holm oaks (Quercus ilex), frame a view of the distant countryside.*

PART II

Paths to Your New Garden: A Way to Unified Design

Introduction

THIS SECTION OF MY BOOK is designed to inspire and inform your think-ing about garden paths and their role in the garden. A path can be the spine of your garden, as illustrated by the main path at the Hid-cote Manor Garden in the previous chapter. Once the main path is established, subsequent problems will be easier to solve. The path will give you the confidence to design your own landscape because it will help to break the design problem into related parts. Paths, as already shown, can help de-fine spaces and create many areas that can be treated in different ways.

Well-designed paths will then suggest places for trees, shrubs, perenni-als and annuals. That teak bench you bought and plunked under the apple tree could go at the end of a long, straight path, or in the widening of a nar-row pine needle path through the woods. Where two paths meet, you could plant the yellowwood tree you've wanted for years, thus providing a logical explanation for why the path splits just there. If two perennial beds are near one another, but they do not relate to one another, you could take up just enough of the lawn at the inside edges of both so that the lawn left between them would become a 5-foot-wide path that wanders or follows straight through what will now look like one big bed. Where the lawn was removed, there is space for the new perennials you have wanted.

Paths will also help you break through many of the old limiting ideas that have held you back from making a garden that really works. For exam-ple, you don't have to stick with the time-worn notion of semi-public lawn on either side of the slightly curved path from front door out to the sidewalk, with a collection of yews, rhododendrons and junipers tight against the house foundation. Take up some or all of the lawn, transplant those shrubs out to the edge of the sidewalk, and then add more shrubs, trees or even a fence to create a screen from the sidewalk. Run a broad, logically curved path from the front door to a gate at the sidewalk. Partway along that path, create a sec-ondary path that leads to a private sitting area surrounded by gardens. That path to the sitting area can also branch off and become a tertiary path that leads through a narrow garden at the side of the house to the back patio, where the possibilities multiply further.

SITE ANALYSIS

Before reading Part II and planning any gardens and the paths through them, though, you need to be clear about your present situation. Take sev-eral sheets of paper and a pencil, sit down at your front or back door—

> *A path leads to the mystery beyond.*
>
> DAN KILEY
> a Vermont landscape architect
> since 1935
>
>

whether you are in a tiny urban backyard garden or in the Rocky Mountains—and ask yourself the single most important question: What impact the style of your home has on the design of your gardens, for most often it is your home that establishes the dominant mood of your property. If it is a formal Georgian home, symmetry and formality might be called for in an overall garden design, especially near the house. If it is a simple rural home or summer retreat, perhaps the cottage garden might be the dominant theme. If it is in the desert of the Southwest, perhaps the theme can come from plants, materials and colors indigenous to the Sonoran desert landscape.

Once you have thought about your home, imagine your garden, whatever its size, in three zones: the one nearest the house; the middle ground; the distant ground. What do you see in each of those zones? Is there a graceful transition from one zone to the next? Is there any transition at all? Look at light and shadow and views, good or bad, and see how those elements help define the differences between and similarities within the large areas of the garden. Look at plants for further clues about the specific qualities inherent in each area. Notice how the land changes where rock outcroppings are, or where and how water flows. Look at any neighboring buildings and any plants you can see that break up the visual impact of the walls. Look at the structure and lines of trees and shrubs. Is there an imbalance of deciduous or evergreen plants? Or no evergreens at all?

Also, during this site analysis, make note of how you have used the property and which, if any, of those uses are outdated. Are your kids out of college, so the space reserved for volleyball is no longer necessary? Did you always say you would make compost in the bin you constructed years ago but never did? Should you refurbish the compost bin and begin using it with resolve, or abandon the idea and open up the space for something else? Are there any trees and shrubs that really don't satisfy and should be cut down or transplanted? Would screening anywhere mask sights or soften unpleasant sounds?

Then get away from the house and look back at it. Notice its shape and how it relates to any outbuildings. Look long and hard at the plantings around it and decide what you like and don't like. Could any plants along the foundation, or anywhere else on your property, for that matter, be transplanted elsewhere to better effect? Talk to your spouse, children, friends, anyone with whom you can be comfortable and honest. Ask for their thoughts about what they see, or how they would change things.

Make notes about colors. Do you like the color of the house, outbuildings, the foliage of trees and shrubs? Do the plants look good against the house? Could the plantings be simplified, or changed utterly to improve color combinations? If you have solid evergreens, would transplanting some and replacing them with lighter, flowering deciduous plants help?

And listen. Listen to the sounds. Pay attention and decide which you like and don't like. Pay attention to fragrances or odors, too. Look, listen, smell and then finally notice what textures there are in your garden—foliage, stones, the barks of trees. Keep orderly notes on all these observations.

Once you have all this in mind, move about your entire property, even those areas you never go into, like the woods or meadows or back corners.

BEADS ON A STRING

I N OLD COLONIAL HOUSES we frequently find that a straight path leads from the street to the front door, where one can see through the middle of the house and out to the garden door. Further beyond began the central garden path, which continued out to the end of the place. Thus, in many good colonial examples, balanced front-yard, house plan and garden plan were all strung like beads on one straight string, which is called the axis. This is a simple and agreeable scheme on which to build the small garden to-day. . .

The principle of the axis depends, in analysis, on the natural and human desire that there be a beginning and an end of a work of art—which a garden must be. It promises also that somehow we can get from where we are to what we see in the distance. An open path is the simple fulfillment of that promise. . . .

The principle for axial arrangement holds on cross views and paths in a minor way. They should have a beginning and an end. Where cross paths meet lengthwise paths, one is inclined to elaborate the intersections by enlargement into little squares or circles, or by marking with conspicuous plants at the four corners.

— FLETCHER STEELE, *Design in the Little Garden*

Be aware of microclimates, temperature changes and the movement of air, for all will give you clues about how your mood changes from space to space. Be sensitive to how you feel in different spaces, and try to form a sense of where entrances to those spaces occur and how you might emphasize them.

Walk established paths slowly and note how the picture changes as you move. Walk familiar routes across the lawn that are *de facto* paths but have never been acknowledged as such. Are there any existing paths, or parts of them, that do not need to be there? Are people taking shortcuts on areas where paths should have been installed? Question the site, shape and surface material of every path. Where might you create a break in a wall or hedge to make a gateway? If you have existing steps, could they be used as a starting point for new paths? Think about how you show guests your property when they arrive. Might you have an existing itinerary through your garden but have just never thought of it that way?

If you can make these observations two or three times, at least once alone and again with one or two people, you can come to a good understanding of your property. Again, all of these suggestions are relevant no matter what the size of your property. It is at this point, after careful site analysis, that the concept and the reality of the path can really begin to make a difference in how you see your land.

ESSENTIAL PATHS

Once you have a clear understanding of your property, look carefully at the existing paths in the light of what you have learned from the site analysis, especially as it relates to the architecture of your home. Whenever you

PATH MATERIALS–A Glossary for Part II

AGGREGATE

Small loose stones, typically rounded, such as ⅜-inch peastone, that can be used loose or embedded in concrete to form a path surface.

COBBLESTONE

Cut granite cubes, typically 10 inches long, four wide and four deep, once used for city street paving.

CUT STONE

Any relatively soft limestone, sandstone or bluestone that is flat on one or both sides and has been sawn into rectangles or squares.

FIELDSTONE

Naturally occurring flat stone that has been collected from fields or dry-laid walls and is flat on at least one side. Typically, it has an aged look and random shape.

FLAGSTONE

A generic term that includes stones, random or geometrically shaped, usually 3-to-5-inches thick, that are laid on the ground to ease walking. A fieldstone, for example, could be considered a flagstone.

HARD LOOSE MATERIALS

These include naturally occurring gravel, decomposed or crushed granite, crushed stone and crushed seashells that come in many colors. No pieces are bigger than ½ inch across. Larger crushed stone is appropriate for the base of walkways, whereas these more refined hard loose materials are appropriate for top-dressing walkways and paths.

QUARRIED STONE

This is dynamited from quarries, split, sorted and sold as randomly shaped paving material with at least one flat side. It can have a new look and a size ranging from 2-to-6- or more square feet.

RIVER STONES

Smoothed and rounded over time by being tumbled against other rocks and by water eroding their rough edges; they come in many different sizes, typically ranging from ⅜-inch peastone up to 8-to-10-inch diameter rocks.

SLATE

Although it is a form of quarried stone, slate is not mentioned as a paving material in this book because its surface sloughs off over time, and it is so slick, and so very slippery when wet that it is, in the words of Willem Wirtz, "the best paving material of all for bringing lawsuits down on yourself."

SOFT LOOSE MATERIALS

Needles from coniferous trees, bark mulches from lumber mills, fallen leaves, or soil; that is, any organic material that can be used to cover a walkway. 🪶

---

are working on a design, start from those elements in the garden that are absolutely necessary. You need to get from the driveway to the house, for example. You need to get from the front door to the mailbox once a day. Determine which paths are essential. Start thinking about them first, and keep in mind that these utilitarian paths may strongly affect how other paths will flow. What do you like or not like about those essential paths? Should they be changed completely? What changes in direction, paving material or plantings might improve the flow or the beauty of the paths? How wide are the paths and how wide should they be in the light of their present or planned uses?

SECONDARY PATHS

Begin to consider how a path could move from the back door into your present garden. If your home is formal, it might echo the English tradition of a broad lawn path between two perennial beds that would lead directly to a particularly fine group of trees or a break in a hedge. If you have a hedge, consider how you could make an opening in it to provide access to a previously unused part of your property. Perhaps you could set a rustic gazebo or grape arbor on the rise of a hilly meadow and then mow a path from it down through the meadow to connect with an existing woodland path.

Once the character and direction of the paths are established, you then have numerous places for plants, benches, gates, hedges, and so on. These places then help you determine plant choice and location. Path design creates a structure in which to make many decisions, which should be arranged from large to small:

- where an arbor, bridge, terrace, patio or wooden garden structure such as a gazebo might be placed so as to draw people into an area;
- where paths might turn into steps to signal a change of level or to draw visitors into a new space with its own mood and structure;
- where trees might create a shady area or punctuate the curve in a path;
- where garden ornaments, potted plants or garden artifacts might be placed, again, not simply to decorate, but to draw people toward them into new garden spaces;
- where shrubs might be placed: to underplant trees; to provide screening from one section of the path to another; to mark entrances or transitions to the next area; or to provide backdrops for garden ornaments;
- what the path proportion will be—they will be different in a long narrow lot as opposed to a square lot, and will be affected by the position of the house on the lot;
- where perennials, annuals and bulbs might provide ground cover under shrubs and/or trees, cover the trunks of leggy shrubs, enliven steps or path edges, or complement garden structures or sculptures;
- where ground-hugging plants and low ground covers might soften steps or the edges of patios and terraces.

QUESTION EVERYTHING. Consider all the possibilities. Be prepared to take risks. Then, with an open mind, consider the photographs and text in this book. They should inspire you, for they are images from gardens around the world whose designers have created paths to solve practical problems in aesthetic ways.

And as you look at these photographs, notice how the garden path is linked to prepositions; how it leads under, within, through, next to, across, over, behind, up, down, and around trees, shrubs, perennials, annuals, bulbs, rocks, gravel, brick, pergolas, benches, birdbaths, garden statuary, water, rock gardens, perennial beds, garden sheds, light, shade and even different temperatures. At the center of it all is the home from which all paths lead. ఠ

Chapter Two

CUT STONE:
The Most Formal Paving Material

CUT STONE IS MOST APPROPRIATE for creating straight, or at most, broadly curving paths that lead to the front door of the house, at which point they can be extended to form broad steps or a generous landing. Cut stone can be used to create subordinate paths or patios off other doors of the house, such as a sitting room or library. From there, steps and paths of less formal materials can lead out into the garden. In *The Education of a Gardener*, Russell Page explains why such a use of cut stone is especially appropriate: "Most houses need anchoring to their setting, and for traditional houses some formal extension of the straight lines and rectangular shapes of the building is usually the most effective way to do so. The shapes and even the volumes of the interior of the house should find some echo on the larger, outside scale." A cut stone pathway leading from the front door or from a broader cut stone patio or terrace can help tie the garden to the architecture, and act almost as part of a platform on which the house appears to rest.

Christopher Lloyd, whose home is surrounded by gardens with a sequence of cut stone paths, adds: "As a fact of general practicality, I would say that paths which are used much (such as the one to the front door) should be as direct as possible and to remember that if short cuts can be taken they certainly will be, path or no path." The cut stone path to Lloyd's front door (Figure 2.1) is one such direct path, and it has "meadow either side and this is tall from May to July, overhanging a good deal especially after rain. We do not cut the meadow areas until the last week of July and through August because we want all the flowers established to have had the chance to ripen and scatter their seed. The path's width allows for this." The welcoming, informal wildflower meadow softens what could otherwise be an imposing entrance; however, as you can see in the photograph, once you are halfway to the house, the path passes through a closely mown lawn that makes the mood more formal before you enter the porch that leads to the front door. It also makes the unmown meadow appear intentional.

And here is a cue as to how this main path can be used to help you design subordinate paths, and thus new garden spaces. Just before arriving at the portico, you can turn left or right on narrower stone paths, either of which would lead you onto other stone paths and on into gardens that surround this medieval home. As such, this York stone path to the front door establishes a motif that is repeated throughout the acres of gardens.

> *The path and entrance to a house can determine how much a house feels like an inner sanctum, like an inviting shelter. A good entrance creates a feeling of a private domain, a world apart.*
>
> CHRISTOPHER ALEXANDER,
> ET AL
> *The Pattern Language*

FACING PAGE: A sitting/dining area in the Hayward's garden.

FIGURE 2.1: Christopher Lloyd's home, Great Dixter, in East Sussex, England. *Guests should pass through a series of increasingly private "zones" to arrive at the front door. Here, visitors pass first through an informal, welcoming wildflower meadow, past a formal section of yew hedge, then between panels of tightly cut lawn before going past the boxwood (Buxus sempervirens) topiaries and between potted plants that lead to the entrance portico and the front door.*

Such a broad cut stone path is particularly appropriate as the material for your main path to the front door because you don't have to think about where you will put your feet. You can walk along a cut stone path conversing with a friend while knowing your feet will land on a firm surface every time. With a stepping-stone path, your attention must stay glued to the ground, and you have to stop to notice what's around you. Gravel, also inappropriate, tracks into the house, marring rugs and floors. Brick or randomly shaped fieldstones set out to form tightly laid walks will also work (see the next two chapters), but they are better associated with less formal rural or suburban homes.

CUT STONE TO THE FRONT DOOR

The Japanese regard a cut stone path, *shin,* as the most formal of walkways and compare it to very formal evening attire. In Japan, straight cut stone

FIGURE 2.2: **The Japanese Garden in Portland, Oregon.** *Precisely crafted cut stone paths can become distinct garden features in themselves. Here, the granite walkway leads next to a magnolia on the right and clipped holly (Ilex crenata) mounds on the left, both underplanted with moss.*

paths typically lead to certain homes, temples and shrines rather than for general garden use. Sometimes the cut stone path such as the one in the Portland, Oregon Japanese Garden (Figure 2.2) can lead to side entrances to the home as well. Its formality can be reduced by informal planting on either side.

The entrance garden designed by Donnelly, Everts and Associates for a Washington, D.C. home (Figure 2.3) includes a straight bluestone walkway and steps that lead from the sidewalk directly to the front door. While the home and walkway are formal, the plant choice—flowering dogwoods, mugho pines, tulips, columbines, et cetera—and planting scheme are informal, so the path does not appear too severe. Clearly, the steps and path create a context for all the plants set out on either side. Notice how you walk along the path, up steps between and under the flowering dogwoods and then onto the upper walkway before stepping in the front door. A rich sense of arrival comes from all those prepositions—along, up, between, under, onto and in. The placement of the trees (the primary level of plants) on either side of the steps, but not opposite one another, preceded the even more informal layout of the mugho pines and other shrubs (the secondary level) that lend permanence and winter interest. The more evanescent columbines and tulips (the tertiary level) were planted last.

Notice, too, that just as you arrive on the upper landing, you are offered an alternative: a tiny suggestion of a path that invites you through the gar-

FIGURE 2.3: Florence Everts' design for a garden near Washington, D.C. *This welcoming cut stone path leads from the sidewalk between informal gardens of* Cornus florida *'Rubra',* Pinus mugho, Dicentra eximia, *columbines and tulips and past a low hedge of Japanese holly* (Ilex crenata *'Helleri') on the way to the front door.*

*Large cut stones
can provide access through, as well as
give form to, a garden space. Here coquina stones lead to a side door but at the
same time provide a structure to the space
between the trunks of two melaleuca trees.*

den on stepping-stones, across the implied path of the lawn and on around
the side of the house. The garden, then, is a place to explore, not simply a
screen to look at or a collection of plants to make the house look pretty. That
little opening on the left makes all the difference.

The soft gray color and uniform texture of bluestone is a surface on which
fallen petals look especially beautiful, so constructing such a path and then
planting flowering trees along it might be a good starting point for a design.
Ryan Gainey showed me a garden he designed in Atlanta, Georgia. He pointed
out that the pink Yoshino cherry blossoms fall on the surface of the bluestone
walkway and each makes the other more beautiful, if only for a few days. If
the path were aggregate or gravel, the effect would not be as pleasing.

CUT STONE TO A SIDE OR BACK DOOR

Cut stone is clearly the most appropriate material in highly formal settings, as I saw in the back and front gardens of a French-style home in Palm

CUT STONE FOR THE ELDERLY AND DISABLED

WILLEM WIRTZ, AN EAST COAST landscape and garden lighting
designer in his eighties, makes an important point regarding paths, paving material and the elderly: "We are developing a bigger census of elderly people worldwide, and security of footing is an important element in their lives. They don't like any kind of
insecurity underfoot because they are insecure enough in their own
fragility." Clearly, one of the best paving materials for paths for the elderly is cut stone. It has texture to provide traction, yet at the same time
is flat, and the stones can be fitted together tightly, so they don't catch
shoes. If the stones are large enough, and properly laid, they will not shift
with time and thus provide predictable, stable footing.

Beach, Florida (Figure 2.4). Four-foot-square coquina stones (cut coral reef that can no longer be removed from reefs) create broad steps that lead down to a 40-by-60-foot rectangle of immaculately maintained zoysia grass, the outer edge of which is maintained by a rectangular path of the same 4-by-4-foot white stones. In many old southern Florida gardens and homes, this coral reef coquina stone (and nowadays a convincing and more environmentally acceptable concrete copy) was used a great deal as a building material in the house and garden. This tawny buff-colored stone and its modern concrete equivalent are porous and pitted revealing brain coral patterns that enliven the surface and give rise over time to tiny ferns, algae and mosses that provide the ultimate integration between garden and paving material. The 2-inch gaps between the stones in the front lawn are filled with the zoysia to create a geometric, minimalist garden, punctuated here and there by melaleuca

FIGURE 2.5: Madame Mary Mallet's garden in Normandy, France. *Consider installing a formal or rustic pergola along any path. Every brick pillar of this pergola, designed by the late Edwin Lutyens, provides places for vines and perennials. The purple-leaved grape vine* (Vitis vinifera 'Purpurea') *grows up and over the pergola while* Hydrangea macrophylla *and* Astrantia major (on the right) *bloom in the garden in early July.*

trees and 18-foot *Ficus benjamina* hedges, whose shapes echo the shapes and proportions of the paths. The stone, then, acts both as a path and as a decorative extension of the architecture.

In this example, the paving and associated hedges define the outdoor space. The zoysia grass, while requiring a great deal of maintenance, echoes the flat surface of the stone. In the slightly less formal garden at the back of the house, terra-cotta urns with terra-cotta oranges and lemons are situated in relation to corners of the paths or near entrances to suggest the real oranges and lemons hanging from citrus trees planted nearby, thus forming a gentle link between planting, path and garden ornament. The result is a spare, French motif around a home that is highly influenced by French design and as such is reminiscent of a painting from the Middle Ages titled "Emilia's Garden," which shows paths dividing grass into similar green panels.

In Madame Mallet's garden, Bois des Moutiers, in Varengeville-sur-mer, France, the cut stone path to the front door also leads off to other parts of the garden, but in a less formal way. As you are just about to reach the front door of Mallet's classic Edwin Lutyens home, the only one he ever designed in France, you look right through an archway in a wall. There you see the cut stone path under a pergola covered with purple-leaved grape vines whose color echoes the brick (Figure 2.5). That path and the brick uprights create a context for perennials and vines, and lead the visitor onto paths of other materials and into gardens of other moods.

For this photograph and the others in this book to become useful examples for you to work with, look not only at the fact but the spirit of the work. Imagine a much simpler rustic pergola, for example, running between your garden shed and another outbuilding, or directly through the center of a broad garden area. After my wife Mary and I returned from a trip to France, during which we visited Madame Mallet in her garden, we decided to put in a pergola that followed the lines of an already-existing brick walk through a 60-by-80-foot perennial and shrub garden (see page 50). Next to our old Vermont farmhouse, the formality of the Lutyens design would look out of place, so we made the uprights and crosspieces out of black locust saplings. The whole garden now has a firmer structure than was provided simply by the brick walkway, and the pergola gave us many clues as to how to reorganize the garden. We are now training a variety of fragrant honeysuckle vines up the posts and along the crosspieces so they will hang down. At the base of each post, we've planted day lilies and miscanthus grasses—whatever strikes our fancy—and the strength of the pergola holds the design together. Because of the firm structure provided by both path and pergola, the whole garden makes a lot more sense than it did when we had neither.

FIGURE 2.7: **Part of landscape architect Dan Kiley's design for a southern Vermont garden.** *Kiley designed this Vermont marble walkway on axis with the door to give form to this apple orchard, to link it to the house and to provide easy access from the parking area to the front door.*

FIGURE 2.8: Landscape architect Peter Curé's design for a Phoenix, Arizona garden. *In warmer climates, the same cut stone can be used inside and outside the house to visually link the two.*

Ohme, vanSweden and Associates, landscape designers in the Washington, D.C. area, have created a garden in a somewhat similar way, though it is considerably less formal (Figure 2.6) and lacks the pergola of Mallet's garden. This bluestone pathway leads you along the side of a home in the Baltimore, Maryland suburbs, and in doing so creates the spine of an ornamental grass and sedum garden, a rich year-round alternative to lawn. The bluestone pathway interjects a note of formality into this otherwise wild garden, but on more practical terms, it also offers sound, dry footing from which to see the plantings or carry in the groceries.

Cut stone is an excellent material to create a strong line out from the house into nearby gardens or even an orchard, and thus to pull house and garden into one coherent image. Dan Kiley, an internationally known landscape architect in northern Vermont, did just this in his design for the Currier Farm in Danby, Vermont (Figure 2.7). He designed a cut bluestone path that leads directly from a pair of French doors, across a simple patio of the same material into and through an orchard laid out in a typical grid pattern to the parking area. He alternates 18-by-36-inch pieces of stone with a pair of 18-inch squares. This regularity tends to make the orchard seem just a bit more formal than if the path was not there, just as in the Baltimore garden described above. By using the Vermont marble steps and the light-colored cut stone, Kiley is able to extend the lines of the house out into the garden, and in doing so reinforce the straight lines of the walls and apple trees. Because

the individual stones are placed in such a way that the grass can grow on all sides of each stone, the path seems less obtrusive; from a distance, it can barely be seen. Without the path, the relationship between the orchard and the house would have remained tenuous at best.

The same would hold true of a 3-to-5-foot-wide cut stone path to a pool or patio a distance from your house; this type of path has the visual strength to link the house to other human-made elements of the garden, while at the same time providing places along the way for trees, perennial beds, shrubs or garden ornaments, or for gateways, trelliswork or archways or any number of other features.

CURVING PATHS AND PLANTED GAPS

Cut stone can also be used to create curving paths, though the shaping of the stones is best left to professionals. Peter Curé, a landscape architect in the Phoenix, Arizona area (Figure 2.8) created such a path for a client. While cutting the Arizona sandstone took considerable time and effort, the result is a set of sinuous paths that lead Curé's clients and their guests from the sitting room into the garden. The logic of the curves and their placement is established by existing and additional plantings of palms. The choice of material was clearly suggested by the existing flooring material inside the house, further blurring the line between interior and exterior living spaces in this warm climate. I should add that a curving cut stone path need not be as sinuous as Curé's; cut stone can be used to make much broader, simpler curves that will require much less cutting.

FIGURE 2.9: **A garden south of London, England.** *There are many good plants to integrate a patio or pathway into the surrounding garden. Here* Alchemilla mollis, *potted pansies and, in the gaps between the stones, artemisia, petrina and lavender are used.*

While cut stones are the most formal and the most expensive of all paving materials, their lines can be softened if the gaps between the stones are planted. Patrick Chassé, a landscape architect in Northeast Harbor, Maine, uses these planted gaps, which he calls "green joints," where he wants to tone down the look of a cut stone path that otherwise might look too tight and formal.

The garden just south of London (Figure 2.9) is a good example of how appealing planting between the gaps of cut stones can be. Where a cut stone path broadens into a patio, or where the path itself is sufficiently wide to allow plantings, perennials such as lady's mantle (*Alchemilla mollis*) and feverfew (*Chrysanthemum parthenium*), woodsy sub-shrubs like lavender or ground-hugging plants can be planted in the existing gaps.

Paths of cut stone are especially useful in gardens, for they help provide structure and a firm geometry to contrast against the forms of plants. They can make a strong statement: gray stepping-stones recede among plants whereas gray cut stones tightly laid are more obvious, although they provide footing that requires less attention.

Cut stone paths can also double as the edging for perennial or shrub borders, preventing nearby lawn from creeping into the beds. At Crathes Castle near Aberdeen, Scotland, cut stone steps lead down to a broad York stone path that edges the large beds (Figure 2.10). Plants in the border flop onto the stone path without being in the way of the lawn mower. In this way, the cut stone paths reduce maintenance and allow for a less formal clipped edge to the beds. Of course, the path in your garden need not be as wide as it is at Crathes Castle; it is all a question of proportion.

Cut stone paths can also run straight through a perennial bed (Figure 2.11). If laid in concrete as in the California garden designed by Ron Lutsko, the path will need no maintenance and the plants can flop onto it, softening the look. In turn, the beginning or end of the path can connect with other paths of similar or different material, thus linking one part of the garden to the next.

For example, you might imagine you have a cut stone patio or courtyard something like Rosemary Verey's at Barnsley House in Gloucestershire, England (Figure 2.12). The courtyard could be thickly planted around the edges, with a gap left in the plantings that leads onto a long, straight cut stone path between perennial beds. In this way, the path system links house to patio/courtyard to perennial beds and onto the far reaches of your landscape.

If properly laid, such a path of closely fitting stones is also among the most maintenance-free of all walkways. It is absolutely flat, providing sound, dry footing that is comfortable to walk on, even barefoot, and it is easily shovelled in those areas of the country where snow falls. It also makes the best surface for wheelchairs. Because it is almost flat, only subtle variations of shadow and light appear on the surface. To increase the texture, you can choose interesting patterns and swirls within the stone itself. Tightly laid, cut stone walkways are also good as routes into major areas of the garden for wheelbarrows and general maintenance equipment, including lawn mowers. When these walkways are near a house, they can act as small terraces or patios.

On the negative side, some cut stone, especially sandstone and bluestone, can become slippery in wet weather, particularly when set beneath overhanging trees where the shade might encourage the growth of mosses. Too much cut stone in a garden can also become monotonous, or too formal; to break up that formality, combine it with brick or granite setts. Gateways or

FIGURE 2.11: A California design by landscape architect Ron Lutsko. *A tightly laid cut stone path between the driveway and the front door runs between a pair of borders, providing access as well as low-maintenance edges.*

CUT STONE TO POINT THE WAY

IT IS IMPORTANT that guests know exactly which door to approach when arriving for dinner or a visit, but many homes, particularly modern ones, lack a front door that is clearly marked by the architecture. An entry garden that is welcoming and provides clear directions to the appropriate front door is one of the first places to start developing a good landscape design.

The owners of a modern house on the coast of Maine asked Patrick Chassé to help create a path and related gardens that would gracefully lead people to their front hallway. As it was, guests unfamiliar with the home would get out of their cars and walk through an opening in a split rail fence to see broad stone steps on their left leading to the only visible door. Many thought, of course, that that was the front door. In fact, it led to the kitchen and den, and several embarrassing moments for the owners. Since the actual front door, further along the concrete path, was not visible from the driveway or along three-quarters of the path that curved through the lawn, no mere architectural change would give guests the right clues.

To solve the problem, Chassé removed the split rail fence, the concrete walkway and the broad steps up to the kitchen door, which he replaced with more delicate wooden stairs and a handrail, enclosing the landing with similar railing to make it look more like a private porch. Then, between the garden and driveway, he installed a vertical board fence with a wooden, 3-foot-wide gate. This opened onto a 3-foot-wide mortared cut stone path that ran straight from the gate and along the side of the house (Figure 2.13) where it made a turn to the left to what was in fact the front door. To further focus visitors' attention on the new destination, Chassé placed a 3-foot-high antique Eric Soderholtz vase in the beds just beyond the end of the path.

To be sure visitors who had just stepped through

FIGURE 2.13: A Patrick Chassé design for a garden on the coast of Maine.
Start your garden design by developing a path and related beds that will lead visitors to the appropriate front door, as does this visually strong cut stone path. The color and material of the fence, gateway and cut stone echo that of the house, thus linking garden to architecture.

the gate would not be tempted to cross the lawn to the new and more delicate kitchen steps, he extended the planting bed on the left just far enough to discourage such a temptation. The owners could still walk across the lawn to their kitchen door, but guests would be just slightly beyond a point where they would be tempted to double back, to follow an S-shaped path over lawn to the kitchen door. As it happened, the end of the newly extended left-hand bed coincided with that point along the cut stone path where the arm of the path to the front door became visible.

Cut bluestone was one of the best materials to use for this task. It can be laid tightly and geometrically to create a strong visual indication of the location of the front door. Unlike lawn, it remains dry and firm underfoot all year long, and in Maine, where it snows, it is easy to shovel. And in the case of this home, the blue-gray color of the stone complements the similar color and formal architecture of the house, thus visually linking home to landscape. In combination with deft planting, framing provided by fence and gate, and the strong straight line of the path, Chassé was able to use cut bluestone to solve a minor but very real and socially embarrassing problem and create more satisfying gardens that had a reason for being where they were.

And other problems were simultaneously solved. The stronger fence and new gate keep deer out, provide a context and a purpose for a private garden space between the kitchen and driveway and screen parked cars from the house. The path also provides an appropriate small garden space and a specific purpose for the fine Soderholtz vase. Finally, the straight cut stone path, rather than the previously curvilinear concrete path, works in harmony with the geometry of the house. No other material could have served all these purposes so well.

entrances are especially good places to make a change from one paving material to another.

And finally, you might want to consider this dictum from Christopher Lloyd: "It is essential that paths should be wide enough for their purpose. 'A horrid bachelor's path' was how my mother used to refer to one that was wide enough for only single file passage. She liked a path to be wide enough for two people to be able to walk along comfortably arm in arm." A cut stone path is usually that kind of path.

THE FORMALITY OF CUT STONES laid one next to the other can be toned down by mixing it with other materials. In the chapters ahead you will see this material combined with brick, fieldstones or gravel in any number of ways. You'll also see cut stone suggested as a material for stepping-stones. Wherever you place cut stones in the garden, you will be introducing a crisp, geometric note of formality that will contrast gracefully with natural plantings, or complement formal gardens and architecture. ॐ

FIGURE 2.12: The courtyard leading to the conservatory at Rosemary Verey's garden in Barnsley, Gloucestershire, England. *A narrow walkway can broaden into an informal courtyard before leading into a house. Verey's informal entrance garden includes bronze fennel, roses and other perennials, shrubs, small trees, potted nasturtiums and ivy on the wall.*

Chapter Three

BRICK: Warmth and Versatility

RICK IS A VERSATILE MATERIAL. A brick path can lead to a door, through an herb garden, or off into a jungle garden such as Yves St. Laurent's in Morocco (see page 55). Brick is inviting, warm and earthen in tone and material, and thus a sympathetic material in the garden. As such, it is less formal than cut stone and being smaller in size, can be used in a wide range of paving styles.

Brick has been used for walkways and paths for at least five thousand years. The clay bricks of the Nile River Valley were handmade and sun dried. The patterns bricks make when set in the ground are nearly as old; the herringbone pattern, for example, can be traced far back into Roman times. Most paths in early Dutch gardens were made of brick, and the same material has been used in cottage gardens throughout England for centuries. Modern brick dates from the mid-1800s, when molding machinery was invented, but there is some variation even in machine-made bricks because the density of the clay and the temperature individual bricks are fired at varies. It is this irregularity that gives life to a brick walkway. On the other hand, molded concrete pavers, the ones that are shaped like bricks, are all exactly the same dimension, their life and vitality having been stamped right out of them.

Handmade bricks, which are still available, are typically rough, sometimes even twisted or "blasted" because they were on the outside of the stack when fired in the kiln. These are prized for outdoor paving because they lend character to a pathway. We have a few such prize bricks. When my wife and I bought our old Vermont farmhouse, we found hundreds of old, hard bricks scattered around the outside of the house. Some were so old that they must have been laid out to bake in the sun, because we found two with cat paw prints in them. André Bernier, a local stonemason who works with me, once found five bricks, each of which had a single fawn hoofprint in its surface; he laid them in a walkway to make it look as though a fawn had walked the path. Old bricks have stories to tell.

Unfortunately, newer brick has been used so often in unimaginative ways that it can become predictable and bland. But if you take your time to look for various sources of brick, you'll find a wide variety of colors, textures and sizes are available for interesting paths. Combine that variety with a far broader range of paving patterns than you ever imagined possible (see Chapter 12) and brick paving can become imaginative, varied, and great fun to design and construct. Furthermore, because brick is baked earthen clay—that is, a very close relative of the clay that perhaps exists in the subsoil of your

> *The path is how the garden is known.*
>
> ROBERT DASH
> painter and gardener in
> Sagaponack, New York

FACING PAGE: **The pergola in the Hayward's garden.**

FIGURE 3.1: Designer Mary Riley Smith's own garden in Sagaponack, New York. *Smith's gray and white house could well have been the inspiration for the theme that helped her choose so many white-flowering, gray-leaved or variegated plants for this entrance garden: Ribbon grass* (Phalaris arundinaria picta), Cornus alba elegantissima, *white birches, white peonies, lamb's ears* (Stachys byzantina) *and, in the background, a* Rhododendron caucasicum *hybrid. The color of the brick could well have inspired her to choose the red-leaved barberry* (Berberis thunbergii 'Atropurpurea') *and* Rosa rubrifolia.

garden, especially if you live in Georgia—its color blends with soils and terra-cotta pots. Russell Page adds in his book, *The Education of a Gardener* that the "close firm texture of brick or stone warmed in the sun or glistening after a shower is (also) a passive foil to the life and energy of plants." Brick is also quick to dry after irrigation or rain, and only becomes slippery when set in shady spots where moss can take hold.

BRICK ENTRANCES

Mary Riley Smith, a garden designer based in New York City who gardens in Sagaponack, Long Island, used old brick to create a warm, wide, inviting path to her own front door (Figure 3.1). But off that main path she created narrower subordinate paths that simultaneously define the shape of and lead through adjacent garden spaces. This entrance garden, which relies on a subtle interplay of plant form as well as foliage and flower color, is a welcoming and rich alternative to the typical straight path through lawn from sidewalk to front door. This garden is a celebration of form and color, and it is the paths and their layout that not only provide structure for the garden, but also invite visitors to explore the space. It is a garden that welcomes people. I can imagine Mary and keen gardening visitors taking 20 minutes to wander around this invigorating space, talking about how lovely the *Rosa rubrifolia* looks near the *Achillea* 'Moonshine,' how skillfully she uses grasses, hostas and shrubs to form variations on the theme of variegation, and how the purple-leaved barberry (*Berberis thunbergii* 'Atropurpurea') complements the color of the old brick, which itself blends so nicely with the color of the house and the other plants. What would they have to talk about were there the typical lawn either side of the walkway with a rhododendron and yew foundation planting? How welcome would guests feel? And the fact that Smith chose brick suggests the warmth and approachable feel this garden has; cut bluestone would have added more gray and greater formality to the picture. Brick here is warm and inviting, lifting the spirit.

Notice, too, how the garden is linked to the house: the width of the main path was clearly suggested by the distance between the columns supporting the portico over the brick landing. And because this main path leads from the parking area straight to the front door, Mary frequently passes through the garden. As she told me, "I go to and from the house and car five times a day and when I do I can keep a close eye on the garden. It's our best maintained garden."

The Charleston, South Carolina entrance garden below (Figure 3.2) offers another example of how brick can be used to create an intimate, inviting but very different "front yard," surely one of the most uninspiring phrases in the American landscape lexicon. This formal herb garden follows an eighteenth-century concept of an elegantly designed practical garden in front of a dignified home. Again, paths of old brick, in combination with a fence, hedge and gate, give form to the garden. Because the plants are generally low, unlike in Smith's garden, the more highly detailed forms and shapes of the beds are not obscured and thus can be appreciated from the street, from within the garden, or from the front windows of the house. The main path is 6 bricks wide, edged with brick, and leads straight to the front door whereas the subordinate paths, 3 bricks wide, are on the diagonal, forming diamond-shaped beds, and are connected to the main and other subordinate paths by little spurs. In this small space, visitors are able to walk on what might be nearly

FIGURE 3.2: An entrance garden in Charleston, South Carolina. *Well-designed walkways provide firm structure and access for maintenance year-round.*

FIGURE 3.3: Nancy McCabe's informal entrance area, *between the driveway and the mud room door, is now a kitchen garden; a macadam tar surface for parking covered this area when McCabe and her husband first bought the house in northwestern Connecticut.*

200 feet of brick paths and not once retrace their steps, in large part because of the nature of the diamond. Such a shape, however, does require that some bricks be cut to create the diamond's points, a task that could well require the assistance of a professional. At the same time, the diamonds provide a shape that can help with design decisions. In this case, the designer placed a clipped yew in the center of each of the two diamonds and surrounded it with English daisies. Mary Smith marked the centers of her two rectangular beds with birch trees, and that decision was the starting point for further plant selection.

Nancy McCabe, who lives in rural northwestern Connecticut, adopted a very different approach when she chose brick paths to give form and shape to her intimate entrance garden (Figure 3.3). She created a 6-brick-wide main path that leads about 30 feet from the parking area at the photographer's back to her front door at the right of the window. Subordinate paths, with their antique terra-cotta edging, form slightly raised beds for rows of vegetables and herbs. The decorative brick placed along either edge lends a note of whimsy and detail to the design, and provides her with several spaces for tiny plants. Again, the nature of the path gave McCabe clues for plant choice.

Where Mary Smith's garden is a subtle combination of trees, shrubs and perennials in a suburban setting, and the Charleston garden is a classic herb garden in an historic town, McCabe's is a vegetable garden, the overall design for which is really very practical: she needed to get from her car to the front door and that fact suggested the placement of the main path. She needed access to the beds for picking beans and weeding cabbage. She looked at the existing feature of the rock outcropping and saw that it could form a kind of destination or conclusion to the first path perpendicular to the main path. She also needed a way into the gardens, behind the house but wanted to separate the vegetable beds from them. Thus the hedge, with its trelliswork archway and its brick path to the front door. The location of the paths are practical and necessary, and once their placement was determined, the shapes of adjacent beds and their planting followed naturally.

The tone of this otherwise practical garden is heightened, however, and made charming and intimate by the use of potted geraniums and vines, antique English watering cans, terra-cotta edging and a low lavender hedge along the main walkway and the honest, unself-conscious use of brick paving. The fact that the bricks are not laid perfectly, that some are broken, others sloughing off their surfaces, only adds to the informality and charm of the picture. McCabe also takes advantage of the fact that terra-cotta pots, made of a material closely related to brick, look especially good on brick walkways, or to mark entrances.

By using brick exclusively as a paving material, and not others such as cobblestones, fieldstone or cut stone in this small garden, McCabe unifies the space, keeps it simple, and in concert with the hemlock hedge and dark green trellis, leads you through it and on to the next part of the garden.

At Lotus Land in Santa Barbara, California, the brick path (Figure 3.4) broadens to encompass a whole courtyard. The plants, unlike in Smith's and McCabe's gardens, have been pushed to the edge, and the water rill runs down the middle of the brick panel to break up the space in an interesting and cooling way. No other material could have helped create such an utterly warm, radiant entrance garden.

Whereas the formal couryard at Lotus Land is elegant and contemplative, Jonathan Plant's design for an entrance path is high velocity (Figure 3.5). This modern entrance garden, designed by Plant for a Stinson Beach, California client, was his first commission, and he would not have designed it this way if he did not have the master bricklayer, Yves Blondel, available for the job. In fact, Plant sees this pathway as a collaboration between himself and Blondel, without whose skills such a path would have been difficult if not impossible. Its design, Plant explained to me, revolves around the fact that it leads to a beach house; so its layout is meant to suggest the flow and eddies of water in the nearby Pacific Ocean. The main "current" leads visitors through a gateway just off the street and along a very narrow section of path between trees to an eddy, a broad, patio-like space but at the same time, by virtue of its flow, leads visitors directly to the front door. A connected side path to the left of the photo and out of view flows, not down steps, but down a slope that leads to, and then disappears into, the beach sand. This set of paths absolutely determines the shapes of all adjacent gardens, and in doing so helps the designer determine where to place trees, shrubs and perennials that in turn help him lend logic to the curves and sweeps of the path. Trees are planted at the point where the path curves inward; shrubs are planted behind the trees to add bulk and weight; low perennials, which are taller further from the path, create detail and color, and soften the edge of the path.

FIGURE 3.4: A courtyard at Lotus Land, Santa Barbara, California. *Because it is warm and welcoming, brick can be used to pave all but the edges of an entrance garden. Details, such as the rill and tiles used here, can be added to break up the uniformity. Bougainvillea adorns the wall.*

FIGURE 3.5: Jonathan Plant's design for an entrance garden on the California coast. *This brick path, which mimics the currents and eddies of the nearby ocean, flows with considerable force from the gateway to the front door, transforming itself into edging, a circular brick fountain and steps before arriving at the front door.*

FIGURE 3.6: Outside the Priest's House at Harold Nicolson's and Vita Sackville-West's garden at Sissinghurst in Kent, England. *Brick buildings call for brick pathways. Here, a tiled house, along with brick walls, walkway and oast houses for drying hops, all pull the garden and architecture together.*

The result is an articulate garden, where path and plants are working in harmony to create a garden of considerable movement and force.

VISUAL AND PHYSICAL PACE

Plant's path illustrates a larger principle about how brick, being so flexible in the way it can be laid out in the garden, can create varied feelings of pace and movement. If you want to slow down the visitor, or at least slow down the feeling, lay the bricks lengthwise across the path to increase the sense of width; to increase a sense of depth or speed up the visual pace, lay bricks lengthwise and parallel with the direction of the path. For example, running bond, the pattern Yves Blondel used to create Plant's "high velocity" path, can be laid, as he did, so that the length of the brick is parallel to the flow of adjacent beds, thus emphasizing length and creating a feeling of speed and a quickened pace. Basket weave, herringbone, running bond or other more complex patterns laid across the path, have a tendency to slow movement, especially if the pattern is varied enough to catch the visitor's attention; for instance, where diamonds or other geometric shapes appear within a field of running bond.

Patterns of brick can also help determine how we perceive space. Simple patterns will unify a large space or enlarge a small space, while an intricate pattern in a small space will give the area special emphasis and hold people's attention while they look at equally intricate plantings. Where large areas of brick are introduced, decorative and detailed panels can be set within the repetition of the primary pattern to break up the monotony of a large expanse of one material. Adjacent planting, then, can be planned to suggest a similar mood or feeling.

Brick pathways can also help extend the architecture out into the garden, thus linking the two. If your home, outbuildings or any freestanding or retaining walls are made of brick, then paths of a similar material make a lot of sense. Brick paths, for example, were an obvious choice near the brick build-

FIGURE 3.7: At Agecroft Hall in Richmond, Virginia. *In this formal garden, the firm structure comes from the tile walkways and brick walls. Notice how, in mid-May, the white blooming redbud (Cercis canadensis alba) outside the wall picks up the white bloom of the candytuft (Iberis sempervirens) inside the garden.*

ings at Sissinghurst in England (Figure 3.6), thus integrating architecture and garden. The paths, in turn, provided a context for the low box hedge, and for the familiar cottage garden style of planting further along. The brick-colored tiles set in concrete in the very formal herb garden at Agecroft Hall in Richmond, Virginia (Figure 3.7) were surely suggested by the brick walls enclosing the garden. In the photo of Lady Mary Keen's garden in Beeham, near Reading, England (Figure 3.8), the brick paving is an echo of architecture some distance from the garden, but in view nonetheless.

Notice in these two herb gardens the relationship between the style of paving and the style of gardening. At Agecroft Hall, the tiles are set out perfectly. Everything—every plant and tile and bee skep—is in the right place. In Lady Keen's garden, the planting is considerably more luxuriant, free flowing and easy. Artemesia billows out onto the bricks, calendulas poke up here and there. This free and easy style is reflected in the way the brick, nearly obscured, is set loosely, with gaps between some bricks but not others, and with the brick set, not in concrete, but most likely on sand or gravel so they can move and shift with time, creating a more relaxed feeling.

Maintenance is also a consideration. If you spend hours and hours or dollars and dollars getting your brickwork absolutely perfect, you want to keep the weeds and grass from taking root between the bricks. There is an alternative: let the grass grow. In his garden in Montgomery County, Maryland, designer Mike Zajic created a brick walkway (Figure 3.9) that leads from a patio across a driveway and through an archway to a gazebo overlooking a

FIGURE 3.8: **Lady Mary Keen's garden near London, England.** *Brick can be used to create walkways through informal cottage gardens. Here roses, poppies, artemisias, rue, dill, nasturtiums and the tall purple* Salvia officinalis *flow over symmetrically laid brick walkways to create a luxuriant garden.*

FIGURE 3.9: Designer Mike Zajic's design for a private garden in Maryland.
*The beginning of any path can be the site
for a trelliswork archway (here covered
with a honeysuckle vine), the supports of
which can become the place to set pots
that further mark the entrance.*

FIGURE 3.10: Bill Willis's design for a
brick ribbon path through part of Yves
St. Laurent's garden near Marrakesh,
Morocco. *A raised brick path such as
this can take you on a magic carpet ride
through palms and jungle-like gardens.*

small pond. He has purposely allowed the grass to grow between the bricks
to reduce the visual impact of the brick, yet retain the solid surface underfoot. In a sense, he has naturalized his brick path just as he naturalized the
grape hyacinth, tulips and daffodils on both sides of the path. He maintains
his brick path with a lawn mower.

The way you design your path, and lay out the brick then, will go a long
way toward helping you determine the mood and feeling of nearby gardens.
Furthermore, the type of brick you choose—glazed or unglazed, new or old,
dark or light—underpins the mood of the space in which the path exists. In
a southern Florida garden I visited, a brick path that led along the side of a
tile-roofed house and then widened out to a patio was made of refined, glazed
brick. At the far side of the patio, where brick ribbon paths led from the patio through a jungle garden, the designer used unglazed, rougher brick to create a walkway that undulated with the natural contours of the land. Both glazed
and unglazed, however, were laid in a basket-weave pattern to assure a coherent look.

Yves St. Laurent's garden in Marrakesh, Morocco (Figure 3.10), has a
similar path that might inspire you to think about how brick could carry you
out into parts of your property where you rarely go—and of course, such a

path need not be of brick. Here, designer Bill Willis laid a brick ribbon atop a concrete pad. This visually strong path would draw, almost compel, one to follow the lead and wander through the trees. Without the path, the existing landscape does not look very inviting, nor does it have any form; this path imbues the otherwise wild area with structure—all trees now relate to the path—and makes it accessible at the same time.

At Great Dixter in England, Christopher Lloyd accomplished the same thing in a much quieter way. His path of bricks on edge, four across, through a meadow and orchard is one of the most charming I know. As Lloyd wrote, "The brick path that crosses the orchard diagonally is basically a service path along which barrows can be wheeled without sinking into the ground. It looks charming, partly because the bricks are set on edge; this also makes for stability. But it is not comfortable to walk on; hence the mown strip along *one* side (I do not allow mowing on both)." This lovely earthen-tone line gives form and shape to the entire orchard through which it winds.

BRICK CAN BE USED IN COUNTLESS WAYS: formal yet inviting walks to the front door; pathways through kitchen and herb gardens; ribbon paths that snake through dunes or meander through an orchard; in combination with cut stone or as edging for a fieldstone walkway. And because brick is small and easy to manage, you can do a lot of the work yourself. Chapter 12 will give you all the information you need to do so. 🐦

FIGURE **3.11**: Margy Kerr Richenburg's site sculpture outside her home in East Hampton, Long Island. *Because brick can be cut and shaped with special saws, the artist was able to create a site sculpture inspired by Persian carpets set within periwinkle (Vinca minor). Climbing hydrangea (Hydrangea anomala ssp. petiolaris) covers the wall.*

USES FOR BRICK

- Rectangular, square or circular paths throughout a formal kitchen, herb or rose garden.
- Paths leading to or from a brick home.
- Steps or walkways through or along brick walls.
- A wide path that doubles as edging along a perennial bed, especially if the background for the bed is a brick wall.
- A small area, where the pattern and form of brickwork will be delightful, while large bluestones would tend to reduce the proportions and make the borders look smaller.
- Paths near brick walls or steps.
- A broadly curved ribbon path through shrub borders, woodland or a jungle garden in southern Florida, especially if the path begins off a brick or tile patio.
- A highly patterned straight path.
- A very narrow pathway through a meadow, with a mown path on either side or only on one side.

Remember that because darker colors recede, brick, as opposed to light-colored gravel, for example, will appear less obtrusive and warmer, and that brick laid in simple patterns quietly calls attention to a space whereas larger materials of lighter colors are more insistent and obtrusive. 🐦

Chapter Four

STONE CARPETS:
Informal Fieldstone Walkways

BECAUSE THE STONE CARPET method of path making is so flexible and adaptable to a myriad of styles, it is appropriate in a range of settings: for a wide entrance walk; for an extension of a similarly constructed patio that leads out into nearby woodland; for a courtyard garden in Japan; for a walk through an English cottage garden to the front door; for a broad, straight path between grand perennial beds in Pennsylvania; for a natural woodland garden in Connecticut, or leading to the door through an adobe wall in Arizona. Outside Japan, the stone carpet is most associated with rural architecture or gardens that emphasize indigenous plantings and informal designs. Broad straight paths 5 to 6 feet wide frequently lead from country houses, gazebos or outbuildings into large gardens, while narrower paths 2 to 4 feet wide, their individual stones "fitting together like seeds in a pomegranate," as the Chinese say, can act as more intimate walkways through smaller gardens. Because these paths are broad and provide firm, predictable footing, they demand less attention than stepping-stones, for example. As such, stone carpets allow you and your friends to walk singly or in groups at any pace you choose.

For four hundred years or more, the Japanese have been creating pathways that look very much like stone carpets, *nobedan,* laid out through their gardens. Slightly rounded river stones or randomly shaped fieldstones from 6 inches to 2 feet wide or even larger are laid close to one another to produce a clean edge and a 2-to-4- or even 5-foot-wide walkway that is straight, broadly curved or meandering. Though these paths are less tightly laid and thus less formal than cut stone paths, they can include cut stones, typically at the edges, or they can be strictly edged to increase their formality. As such, their design can celebrate the hand of the designer even more than a stone carpet made solely of random fieldstones.

The Japanese divide the stone carpet into two levels of formality. In the most formal, *gy,* rectangular, cut stones act as foils to flat-topped but randomly shaped stones. The cut stones are set along the edge of the typically straight or sometimes angled 4-to-5-foot-wide walkway; these flat stones are called *tanjaku* (poetry cards) because they are shaped like the cards in vogue during the Heian Period, from 784 to 1183. A good example of this style can be seen in a section of the path that leads to the tea house in the Japanese Garden in Portland, Oregon (Figure 4.1). As handsome as this style is, it is so strongly associated with Japanese gardening, and so costly to install, that its usefulness to all but the purist Japanese gardener is limited. Furthermore, be-

> *The fairer your walks be, the more grace your garden shall have.*
>
> JOHN PARKINSON
> *Paradisus,* 1629

FACING PAGE: **In Fred Watson's garden in New Hampshire.**

FIGURE 4.1: In the Portland, Oregon Japanese Garden. *Fieldstones can be combined with cut stones to create beautiful paths that become garden features in themselves. Here, a strictly edged Japanese* nobedan *path, a combination of cut stones and fieldstones, passes through rhododendrons, azaleas and ferns.*

cause its edges are typically straight, such a path rarely reaches out to embrace the trunk of a tree or nestle into the shape of an adjacent boulder or bedrock. As handsome as it is, then, the gy stone carpet seems aloof, dramatic in its craftsmanship, and calls a good deal of attention to itself. It is meant for a garden in Japan.

The second style is considerably more flexible and informal, and can be used to create stone carpet paths of any width or shape imaginable. The Japanese call this method *so;* rounded or randomly shaped fieldstones of varying sizes are informally set so as to have straight or curved edges.

A good example of this style is a path A.E. Bye, a landscape architect of international reputation, designed for clients in Ridgefield, Connecticut (Figure 4.2). You can see how the straight-edged stone carpet flows with the contours of the land, so steps are not needed. Because the rock outcroppings on either side are a similar color and texture, and moss grows in the gaps between the stones, the path is a natural, gentle presence in this serene garden comprised solely of *Vinca minor,* rhododendrons by the house and indigenous trees. Notice how the subordinate path leading off to the right and between the end of the house and the pine gives the feeling of intimacy and entrance. If the pine did not already exist there, it would be a perfect place for it. Because it does exist there, this is a perfect place for the subordinate path. The choice of the stone carpet in this case, then, is wholly consistent with the natural, serene feeling Bye wanted to create. Materials such as brick or cut stone would have interjected the wrong mood into this calm landscape. Here, the stone carpet, with its irregularly shaped and planted gaps and its unself-conscious design supports the feeling of quiet and repose.

FINDING THE RIGHT PLACE

In another part of the same garden, Bye created a simple stone pathway that leads from a wooden deck and along a rock outcropping before turning into a narrow, trodden earth path through vinca, over bedrock and on into the woods (Figure 4.3). By nestling some of the stones against the bedrock

FIGURE 4.2: Landscape architect A.E. Bye's design for a rural Connecticut garden. *Because fieldstones are randomly sized and thus more versatile than cut stones, they can follow the contours of existing landscapes—in this case from the driveway to the front door.*

and others against the wooden steps and then planting moss between the rocks, the designer made the stone carpet the link between the man-made and natural worlds, while simultaneously providing an invitation and access to the woodland a distance from the house. The path, then, draws the naturally occurring rock outcropping into a relationship with the house, fusing the two. Had a tree or another mountain laurel been growing at the level of the pathway, the base of their trunks could have been surrounded by paving stone too, thus incorporating them into the path. No other paving material could have accomplished all these tasks so simply, so gently, and so convincingly. Brick, cut stone, cobble, any material manipulated by man would have disrupted this serenity and simplicity.

The edges of beds can help you find places for stone carpets too. In designer Ryan Gainey's own garden outside Atlanta, Georgia, he has created a stone carpet that flows, not with existing rock outcroppings or the contours of the land, but with the shapes of adjacent lawn and shrub borders (Figure 4.4). When you get out of your car at the end of Gainey's driveway, you can either go left into the house or straight onto this path. Because it curves as it does, because of the large pot, and because you can only see the tops of the sculpture and birdhouse just visible over the shrubs, you are irresistibly drawn into Gainey's garden. Once in, you are drawn from one area to the next; in a way, this stone carpet sweeps you up and transports you through the garden.

The way he has laid the stone forces the perspective to create the illusion, when seen from the beginning of the path, that there is a greater distance ahead than actually exists. He did this, and you can too, by making the start of the path quite wide and then very quickly diminishing its width, whereupon it curves abruptly behind a group of shrubs. Manipulating a path's width in this way can create a variety of different feelings, many of which rely on obscuring what is ahead, on tantalizing you. The shrubs and trees are all part of

FIGURE 4.3: **In another part of A.E. Bye's design for a rural Connecticut garden.** *This is the destination for the path through* Vinca minor *shown in Figure 4.2. Moss has been planted in the gaps between the fieldstones, so the path appears to be a natural part of a garden comprised of native plants, such as mountain laurel* (Kalmia latifolia), *columbines and mosses.*

FIGURE 4.4: Designer Ryan Gainey's entrance path into his own garden outside Atlanta, Georgia. *In this tightly woven tapestry of shrubs, trees, perennials and sculptures, the profile of the individual plants is lost as the visitor becomes aware only of the feeling of being swept into the garden by a fieldstone path. White impatiens and* Liriope muscari *grow on the left, to the right, the pink* Phlox paniculata *in front of the grass is* Miscanthus sinensis *'Zebrina.' Arching over the lawn in front of it is* Macleaya cordata.

that process; the path draws you in among them, and sends you on your way.

On the other hand, the stone carpet can remain open, obvious and very simple indeed. Nigel Nicolson knew the easy informality that could be introduced into a garden by creating a stone and brick carpet to the South Cottage at his parent's garden Sissinghurst in Kent (Figure 4.5). Originally nearly all the paths in this garden were lawn, with cut stone paths associated primarily with the more formal main house some hundred yards or so from South Cottage. When the National Trust took over Sissinghurst, and tens of thousands of people began to visit annually, Nigel Nicolson watched the lawn paths disintegrate under the pressure of so many visitors. He took them up—they must have been devilish to maintain anyway in the tight quarters outside South Cottage—and laid simple stone carpets intermixed with brick. Nicolson would be the first to admit that these are above all practical, simple paths that are there to do a job, but that is the other point I want to make. You can make an inexpensive, low maintenance stone carpet out of odd bits of stone and other materials to create an inexpensive, low-maintenance path. Clearly the use of the odd brick or two in this path leading to a brick house was a simple, unself-conscious way to fuse the path with the architecture. The rectangular beds, edged by the main path and subordinate paths perpendicular to it are planted with flowers in brick red, yellow and orange. This was the idea of Vita Sackville-West, Nigel's mother. The family had their three meals in three different buildings, and she wanted this garden outside the South Cottage, where they had dinner together, to capture the reddish light of the setting sun.

FIGURE 4.5: In front of South Cottage at Sissinghurst in Kent, England. *The addition of bricks into this informal fieldstone walkway links the cottage to a garden of reds and yellows that come from species columbines (*Aquilegia canadensis*), golden marjoram, achillea and helianthemums.*

You could introduce any number of other materials among the stones, just as Nigel Nicolson did—brick, tiles, cut stones or small pebbles, or decorative panels built up of pebbles or cobble, the way they do in China—to add to the variety and intricacy of the pathway. But the more detailed the path becomes, the more you draw attention away from the surrounding gardens and toward the path and your role as a path maker. One of the strengths of the stone carpet is its simplicity, and to make a path of this type with too many materials is to run the risk of creating a very busy-looking surface.

Another of the dangers of the stone carpet is that if the shapes of the stones aren't related to one another—if the convex of one does not fit into the concave of the next—the path can look awkward and unsatisfying. Look closely at the stones in Nicolson's (and Bye's) paths and you will see that some stones fit snugly into the shapes of others, while several don't fit very well at all. To lay this type of path takes time, a good eye, and an awareness that the stones look best when they fit snugly together.

Stone carpets look natural in desert gardens, too, where they mimic dry stream beds. But look closely at the path leading to the door in the adobe wall in the Santa Barbara, California garden (Figure 4.6) and you will see this is not a path for the elderly, or those with spike heels. It is a rugged walkway with a very definite destination: the door into a courtyard garden. The rocks comprising the path are set roughly into a bed of gravel, and their shapes—rounded and jagged, smooth and coarse, beige and buff, others approximating the color of the adobe wall—are there to act as a foil to the refined planting of bearded iris (*Iris germanica*), and other purple flowering perennials. Notice how the path provides the garden with structure and places for plants and stones. The two boulders of unequal size mark the entrance as well as the point of the curve halfway along the path. Two groups of bearded iris are

FIGURE 4.6: **A dry garden outside a home in Santa Barbara, California.** *Informal paths of local stone invariably work well with the colors of architecture indigenous to an area. Complementary plant colors come from upright junipers, sea lavender (*Limonium latifolium*), bearded iris (*Iris germanica*), the broad gray leaves of verbascum, the callistemon or bottlebrush shrub on the right and the white blooms of foxtail lilies against the wall.*

FIGURE 4.7: In the Kirstenbosch Botanic Gardens near Cape Town, South Africa. *A rough path such as this leading through native drought-tolerant plants makes more refined parts of the garden feel even more so.*

FIGURE 4.8: A dry garden in Santa Barbara, California. *Unlike at the Kirstenbosch Gardens, plants here are set far enough apart along the path that visitors appreciate their individual characteristics: for example, the boojum tree (Fouquieria columnaris), lower left, the upright cactus (Pachypodium lameri) and the white matileja poppy in the background.*

set partway along each curve but on different sides of the path. The upright juniper works with the upright boulder to help form the sense of entrance and in places, the further you get from the path, the taller the plants become. Drought is the theme of this garden, and this variation on the stone carpet is the perfect choice for such a dry image.

This walkway is very similar in feeling to the rough stone path through a section of the Kirstenbosch Botanic Gardens near Cape Town, South Africa (Figure 4.7). However, in this case the plantings of native shrubs and trees are brought up very close to the path; the feeling is wilder, less refined, more natural, perhaps a bit claustrophobic just at this point. You might regard this path, too, as a naturally occurring drainage swale created by the runoff from seasonal rains. Notice how it runs along a natural low spot, and therefore fits with the existing contours of the land, just as A.E. Bye's Connecticut path does. Also, notice that plants obscure the distant view, yet you know from looking up to the mountains that the view is going to be spectacular. Use that technique in your own garden. Dense plantings close to the path can block sections of the view, but leave just enough to tease people, to draw them on along the path with the feeling that the view will inevitably be unveiled.

In another Santa Barbara dry garden (Figure 4.8), a similar path has been created, but in this case the stones are considerably smaller and rounded, and would not have remained in place unless set in concrete as they were. But notice how inconspicuous the path is. I suspect the concrete was made by mixing the existing sand with the cement to create a mix that closely approximates the color of the sand through which the path runs. The rocks, too, must have come from the site, for they look very similar in color and texture to the large boulders in the garden. All parts of this garden work together: paving materials, naturally occurring boulders and the plant community. The same kind of harmony as in A.E. Bye's gardens results, because paths, their paving materials and the plants are all working together to form a coherent picture. But by setting a stone carpet in concrete, what you gain in solidifying the footing, you give up in the wonderful effects that can result from planting the gaps.

PLANTING THE GAPS

For example, 6,000 miles east of Santa Barbara, California, Rosemary Verey has an equally rough stone carpet path that leads to the front door of her Cotswold stone Barnsley House in Gloucestershire, England (Figure 4.9). Years ago, it was very likely the formal path from her front door into the garden, and as such is a good model to show how a stone carpet can be laid to the front door. Tightly laid, it would form a formal entrance, especially with upright Irish yews every 10 feet.

Over time, however, Rosemary Verey has changed this path so that it is now as much a garden as a path. The English call this crazy paving: irregularly shaped, relatively small stones are set to form regular, straight edges. Verey has taken up many of the smaller stones and planted self-seeding helianthemums in the spaces. As she told me, "They make a vivid carpet when they come into full bloom in May, and last for a full month. They are then pruned back hard to keep them in good shape."

Sir John Thouron has also taken advantage of the chance to plant in the gaps of a stone carpet, not only in a broad path between perennial beds, but also in a rock garden set into steps leading down from his Pennsylvania home called Doe Run on the Brandywine River just outside Philadelphia. The 75-foot-long broad stone carpet laid between a pair of dramatic perennial beds starts directly across the driveway from the front door of his home. It links the garden to the house and provides a sure siting for the perennial beds, which do not feel as though they are arbitrarily situated. They connect, and it is the path that does the connecting.

Walking between the pair of grazing deer, you step onto a stone carpet path recently laid down in place of a lawn path (Figure 4.10). Thouron likes to soften straight lines wherever he finds them in the garden, and the lawn path, with its strict edging, did not allow plants to flop and fall to soften that edge; if they did, the lawn mower stripped the errant leaves and blooms, resulting in a ragged edge. By putting the stone carpet down, Thouron was able to reduce maintenance and achieve the look he wanted. Also, he was able to plant perennials that *do* like to flop and spread onto the stone path, including *Alchemilla mollis*, *Stachys byzantina* and dianthus of various kinds. To further soften the straight line of the path and relate the path to the greenery in the beds, he planted thymes and other ground-hugging plants in the gaps between the steps, creating a lovely patchwork of green and reddish-gray stone reminiscent of the house across the driveway. As a backdrop for the two beds, he planted serpentine evergreen hedges. Because the beds are a distance from the house, Thouron planted perennials whose flowers could be seen from a distance; cherry-reds, pinks, oranges and light blues as well as yellows and golds.

FIGURE 4.9: Rosemary Verey's garden at Barnsley House in Gloucestershire, England. *This walkway is more a garden than a means of access. Irish yews (Taxus spicata) frame the front door and provide a firm structure for planting within the gaps between stone. There is cow parsley in the right foreground, helianthemums and campanulas along the length of the path.*

USES FOR STONE CARPETS

- A path from a patio out into woodland or down a slope to a beach, stream or pond. At any point, the path can "dissolve" into stepping-stones.
- A path from a deck out into woodland that presses periodically against existing bedrock.
- A path cum drainage swale that prevents erosion. This is particularly useful near a driveway, or along parts of your garden where seasonal run-off erodes the soil.
- A broad area that extends out from the back door, with a perennial bed on either side. Side paths can emanate from the main path to link up with other parts of the garden.
- To provide gaps between the individual stones for low and fragrant plants. See Chapter 18 regarding plant suggestions.
- Paths through a vegetable garden, where river stones as wide as 2 feet can be used.
- For negotiating gentle slopes, possibly eliminating unwanted steps;
- A path that flows up to and around rock outcroppings or trees. Large rectangular paving units such as bluestone would not allow such treatment.

FIGURE 4.10: Sir John Thouron's garden outside Philadelphia. *The choice of stone for this low-maintenance walkway, one that replaced a high-maintenance lawn path, echoes the color of the stone house, thus linking garden to architecture.*

FIGURE 4.11: **The steps down from Sir John Thouron's home on the Brandywine in Pennsylvania.** *A set of steps in full sun can display an alpine collection such as this one, which includes* Penstemon fruiticosus *var.* scouleri, Ourisia elegans, Campanula muralis, *and varieties of* Rhodohypoxis, Dianthus, Lychnis, *and* Brodiaea.

On the opposite side of the house, Thouron planted a remarkable rock garden within formal, broad fieldstone steps that lead down to the lawn from a terrace connected to the house (Figure 4.11). Like the stone carpet path, this semicircular set of steps is built up from flat but randomly shaped pieces of stone. Because the material is irregular, Thouron was able to leave irregularly shaped gaps, which he filled with soil. He now uses the steps as a display area for unusual, low-growing alpine perennials that require good drainage. While this garden might be more than you want in both scale and style, it could inspire you to remove stones in existing steps or make new steps with soil pockets to plant with any number of alpines or perennials. (Chapter 18 lists plants for just such a situation.) And what better place to set potted plants than on broad steps leading up to the house? By planting on or in steps, you add a new level of interest to your garden; the simple act of walking up the steps becomes a new experience every day of the growing season.

PATHS FROM PATIOS

If you have a patio of randomly shaped stones already laid at the back of your home, or you plan to construct one, make or leave planting spaces. Wallace Huntington, a landscape architect, did just that at his home in the Willamette Valley near Portland, Oregon (Figure 4.12). As you can see, Huntington planted topiary boxwood, placed potted plants about, and set dianthus and other low and fragrant plants into the gaps in the stone carpet patio. All this makes the patio seem more a part of the garden and a much more stimulating place to sit. Later, when you want to expand the garden, you can create new stone carpets that run out from the patio into other parts of the garden. The direction of those paths could be suggested by existing beds, borders, trees or outbuildings. Consider an existing patio the beginning of a new path, and whole new areas of your garden might be pulled into a relationship with your home.

While we may not all have a landscape such as the Ohmes have in Wenatchee, Washington (Figure 4.13), your patio might overlook open woodland or a beach, or slope down through a meadow to a pond or stream. You could make a ribbon path or a less obvious stepping-stone path of randomly shaped stones such as the Ohmes made that would invite guests to walk from your patio down into the distant landscape. The path would simultaneously link the patio with existing elements of your landscape, and invite guests to explore far more than just the area around your home. The entrance to that path could be marked with shrubs, boulders or a gate, any of which might become the first feature that would help you make subsequent plant and design choices.

The stone carpet pathway is usually wide enough for two people to walk side by side, but it can also be narrow and sinuous, like the Ohme path. Because the stone carpet is primarily a wide path that demands a certain broad physical and visual space, it should be seen as a primary path. For a transition into stepping-stones either at the ends or sides, gradually let the strictly edged path break down into individual stones that disperse until they become individual stepping-stones that wander off into nearby gardens.

ONE OF THE MOST APPEALING elements of the stone carpet is that the edges are so flexible. As you saw in the A.E. Bye photographs, stones can flow out to meet bedrock; they can also reach out to surround the trunk of a nearby tree, pulling it into the path. They can swing around boulders, tiny pools, swell out to provide a space for a bench or chair, or dissolve into individual stepping-stones that wander off into another part of the garden. You can't be quite so flexible with brick or cut stone, but with randomly shaped fieldstone, you can make the edges, and thus the whole path, really come alive. ❧

FIGURE 4.12: Landscape architect Wallace Huntington's home in the Willamette Valley near Portland, Oregon. *If you already have a stone patio, set potted plants on it or take up some of the stones and plant in the resulting gaps.*

FIGURE 4.13: The Ohme garden in Wenatchee, Washington. *A ribbon path of fieldstones winds down among fir trees and a carpet of thymes, splits around a pool and converges again at a great boulder and outlook.*

Chapter Five

LAWN: The Living Alternative

Surely the lawn path is the most lush, and most refined of all. Grass is soft, rich green and alive. You can walk barefoot on it, lie, play or run on it. Whereas the color of gravel or stone contrasts with nearby plants, defining their differences, the green color and uniform texture of a lawn path acts as a more subtle foil for a multitude of textures and colors in foliage and flower. Lawn paths are also visually and physically linked to adjacent expanses of lawn, thus adding a coherence, particularly to a small garden, that can often be broken when too many materials are used.

But, as Russell Page wrote, "Grass is one of the most sumptuous and extravagant materials for a wide path . . . (and as such is) a highly perfected invention from rich nineteenth-century England." And that's just the point: grass is a great path material in England, the northern two-thirds of America or anywhere else where lawn grows well naturally, without vast outlays of money for irrigation, seeding, fertilizing and constant pampering. But even in England, a lawn path requires fertilizing, watering during dry spells, frequent mowing, edging and raking.

A lawn path that is not well maintained can look pretty awful, and it can go from bad to worse in three weeks or less. Don't plant a lawn path if you can't see to its weekly maintenance.

Another problem with lawn paths is that you cannot use them when dew is on the grass without getting your shoes wet unless, as Gervase Markham wrote in 1613, you "provide shoes or bootes of extraordinary goodnesse."

A lawn's dense root system prevents erosion and if the soil underneath is easily drained, or the path is slightly sloped or crowned in the middle, it is walkable even after a heavy rain. But there is no question that a lawn can get muddy during the rainy season or when the spring thaw takes place.

While grass can sustain a great deal of use, it can wear down in heavy traffic places such as main paths, gates or breaks in hedges, which should be made of a harder material such as cut stone or brick. Although lawn paths are easy to restore, Christopher Lloyd feels that you should not create mown paths "if traffic is so heavy as to wear them to mud."

This fact alone argues for the lawn path being used only in relatively low-traffic areas such as between perennial beds, as implied paths in existing lawns, or in those areas where lawn mowers can be used to maintain the edges. To put lawn paths in intimate herb or rose gardens, for example, is to ask for a great deal of fussy work. We recently took up all the lawn paths through our four-quadrant herb garden, laid down porous landscape cloth where they had

> *In a path is the beginning of narrative, that sure and welcoming sign of human presence.*
>
> Michael Pollan
> *Second Nature*

FACING PAGE: **In the Hayward's garden.**

been to prevent weeds from coming through, and then covered the cloth with 3 inches of crushed stone. In doing so, I reduced the amount of lawn edge I have to maintain by a surprising 335 lineal feet. Now plants can spill over onto the gravel and I'm not spending an hour or more a week mowing and edging this one part of our garden.

THE VERSATILE LAWN

In places where it is appropriate, the lawn path is surely one of the most versatile and fluid in terms of design. It can be straight or curved, narrow or wide, sloped or flat, formal or informal, and all for the minimal cost of seed and some fairly simple work. Lawn can be edged to form any shape imaginable, though the rectangle is the most formal and is perhaps most appropriate near the house. You can easily set other materials such as cut stone, stone carpets or stepping-stones into existing lawn paths. They can even be mowed in several ways so that the lines left by the mower form subtle patterns that reinforce, albeit temporarily, the lines of adjacent beds. The 8-foot-wide lawn path between our pair of 110-foot perennial beds is three widths of the riding mower; I mow the two sides the same way, shooting the grass into the middle, and then mow the middle strip the opposite way, catching the clippings. The pattern is very appealing for a day or two at the most.

A California Path

The owners of a home in Woodside, California (Figure 5.1), created a lush green rectangular lawn path between two summer perennial beds, based on a design by the late California landscape designer Thomas Church. The idea may well have developed from the existing set of brick steps within the brick wall, behind which was featureless lawn. If you have a wall anywhere near your home with steps through it, look at those steps as a cue for how to develop your garden beyond the wall. Here is the sequence of thought.

In this California garden, something was needed for the steps to lead to: a path with a chair or bench at its top. What should the path be made of? Well, the lawn is already there. Why not simply leave a panel of it to form the path and remove the lawn on either side to create perennial beds? But are there other, more suitable materials? In this case, the lawn is particularly appropriate. It's already there, and creates a comfortable slope to walk on; a sloping brick, cut stone or stone carpet path would feel much less natural, look much heavier, and would be very costly to install. Steps would look heavy too, and would require costly professional help. The lawn is so monochromatic and unself-conscious that it almost disappears from your attention once you are between the beds; the artistry of stone or brick is not the point, the gardens are.

How wide should the path be? In this case, the width of the existing steps suggests the width of the path, which in turn sets up a standard for the proportions of adjacent beds.

But what to plant on either side of the path? If it were far from the house, large-scale shrubs and trees might have been appropriate, but nearer the house, more intimate plantings such as this carefully designed perennial bed feels right; the fragrances, colors and subtleties will be appreciated close to

the house and along this relatively narrow path. Lower perennials that will not flop significantly beyond the relatively narrow brick edging will make most sense along the edge of the bed. Taller perennials will be gathered primarily in the back part of the border, but not slavishly so; some could be brought right up to the edge. And what about a background for the beds? In this case, the designer chose a variety of shrubs and trees, including an orange tree, to introduce a larger scale with varying colors and textures. A more formal design might have included a clipped hedge.

And how could you create a feeling of entrance to the garden? In this case, the owners chose two large terra-cotta pots, whose shape was suggested by the detail work in the wall where they would be set. To echo their symmetrical placement, the designer planted lamb's ears (*Stachys byzantina*) on either side of the beginning of both perennial beds. Beyond those two elements of formal symmetry, however, the feeling becomes more relaxed, although the brick edging maintains the symmetry and unity of the garden. It also reduces maintenance by keeping the lawn from encroaching into the beds and providing a surface for one of the wheels of the lawn mower.

And what is the destination of this path? Ostensibly, it is the chair, barely visible at the very top of the path, but it is also the four subordinate paths that lead away, one to the left and one to the right at both the top and bottom of the garden. These, in turn, lead off to other parts of the garden and

FIGURE 5.1: **The Hunter garden in Woodside, California.** *A pair of beds can be cut out of existing lawn, leaving a straight panel of lawn between them as a central path. Here the path leads between mixed perennial borders of yarrow, day lilies, lamb's ears and poppies. There is an orange tree and a pittosporum shrub just behind the gray-leaved artemisia on the left.*

FIGURE 5.2: **Garden House, Buckland Monachorum in Devon, England.** *Narrow lawn paths can widen out into broad lawns that can act as implied paths that link with other lawn paths. Here mature dwarf Alberta spruce (Picea glauca conica) form a garden theme framing the entrance to subordinate walkways off a swooping lawn path.*

other destinations, so in a way this formal perennial bed and its lawn path are the jumping-off point for a whole series of related gardens.

PLACES FOR PLANTS

The swooping path at Garden House, Buckland Monachorum, in Devon, England (Figure 5.2), also takes particularly good advantage of grass as a path material. This is the main path that leads right through the entire garden; it is the spine of the garden, and as such is a very useful model for your own garden, whatever its size. Subordinate paths, whether to the garden shed on the right, to the house on the left, or into other parts of the garden, form the ribs, if you will, of the garden. Wherever subordinate paths lead off from this main path is an occasion for a large upright conifer, which acts as an entrance post. To differentiate between secondary and tertiary paths, their surfaces can change, as they do when the stone carpet path crosses this main lawn path at the halfway point, thus drawing guests off into other parts of the garden. Where the path leads up steps, trees, shrubs or large potted plants can mark the change. In short, an entire garden design can develop from one forceful gesture such as this lawn path, which feels so right and so comfortable in a watery climate like that of England. Set this path in a dry garden where constant irrigation and spraying will be required and it will look unnatural, laborious and wasteful.

FRONT LAWN PATHS

Many of us have a front lawn through which a stone, brick or concrete path leads from the sidewalk to the front door. While hard paving to the front door is clearly practical and appropriate, your existing lawn can be turned into subordinate paths that lead off that main path into other parts of the garden. What Dr. and Mrs. Howard Minners of Bethesda, Maryland, did with their front lawn is a good example of how an expanse of lawn with foundation plantings along the house can be changed from a cliché into an interesting, inviting garden (Figure 5.3).

To the right and left along the main walkway of your own lawn, lay hose or string to determine what part of the lawn should be used for a path, and what should be taken up to make way for beds. Notice how, for example, the Minners used the big cherry on the right as the center for a bed, around which the path curved. Notice how they allowed the foundation planting to flow out into what must have been lawn, and then how they ran even narrower paths through the shrubs and perennials to encourage visitors to explore the gardens. Those paths could curve around either or both sides of the house and out to a set of paths at the back. In shady areas, you might want to shift to stepping-stones, a stone carpet or brick; under pine trees you might want to shift to pine needle paths. The point is that once you give up the sacrosanct front lawn and see it as the beginning of your path, there is no limit to where your garden can lead. In the Minners' case, the lawn path at the front of the house leads to a side garden of wildflowers and down a hill to the left of the photograph. Notice, too, that trees and large shrubs help lend a logic to the curves, so they don't appear arbitrary.

LINKING SPACES

The lawn path can also be cut from existing lawn at a distance from the house, making way for new beds and defining sitting areas under grand

FIGURE 5.3: **The Minners garden in Bethesda, Maryland.** *In May, azaleas, pale blue* Phlox divaricata *and the dark red foliage of the Japanese maple (Acer palmatum 'atropurpureum') are knitted together with lawn paths.*

spreading trees. For Dr. Geoff Beasley, who lives in the Willamette Valley near Portland, Oregon, Michael Schultz designed this path (Figure 5.4) that leads from a garden shed and greenhouse out into the garden. The tree was clearly the destination, and that fact is underscored by the lawn chairs set under it. The sinuous ribbon path created a variety of places for perennials and shrubs on the way to the sitting area under the shade of the mature hardwood. Joining lawn to lawn, the grass path forms a quiet link between different parts of the garden.

Princess Greta Sturdza uses lawn paths in a very similar way but on a much larger scale to help her organize her 11 acres of gardens (Figure 5.5), Le Vasterival in the village of Sainte-Marguerite-Sur-Mer on the Normandy coast in France. But even though her garden is so large, the lessons you can learn from it can be applied to even the smallest of lawns that you want to transform into gardens.

Whenever Princess Sturdza clears woodland and underbrush for future gardens, she seeds the open soil, which can be maintained easily by weekly mowing. When she is ready to create new garden spaces where lawn grew, she first designs the paths, by staking them out. In designing a path, the negative space, she is simultaneously designing the adjacent garden, the positive space. Once the paths and thus garden spaces are designed, she takes up the necessary sod and plants trees and large shrubs to help lend a logic to the placement of any curves in the paths. She then double-digs the open soil, incorporating well-decomposed cow manure and compost. Only then does she plant smaller shrubs, perennials, bulbs and annuals.

Her 11-acre garden, then, is a collection of island beds, the shapes of which are related to one another by adjacent lawn paths. At times, these paths broaden out to form grassy quiet areas where the eye can rest before being stimulated again by the intensely planted beds. Lawn is clearly the very best material for the paths in this situation; the climate on the coast of Normandy encourages lawn. The shapes of the garden beds can be changed easily. If Princess Sturdza wants to add beds she takes up another section of lawn and plants the area; if she wants to remove a bed, she simply takes out the plants and seeds the area. It is the ultimate in flexible garden design.

To use her method of designing gardens, see if there is a clear line in your lawn between a back door and some feature such as a swimming pool, tennis court, garden shed or even a large tree where you might set a bench. Lay hose in a straight or curving line between the two points so as to mark the edges of a main, 3-foot-wide path, remembering that straight paths emphasize what is at their ends, while curved paths build suspense. Gaps in the plantings along either side can frame interesting views. Lay hose to outline subordinate paths that lead to other points of interest, always keeping in mind that the spaces between any two nearby paths might become planting beds for small trees, shrubs, perennials and annuals.

Cut saplings and set them in the ground to simulate trees. Big cardboard boxes can simulate shrubs. Once you have created a flowing set of paths (and beds) that satisfies, you can take up the sod and prepare the soil for planting. When you are ready to plant, start, as Princess Sturdza does, with the large plants first—trees and shrubs—and then decide where to put which

FIGURE 5.4: Dr. Geoff Beasley's garden in the Willamette Valley near Portland, Oregon. *Free-form beds can be cut out of existing lawn, leaving curving lawn paths to provide access to a sitting area under a grand spreading tree.*

perennials. Existing gardens, shrubs, trees, buildings, doors into the house and good distant views can help you determine where the paths and their twists and turns or straight runs should be. Develop a broad outline for a garden in this way, and the plant choices, always the most difficult aspect of design, will become much easier, for you will have created a multitude of places with their own special characteristics.

The lay of the land, and existing features on it, can also help. In the late fifties, Thomas and Mary Hall of Mount Desert Island in Maine hired landscape architect Howard S. Kneedler of Philadelphia to help create gardens around their recently built home. The structure for the garden was in large part determined by the foundation for what had been a 29-room cottage and the slopes that run away from it.

The interior structure of the garden emanates from the broad steps out to the sunny border and also from the oceanside door of the house that leads to the upper terrace held in place by the old foundation walls. The lawn in the sunny border area acts as an implied path that leads one along its edges and then through a narrow passage to three other routes: a visitor can turn right onto the upper terrace, go straight ahead to the outer terrace where the bronze "Three Graces" stands, or to the left and down to the sunken garden (Figure 5.6). The lawn embraces all elements of the garden; it is a green carpet laid throughout its corridors and foyers.

There are two points where the lawn makes a transition to other materials. First, if you choose to take the route to the sculpture, you will find that the lawn flows right up to bedrock, which you must walk over before step-

FIGURE 5.5: **Princess Greta Sturdza's garden in Normandy, France.** *Princess Sturdza designed 11 acres of gardens by cutting the beds out of existing lawn so as to form—simultaneously—sinuously curving beds and paths, always designing the paths, not the beds, first.*

FIGURE 5.6: **The late Thomas Hall's garden on the coast of Maine.** *Like Princess Sturdza's garden, this one has lawn paths that provide coherence throughout this graceful garden. The "Three Graces" by German sculptor Gerhard Marck and the view of the ocean are two destinations.*

ping again onto the shady lawn under the great white pine. The bedrock is incorporated into the path. If you follow the sweep of lawn path down to the sunnier sunken garden, you will come to a place near the bottom where the grade is a bit too steep for lawn (Figure 5.7). The Halls had stepping-stones installed to ease the final descent. Further down the garden you can walk dry-shod through a small reflecting pool to rejoin the lawn path that in turn leads you on to the moss garden and dwarf conifer collection. Such use of stepping-stones provides an excellent way to make a transition from lawn to another material.

While the lawn clearly requires a good deal of maintenance, it is nevertheless far preferable to any other paving material here. Only gravel or crushed stone could have replaced all the lawn in this situation, but how dry and arid it would have felt in this seaside home. Stepping-stones could have been set down the slope from the upper terrace to the sunken garden, and plants set within them, but the flow of grass acting almost like water, is far more appealing to my eye.

CLIMATIC CONSIDERATIONS

For all their beauty, you have to be careful about lawn paths; some climates, such as Great Britain and the Pacific Northwest, are superb, given reliable rainfall. On the other hand, Willem Wirtz, a garden designer who has lived in Palm Beach, Florida, for many winters, told me, "I would never have a lawn path in this or any other climate like it. Such a path is an artificial notion handed down from the great English gardens, but Florida's climate is certainly not England's. A lawn path in this climate can only be maintained at great cost."

Linda Grotzinger concurs. Her father was in the golf course industry all his life, and she works with landscape architect Steve Martino in Phoenix, Arizona. When Grotzinger and I were visiting gardens in the Phoenix area together I asked her about lawn paths in an arid climate. She talked for almost 10 minutes about what it would take to create a lawn path in Phoenix: how to prepare the soil, install an irrigation system, sow Bermuda grass in spring, water it twice a day for months and fertilize regularly; how you have to overseed with rye grass in the fall so the lawn stays green, and change mower heights in relation to rainfall. She also talked about fertilizer content for different grasses and the pros and cons of alternative seeds. The list went on. When we arrived at one of Martino's gardens, she pointed to a subtly planted desert landscape through which ran a very appealing gravel path: "Now, you see those gravel paths? All we had to do was rake the rocks out of the way, and we had a gravel path. Steve's whole point as a designer is that we all have to work with, not against, nature."

But in the Northeast and many other parts of America, lawn makes a lot of sense. For one thing, it is a relatively inexpensive surface that gives you time to prepare for a longer-lasting, lower maintenance, but more expensive solution such as brick, cut stone or fieldstone. If you think you might want to change your design later, or if you have a tight budget for the garden now, lawn is a good substitute for the more expensive path materials. Lawn seed is inexpensive and with attention to detail, you could lay the path yourself following the information in Chapter 13 of this book. Later, when your budget allows, you could take up the lawn path and lay down a more permanent hard materials.

THE MEADOW PATH

Perhaps the easiest lawn path to create is one through an existing meadow. It will not cost you a cent, yet its impact is remarkable. All you need

FIGURE 5.7: **The late Thomas Hall's garden on the coast of Maine.** *This sunken garden, hedged by trimmed white pines (Pinus strobus), provides a striking setting for pink astilbes, lilies, meadow rue (Thalictrum), the low pink Geranium sanguineum lancastriense and yellow snapdragons.*

FIGURE 5.8: A meadow path in southern Vermont. *This simple path through an existing meadow links lawn to meadow and encourages exploration.*

to do is set the rotary blades on your lawn mower at their highest level and pay attention to the natural contours of the land (and your destination) when you drive into your meadow or field in early spring before the grass is too high. This is just what clients of mine did years ago in a meadow that separated their house from the guest house several hundred yards away (Figure 5.8). One day, their caretaker suggested he mow a path between the two homes so guests could easily find their way to the main house and have a pleasant walk through the meadow while doing so. Following the contours of the meadow, he took four passes with the riding mower, resulting in a path the width of the old rusty gate. The path, just as he mowed it that first time, has been maintained by the same caretaker for about 20 years. The result is a useful and inviting path wide enough for three or four people to walk side by side. It simultaneously defines the sweep of the land and draws people up into the meadow where there are wonderful views of the distant Connecticut River valley and New Hampshire. Because the ends of the path flow gracefully into the lawn around the two homes, the houses are related to one another, so the meadow is a link rather than barrier between the two. This meadow path, then, is a simple, pragmatic feature with many subtle results.

An even narrower path through Christopher Lloyd's wildflower meadow at his garden in Great Dixter in southern England is equally inviting (Figure 5.9). Again, the path enables people to walk through the meadow. It is a gentle and equally unself-conscious path although in this case people must walk single file. When I asked Christopher Lloyd about it, he told me that,

> Through the orchard meadow area itself there are a number of mown paths. These allow access in an intimate way. They also demonstrate, by contrast, that the wildness of the meadow is intentional. Here it should be noted that the curves in the paths appear entirely natural, being made obligatory by orchard trees. I take strong exception to paths (or border margins) that wiggle for no better reason than that the owner is striving for informality, but is fussy in doing so.

LANDSCAPE ARCHITECT PATRICK CHASSÉ told me that he finds it helpful when designing paths to think of them as running water. A natural flow with the existing contours of the land invariably results. Lawn paths are a good example of this. In our own garden in Vermont, as in Princess Sturdza's in France and in the Hall garden in Maine, lawn paths predominate. They flow down and around beds, up gentle slopes, straight between perennial beds and around trees and shrubs where they open out into broad panels, much as water would. Along the way, they direct us to the subordinate paths of cut stones, gravel, stepping-stones and bark mulch that take us into detailed areas. But it is lawn paths that link our gardens, and introduce a strong level of coherence. ꙮ

FIGURE 5.9: Christopher Lloyd's meadow path at his home in East Sussex. *A mown path through a wildflower meadow makes each look intentional.*

THE POLLAN PATH

SO IT WAS A LUCKY DAY for me when I discovered I could put the lawn mower blade on the highest setting and cut a path through the tall grass that, at a stroke, transformed that sorry patch of grass and weeds into something altogether different—into a meadow. . . . That path, in my eyes anyway, is a thing of incomparable beauty, especially right after it's been mowed. I don't know exactly what it is, but that sharp, clean edge changes everything; it makes a place where there wasn't one before. Where before your eye sort of skidded restlessly across the tops of the overgrown grasses, in search of some object on which to alight, now it has an enticing way in, a clear and legible course through the green confusion that it cannot help but follow. The path beckons, making the whole area suddenly inviting. (Even my cat, whom the tall grasses never bothered, now makes a point of keeping to the path.) New possibilities have opened up; there's now the prospect of a little journey.

. . . . A path through the (meadow) grass is an entirely different thing than a lawn. True, I have to mow it again every week, and yes, the grasses seem intent in erasing my cherished line. But still, this is no pitched weekly battle, Mower vs. Grass. It's more like an argument of old friends, or husbands and wives after long years, a quarrel renewed week after week with no end in sight, and no end sought.

Am I making too much of my meadow path? Perhaps. But the longer I mow it, the more I can see my whole garden in that simple footpath, in the way that it seems to inflect the land, to give it something of ourselves without diminishing it. On days when I've mowed, the path seems as lucid and convincing as geometrical proof, like some fine Appolonian line drawn against all that's inchoate and polymorphous in the world, a stay against entropy, a proud declaration of identity in the face of so much grassy indifference. . . .

To look at a freshly mowed meadow path, the way it draws such a crisp, syntactical, human line through the soft, billowy, heedless grass is, I think, to understand the gift of the garden to the wilderness, and its dazzling reciprocation.

— MICHAEL POLLAN, *Second Nature*, 1991, p. 252 ꙮ

Chapter Six

CONCRETE: The Liquid Material– Plain, Embedded or Precast

IN 1924, FLETCHER STEELE, an influential American landscape architect wrote, "A concrete walk need not be ugly, but it generally is." Most people agree; we regard concrete as harsh, as having an unappealing color and texture, as being unsympathetic and lifeless. We will admit that it makes a durable, no-maintenance walkway from the parking lot to the dentist's office, from the sidewalk to our front door or from the garage to the mud room, but these are the only kinds of concrete "paths" we think of. I felt the same way until I began to visit gardens across the country for this book and until I began to peer at hundreds of slides of satisfying paths and walkways in which concrete figured. When used imaginatively, concrete can be handsome, enduring and, most important, one of the most versatile of paving materials.

You can cast concrete into any shape imaginable or purchase large precast rectangular, square, or circular pavers to use as stepping-stones or in the creation of straight or curving, narrow or wide paths from the house into the garden; you can make decorative panels or *faux* millstones to place at a gateway or break in a hedge; you can tint, paint or stain the wet cement so the color of a walkway blends with that of nearby architecture; you can give concrete innumerable finishes or patterns. It can be scored to look old; modern compounds can retard hardening so you can take your time embedding pebbles or tiles to form decorative patterns in the path; the surface of a walkway leading from a loggia out into a garden can be marbleized or polished as in the Italian terrazzo finish or made into false coquina (coral reef) stone, as is done in Florida, so as to link architecture to garden. Concrete can be combined with any number of other materials to form steps or ramps into which planting pockets can be built. In the hands of an artist, it can mimic rock outcroppings and boulders through a garden; it will take any form, such as water rills and channels the length of walkways. No other paving material is so fluid; no other paving material is, in fact, a fluid.

Like brick, concrete has a long history. Concrete paving has been discovered in excavations in ancient Pompeii. There, artisans pounded tiles mixed with lime to create a reddish base into which they set black and white marble pieces for decorative patterns along walkways near homes or buildings. In China, path mosaics of colored pebbles, stone chips or roofing tiles on edge have been set in concrete-like materials along garden walks for centuries. These can be seen today in The Summer Palace, Chung-shan Park and the back garden of the Imperial City in Peking. The ancient Greeks used peb-

Is it not so much more enjoyable to travel than to arrive?

LIU TUN-CHEN
Suchou Gardens

FACING PAGE: The late Thomas Church's entrance garden in San Francisco.

bles set in a kind of concrete to pave paths, and in doing so created images of birds, leaves and scrolls.

WHERE TO USE CONCRETE

But as appealing as concrete can be, it is not for every garden or house. It is a contemporary product most appropriately associated with modern homes in warmer climates: stucco houses, Spanish Revival or International Style architecture in Florida, the Southwest, or on the West Coast. Russell Page, the eminent English landscape designer, wrote that, "Precast cement slabs with a stone finish can be quite pleasant in colour and are very well suited, for instance, to the painted stucco houses you find in London. In such a context the smooth surface and rather sophisticated appearance of cement may look well as long as it is kept apart from real stone."

As Page implies, the decision to use concrete or not is based on the material and style of your home. Next to a white clapboard house in New England, a brick home in South Carolina or a stone house in Bucks County, Pennsylvania, concrete would look flat, cold, utilitarian and wholly out of place. In colder climates, too, concrete can be heaved about and broken by alternate thawing and freezing, and thus requires considerable reinforcing and adequate drainage underneath in order to hold up over time.

A Welcoming Carpet

When I was working on this book, the most frankly concrete path I walked on was the entrance to the home of the late California landscape designer (Figure 6.1) Thomas Church, who designed this garden in the mid-thirties, shortly after he and his wife bought the then 60-year-old house. Its present shapes and forms were set out during the forties and fifties. Even though the path through this entrance garden is concrete, unadorned and gray, it is utterly welcoming; it is, as Church so often wrote, a carpet that he laid out for his guests. To Church, a man who welcomed guests often, the entrance garden was the most important part of the overall design.

FIGURE 6.1: The late Thomas Church's design for his own entrance garden in San Francisco. *Serenity can be created in a garden by repeating the gray of concrete, or any other muted color throughout the human-made elements of the garden. The color here provides a backdrop for the dark greens of the Tasmanian tree fern* (Dicksonia antarctica), *Algerian ivy* (Hedera colchica), *the camellia in the pot and the aspidistra ground cover under the trunk of the pollarded sycamore.*

When my wife Mary and I walked through the gray door in a high wooden fence that screens the garden from a busy San Francisco street, we felt immediately welcome. There was the weathered teak bench on our right where we could sit for a moment under one of several pollarded sycamores along the inside of the fence, and behind the bench was a concrete and metal sculpture. The greens of the lush, semi-tropical plants, including pittosporum, pieris, clivia, aspidistra and agapanthus, glowed in contrast with the gray concrete ribbon path that wound up the gentle slope to a pair of wooden staircases to the front door. (See page 115 for a photograph of the stairs.) This main path is 5 feet wide; wide enough to allow two people to walk side by side comfortably; Church always maintained that a narrower entrance path was a "mean dimension," Mrs. Church told us.

The main path (and two subordinate paths) (see illustration on page 82) also divides the 25-by-50-foot space, which is enclosed by the fence, the walls of two adjoining houses and the front of Church's home, into handsomely proportioned garden spaces that have been planted with those proportions in mind.

As you can see in the same illustration, the two subordinate paths lead off the main one at different points. The first goes to the left through lush plantings to a secret enclosed garden with a rustic cast iron bench and two chairs where I sat and listened to the palm leaves rattling in the wind. Further along the main path, and just past the first of many Tasmanian tree ferns (*Dickso-*

FIGURE 6.2: **A design by Bill Hays for a private garden in Albuquerque, New Mexico.** *Concrete embedded with aggregate that echoes the color of architecture can fuse the garden to the house. The line the owners naturally walk from the street to the back door may well have suggested the route for the path, and thus the form of the beds on either side of it.*

nia antarctica) there is another secondary path that leads off to the right to the apartment. Further on, the concrete path leads you to the base of the wooden steps where you can turn right or left up the stairs to the front door.

At certain points along the path, rocks are laid so that they are at once in the adjacent garden as well as on the path. At other places liriope creeps up to and over the edge of the concrete to soften the look, and mask the hard edge of the formed concrete walkway. Expansion lines across the path reinforce its curve and add subtle rhythm.

In part, the concrete walkway feels so right because the consistent color of the wooden walls, stairs and metal railing is close to but not the same as that of the concrete. The color gray, then, becomes a theme throughout, linking architecture to path and thus garden, and providing a uniform background for the dark green foliage that predominates. Furthermore, the concrete path calls little attention to itself. It provides a generous and predictable surface on which to walk, so guests need not look down to negotiate the walkway but can pay closer attention to the garden. In a way, the path disappears from view the minute you enter this lush, quiet, shady, secret world. By the time you arrive at the front door, you feel as though you have travelled a great distance through a calm and gentle world, during which you sloughed off all your cares. You arrive at the front door refreshed, enlivened, welcomed; I know we did.

More recently, designer Bill Hays was asked to create a garden behind a modern adobe house in Albuquerque, New Mexico, and he too designed a

FIGURE 6.3: A garden near the Rio Grande River in Albuquerque, New Mexico. *Being so versatile, concrete can bring people and water into the heart of a garden.*

concrete path to allow access through, provide structure for, and create an appealing element within the garden (Figure 6.2). Hays wound the path through the space and then planted pines and junipers on either side to give people the feeling of walking through a garden while getting from point A to point B. Furthermore, he embedded the concrete with aggregate indigenous to the area to echo the color of the adobe. To link the path to the garden, and to justify the curves in the path, he used indigenous boulders of a similar color to the architecture and aggregate. Being partly in the path and partly in the gravel garden, they fuse the two like keystones. The boulder in the lower left corner of the photograph is another key element of the design, in that it echoes the path boulders but is situated separately in the garden: coherence is the result. The boulders in turn have other roles. They contrast with the gray junipers, mark the steps so that people are certain to see them, form planting pockets for marigolds, and introduce a sense of time and maturity into the garden, something also done by the aged wooden ties, used here as risers in the pathway. The result is a very useful, durable and appealing pathway that not only invites Hays' clients and their guests out into the gravelly garden, but also provides a whole series of cues for plant choice and placement. Very clean lines result; had Hays wanted less definition in the path, a stone carpet would have been a good alternative.

Even though this particular concrete path leads to an adobe house in New Mexico, it could inspire you to create a stone carpet path through the woods in the Northeast, with great mossy boulders similarly positioned. It can even become the cue for a path up a more gentle slope in the Berkeley Hills. Work with these photographs. Think about what they have to teach you about your own garden. Within every garden pictured in this book are universal design principles that you can turn to advantage in your own garden. The path is the starting place to unravel those principles.

Water Rills and Steps

In another Albuquerque, New Mexico garden, embedded aggregate and concrete create an acequia, an irrigation ditch that runs nearly the full length of the main path from the house into the garden (Figure 6.3). The acequia or rill, reminiscent of those in the old Moorish gardens throughout southern Spain, is fed by water from the Rio Grande, to which this long-established ranch has water rights. The water not only irrigates this and other parts of the garden, but also cools the surface of the walkways in this hot climate and provides the cooling look of water throughout the garden. Children could play for hours on such a pathway. Notice, too, how the formal quadrants of this garden, established by the embedded concrete paths, contrast with the almost wild look of the herb garden. Again, the paths provide the structure for this garden, while the paving materials and their colors and textures tie the garden to the house. This four-quadrant herb garden is based on a classic design used for herb gardens worldwide, the hedge. The design echoes the structure of the paths and thus helps give form to the space, helps create the feeling that this garden is a world apart.

Because concrete can be formed to any purpose, it is also a very good material for the risers and treads of steps. Ron Lutsko, a landscape architect

FIGURE 6.4: A design by Ron Lutsko for a Walnut Creek, California residence. *To reduce the massive feeling of concrete steps, spaces can be left within or along the sides for plants such as those you see here: fountain grass (Pennisetum alopecuroides), lavender and the Chinese pistacia tree staked at the top of the steps.*

FIGURE 6.5: A design by Robert Fletcher for a garden in the Los Angeles area. *A white, clean-edged ribbon path gives form to everything it passes through.*

who teaches at the University of California at Berkeley, designed a set of aggregate-embedded concrete steps that lead from the sidewalk up to a modern home in Walnut Creek, California (Figure 6.4). Lutsko took advantage of the flexibility of the material by leaving planting holes at alternate sides of the steps for lavender, a plant that tolerates the heat and drought of such a site. The result is that you have to pay attention to where you're walking and so enjoy the color and fragrance of lavender as you brush against it. At the same time, the plants and the aggregate add variety and break up the massive look of the steps. Walking up to this house, then, becomes an exploration of a garden rather than a prosaic walk to the front door. To give the walk to the front door even more interest, Lutsko put in plants such as fountain grass on either side of the steps, and marked the very top of the steps with a tree that signals the arrival.

Aggregate-embedded concrete stepping-stones could well have been set into the lawn on the left at the top of the stairs to invite visitors to explore side gardens; such a path could then link up with other paths or a patio at the back that in turn could lead around the house to create a full circuit, much like the Plant Garden described in the first chapter. Each of these paths could in turn suggest places for trees, shrubs or perennial gardens.

CONCRETE WITH AGGREGATES

Concrete can also be combined with aggregate to create a dramatic and sinuous ribbon path that winds throughout a level garden. Los Angeles landscape architect Robert Fletcher designed such a path that serves many purposes (Figure 6.5). First, it provides a clean, smooth dry surface on which to walk along the edge of the lawn and through the evergreens to a pool surrounded by the same material; the cue here is that your choice for paving materials can be suggested by what materials already exist in your garden. Second, being a color dramatically lighter than the dark green lawn, the path gives form and shape to everything it runs through. Third, it prevents the lawn from encroaching into the ground covers under the birches and pines. Fourth, it visually links the pool and garden to the house where it begins. No other material could have provided such a clean-edged, unbroken ribbon whose color echoes the white of the birch trunks. It is perfect in its curves, and practical; it can be seen easily at night when people go for a moonlit swim. Again, this photograph can inspire all kinds of paths: a gravel path that winds along the edge of a shrub border and leads to a pine needle path into the woods; a sinuous stone carpet path from a patio, across a lawn and along the edge of a woodland garden to a pond. The principle here is the ribbon path that doubles as edging; the idea can be turned to innumerable uses.

EMBEDDED CONCRETE

At another end of the spectrum, Rosemary Verey's laburnum walk in Barnsley, Gloucestershire, England (Figure 6.6) is a fine example of how delicate and charming a concrete walk can be. Verey and her late husband David

FIGURE 6.6: Rosemary Verey's laburnum walk at her garden at Barnsley House in Gloucestershire, England. *The simple, pebble-embedded concrete walkway provides access, and perhaps the inspiration for the long, narrow shape of this tunnel garden. The yellow blossoms of the golden chain tree hang down while the* Allium aflatunense *flowers reach up.*

FIGURE 6.7: **A garden in Johannesburg, South Africa.** *Tile inlays arrest people's attention in the garden, slow their pace, or create intricate and charming patterns at ground level.*

may well have taken a cue from the Chinese (who embed concrete with many materials to wonderful effect) when they collected pebbles on the Welsh beaches over the years and then one weekend created this walkway that barely calls attention to itself and concludes at a concrete pedestal. Ryan Gainey, an Atlanta, Georgia landscape designer and a good friend of Verey's, refers to this path as one comprised of "collected thoughts." We all gather small stones, tiles and found objects that help us recall certain moments. To embed them within concrete to make a decorative panel in a walkway is to add great interest to a garden on even the dullest of overcast days, not to mention bright summer days. Concrete will allow us these flights of fancy, these paths of collected thoughts and memories, and enable us to make them ourselves (see Chapter 14). The path also forms a place to create an allée, as Verey did when she planted the laburnum and later trained it into the remarkable arched tunnel. The sides, here planted confidently in *Allium aflatunense,* and other perennials, results in a remarkably simple, intimate and very beautiful garden picture. The delicacy of the embedded concrete walkway feels right. On either side of this laburnum walk are two other long, narrow gardens; on the left, a brick walkway passes through a shady woodland garden; on the right, a lawn path follows along a shrub border. It is a brilliant use of a piece of land about 30 feet square.

As you can see in Rosemary Verey's laburnum walk, one quality of concrete is that it can hold very small paving materials like pebbles and other small materials firmly in place. Throughout Spain, Portugal and many other Mediterranean countries, the practice of embedding pebbles in a mix of sifted clay, soil and water is very much a part of the national style of gardening. Look through a book such as *Los Jardines de Granada,* published in 1952, and you'll see hundreds of examples of embedded pebble walkways and panels (*los pavimentoes decorativos*), all of which can suggest ideas for your garden. There are circular panels off loggias, from which four paths emanate into other areas of the garden. A panel can form the center of an herb garden, or a decorative element around a small circular or square pool set within a path, or at the confluence of four paths that come from the four points of the compass,

MOCK MILLSTONES

FOR YEARS, THE EPSTEINS, whose garden just outside Atlanta, Georgia is described in Chapter 1, had wanted a millstone at the entrance to an intimate garden space near their home. But because a grist mill is so very heavy, and because the part of their garden where they wanted the stone was on a hillside that was wholly inaccessible to heavy delivery equipment, they made their own stone out of concrete.

Mrs. Epstein told a worker how much she would like a millstone at the entrance to the Pegasus Garden. He took it all in and a few days later, unannounced, returned with two buckets, a cement mixing trough and some sand and mortar and said he could make the grist millstone in place. He dug a 6-inch-deep, 3-foot-wide circle in the ground, mixed the concrete and poured it into the hole. He then threw gravel from the adjacent garden path onto the cement and roughed it into the surface of the still wet concrete to blend its color with that of the existing garden path surface. As the cement began to harden, he scribed the radial lines of a grist millstone in the surface and scooped out the center hole. The next day the Epsteins walked atop their new "*faux* millstone" into their garden, pleased as punch. 🐦

the base of steps or an entrance courtyard. Notice that all these are places where people will pause, where the space is intimate, or where several paths come together. Equally intimate or very simple gardens can be designed next to such highly detailed panels in a walkway. These panels can also be used to slow or even stop people at points along the path where you want to concentrate their attention not only on the embedded panel, but on some other element in the garden: a special view, an unusual plant, a bench, chair or sculpture.

Maggie Keswick, an expert on Chinese gardens, notes that what distinguishes embedded pebble paths (called *luan shi pu di* or "pebble flooring") in China from those found in the West is:

> . . .the constant change from one pattern to another, with a change in rhythm to announce a change in function. In a Chinese garden, even if the visitor walks around looking only at his feet, it is easy to see when the scene has shifted. Pebble mosaics define different spaces and emphasize the alterations in mood. One pebble mosaic may be formal and geometric, and the next one gentle and feminine, achieving the intimate mood of an embroidered carpet.

In a sophisticated garden in Johannesburg, South Africa, a section of concrete path has been inlaid with tile (Figure 6.7) to suggest flowers and leaves, perhaps reminiscent of those that grow near this spot in the garden. At Lotus Land in California, (Figure 6.8) pebble mosaics reminiscent of those found in Spain are embedded in concrete. In this case, the panels are juxtaposed with a brick walkway. The color of many of the pebbles is brick-like, thus forming a pleasing unity of color and contrast of form. Again, these are

FIGURE 6.8 : **Lotus Land in California.** *The Chinese and the Spaniards have traditionally used pebble inlay to create beautiful swirling images that can ornament the garden. These are typically inlaid near architecture.*

tours-de-force, so the site for them must be carefully chosen or they will appear self-important.

PRECAST CONCRETE

In another part of Verey's garden she has used precast concrete pavers to create a utilitarian path through parts of her extraordinary potager (Figure 6.9). Here, the paving material is far less important than the shapes the pavers established. Verey, highly influenced by the gardening style of the Middle Ages, began by setting out her paths. Once the shapes of the paths, and thus the beds, were established, she had countless clues as to plant choice. The junctures of all the paths are marked by the miniature boxwood topiary cones. Apple trees form allées that run parallel to the paths. The structure of the garden is formed by the structure of the paths. The utilitarian concrete blocks confirm the practicality of this garden, which is the source of fruits

FIGURE 6.9: **Rosemary Verey's potage in Gloucestershire, England.** *Simple concrete or tile blocks can be put to good use to create pleasing walkways among apple trees, variegated strawberries and hollies, leeks, cabbages and low boxwood hedges.*

and vegetables for Verey and the many people who help tend her gardens.

Verey's friend, Ryan Gainey, also used precast rectangular concrete panels to create a strongly patterned walkway in his own garden outside Atlanta, Georgia (Figure 6.10), but the reverberations and metaphors go well beyond the practicality of Verey's potager. When Gainey bought his home several years ago, he discovered that the previous owners had precast almost 100 1-by-4-foot 2-inch thick concrete panels, which were set on edge to create 8 raised beds. Gainey used the panels to create this 75-foot-long path in the shape of a cross. As I stood looking at this path, Gainey told me:

> The idea of paths with these stones started me off with the design of this whole garden. [Because the concrete panels are so light] you can see the pattern, especially from the upstairs porch. It looks like the spine, the backbone, the vertebrae, the bones of the garden. It holds it all together. And it creates four quadrants. The cross creates a double axis, one short, one long, with hedges on both sides, making the classic *Hortus conclusus*. The short and long axes come together and radiate like the sun, with four small curved beds that define the radius around the center of the cross. When I built this path, I thought of the book of Genesis, in which a river flows out

FIGURE 6.10: Ryan Gainey's garden in Decatur, just outside Atlanta, Georgia. *Concrete panels can be used to create highly patterned gardens. Within Gainey's radiating concrete panels there is an Italianate glazed jardinière surrounded by variegated ivy (Hedera helix), Alchemilla mollis and the purple ball-shaped flowers of Gomphrena globosa. Outside the radiating concrete panels, Gainey planted Hydrangea paniculata grandiflora, Madagascar periwinkle (Catharanthus roseus), which has white, star-shaped blossoms, and just behind the low boxwood hedge, Rosa 'The Fairy'.*

FIGURE 6.11: **Harland Hand's garden in the Berkeley Hills of California.** *All the "stone" in this picture is concrete that Harland Hand formed himself. He also designed and planted the extraordinary garden, which includes a firecracker plant in the foreground and in the middle right, the dark purple of Aeonium arborescens.*

of paradise and separates itself into four quadrants, which relate to the four seasons and our heart's four quadrants. In the four quadrants I have planted the four essential trees: apple, peach, pear and quince.

In Ryan Gainey's garden, then, the structure of the path—the cross—is the structure and the central metaphor of the garden. The glazed Italianate urn, the signature piece of Gainey's garden, then acts like the sun at the center, around which the concrete panels radiate. In concert with cherry laurel hedges parallel to the main path, Gainey has created a long garden room. One cross path leads just a few feet to an ornate cast iron bench; sit on that bench and you can look over the urn and down the other cross path that leads into the Oval Garden. From there, other paths lead out into other gardens. Such a paving system, using simple concrete panels, sets up an unusual rhythm and pattern throughout the garden.

CONCRETE AS NATURAL-LOOKING ROCK

Concrete can also be used to create stepping-stones, boulders and walkways that mimic naturally occurring rock. Harland Hand, who lives in California's Berkeley Hills, showed me how he has used concrete to sculpt benches, pools and steps throughout his small sloping garden (Figure 6.11). Because Hand's inspiration came from the rock formations and natural ecology of the Sierra Nevada near Carson Pass, he did not want to use the small indigenous rocks on his steep hillside property. They had neither the scale nor form he wanted. Instead, he decided to make the stone with concrete, more than 200 cubic yards of it.

The garden is organized roughly as a series of areas, each inspired by a distinct plant and rock community he saw in the Carson Pass some 150 miles from his home. He molded and formed the concrete stepping-stones to reflect the spirit, if not the fact, of the bedrock over which he walked when exploring the Carson Pass. In ledges of the same material, he molded benches, pools and rock outcroppings. Every rock was made to satisfy a certain need at a certain juncture in his paths. Where paths narrow and wind down around ledges, the stones are smaller, the plantings more intimate; when the paths

---

USES FOR CONCRETE

- Plain walkways to the front or side doors.
- Paths laid wet and then embedded with pebbles or tiles, near a building or for some point along a walkway that deserves special attention.
- Stepping-stones, as precast rectangular, square or circular pavers.
- Steps with gaps that can be backfilled with soil and planted with drought-tolerant plants such as lavender.
- Walkways to houses or through gardens near stucco houses in the Southwest, or near modern concrete houses or Spanish Revival houses in which concrete figures.
- Works of art, as in the garden of Harland Hand. ✿

move through broader areas, the stones become broader. When all these paths are seen from the deck of the house well above the garden, the structure of the paths, and thus the garden, becomes very evident, and conveys the message that this is a place to explore. The first path leads directly from the wooden steps of the deck.

The stepping-stones also form niches, nooks and crannies for thousands of plants that turn this garden into one of the most extraordinary on the West Coast. And by allowing the concrete to crack, or by scoring it intentionally, Hand has been able to make the material look stone-like and old. While this system would not be possible in significantly colder places, it is feasible for temperate places, but making it look convincing is the trick. Hand has accomplished this with remarkable dexterity.

CONCRETE, THEN, NEED NOT be the bland, lifeless material that leads only to the dentist's office. If carefully conceived and appropriately used, concrete paths, walkways, steps and embedded panels can become an integral and exciting part of many different kinds of gardens. ɜ

Chapter Seven

STEPPING-STONES:
Determining Pace

F LAT FIELDSTONES USED AS stepping-stones are appropriate for paths through gardens, woodlands or even areas of lawn. Because they are informal and demand that you watch where you're stepping, they are best used through gardens that require attention and a slow, considered pace. Unless unusually large and close together, they are not practical as a way to bring you safely from the garage to the kitchen door laden with packages. Stepping-stones create a path for reflection, one conducive to a thoughtful response to its surroundings.

Whereas broad, geometric walkways of cut stone, brick or stone carpet provide access from the house to major garden areas, stepping-stones wander into and through more intimate, informal areas such as rock gardens, wild gardens or woodlands, typically at a distance from the home. If stepping-stones do lead directly from a rural house, they should be 2 or even 3 feet across so you can walk the path frequently and not have to look to see where you're going. Or stepping-stones can lead from a vacation home where the living is casual, the pace slower.

Because stepping-stones are made of a natural material, they blend in with the landscape, hiding the hand of the designer. Their invitation is gentle, quiet and subtle. Stepping-stone paths through most gardens are not straight because such a layout can create an unpleasant, nervous staccato look rather than one that is flowing and gentle. Furthermore, these separately laid stones are best used to make turns around trees or shrubs, to move up and down or across slopes and to encourage people to wander rather than to get efficiently from point A to point B. This wandering quality of the stepping-stone path, then, can tend to make a small garden seem larger. David Engel, a landscape architect in New York City and an expert on Japanese gardens pointed out to me that,

> You can use the path to increase the sense of space in a garden by increasing the amount of time that it takes to get from one area to another. You can slow people down by using stepping-stones that force them to watch their feet. You can plant fragrant plants along the pathway that will cause them to pause, or hang a bird cage along the path. You can set a gazebo along the path, or a bench; you can curve a path all through a small garden so that when you get back to the beginning you feel as though you've been on a long trip.

Japanese legend has it that stepping-stones as a means of providing the visitor to a garden with solid dry footing dates back to the fifteenth century.

> *The way we are enticed into the garden and encouraged to pursue its experience to the end is like the plot of a novel. It is the thread on which the whole story unfolds.*
>
> JOE ECK
> garden designer in
> southern Vermont

FACING PAGE: Part of the Prozzo garden, designed by Gordon Hayward.

FIGURE 7.1: Part of a garden designed by Patrick Chassé for a summer retreat on an island off the coast of Maine. *Stepping-stones set into a carpet of haircap moss take you past boulders and birch trees into indigenous woods. The transition between deck and small stepping-stones is accomplished with a larger threshold stone.*

In a collection of tea ceremony anecdotes published in 1640 titled *Choandoki*, a shogun named Ashigaga Yoshimasa (1435–1490), returning one day from a hawking expedition, stopped for a visit at the home of Ishiguro Dotei, a senior disciple of a famous tea master. As Yoshima walked across the wet path to the tea house, his attendants saw that his shoes were sinking into the mud. They began to throw their garments before him on the ground to prevent him from soiling his shoes.

Dotei, watching the activity from his tea house, knew it contradicted the purpose of the arrival at the tea house. After all, the approach was and is meant to symbolize the journey from civilization to the simple hermit's hut that is detached from civilization and its cares. Only by experiencing this passage toward simplicity and detachment in a thoughtful way could the visitor hope for spiritual rebirth, the true purpose of the tea ceremony. Dotei began to think about a better way to bring visitors from the entrance to the secluded tea house. Days later, he gathered flat stones and began setting them into the soil, conscious of the fact that the stones would be both practical and pleasingly arranged. The idea of *tobi-ishi* or the stepping-stone path—that is, flat stones set separately to match the human gait—was devised, and is as relevant today as it was 500 years ago.

STEPPING-STONES INTO WOODLAND

Patrick Chassé designed just such a path to lead people into indigenous woodland from the wooden deck of a summer home, whose design was inspired by Japanese architecture (Figure 7.1). The island house sits quietly within the woods with a view through the trees and across the bay to the distant coast of Maine. I walked this path one rainy November day, and found that it had much to say about the power of a well-designed stepping-stone path.

I stepped off the deck onto the large landing stone and then onto the much smaller stepping-stones. They took me through the haircap moss, between the birch and the boulder and on up the slope into the woods of spruce, fir and rock outcroppings. Every turn the path made was natural, between the birch and boulder and then toward and then around a mossy rock outcropping. Soon the placement of the stepping-stones became less regular. A low, flat section of granite outcropping took the place of a stepping-stone; niches in the outcroppings became natural sites for four 18-inch-high, lichen-covered Korean tomb figures that appeared to be disciplined manifestations of the wild bedrock. Then one or two steps were missing, and I had to step on the forest floor before the next, considerably smaller, less regularly shaped stepping-stone appeared. The next few stones, now well in the woods and out of sight of the house, were set obliquely so I had to search just a second to find them. Then the stones disappeared altogether, and I was at the beginning of a spruce needle path that had been made by simply pruning dead wood from the base of trees along the path as it wandered into the woods.

There are several elements of this deceptively simple path that can inspire your path making. First, its twists and turns all appear natural: as J.C. Loudon wrote in 1822,

> The principle of sufficient reason should never be lost sight of in laying out walks . . . that is, no deviation from a straight line should ever appear, for which a reason is not given in the position of the ground, trees, or other accompanying objects.

Second, because the end of a stepping-stone path can so easily scatter and dissolve into other materials (in this case, spruce needles) it is an excellent material for making the transition between the garden and the woodland. Third, the gap between the stones is no more than 6 inches or so at the outset, so you are forced to walk slowly, to keep your eyes to the ground. If you want to look around, you must stop. Any garden designer can thus manipulate a visitor's pace, not only by altering the gaps between the stones, as well as the size of the stones.

DIMENSIONS

The stepping-stone path is typically comprised of stones that are around 18 inches across, though there is no rule to say they can't be considerably larger or slightly smaller; the scale of the garden and the pace you want to establish will give you clues as to the appropriate size. At the beginning or end of the path, or at a place along the way where the path branches, a significantly larger "double stone" may be used to enable one to stop on both feet. But in order for all of these individual stones to work together, they should

FIGURE 7.2: **A home on the coast of Massachusetts.** *This entrance garden, with its stepping-stones through pines, sedum and broad-leaved* Bergenia cordifolia, *keeps your attention on the ground until you come to the portico, and the dramatic view.*

FIGURE 7.3: **Harland Hand's garden in the Berkeley Hills of California.** *Stepping-stones, especially in a garden that can be seen from above, provide a subtle structure and form.*

be arranged so that their shapes relate one to the next. In Japan, this method is not only an aesthetic dictate, but also reflects the Taoist spiritual belief that the world is made up of positive (*yo*) and negative (*in*) influences.

While geometric materials such as cut stone and precast concrete pavers are appropriate as stepping-stones, they can't be knit together in this way. Fieldstones can be made to fit together, especially when interplanted with moss, to give the impression that the stones were touching long ago, but have since moved apart.

PLANTING THE GAPS

Far more than other materials, stepping-stones can be subtly integrated into the garden. In a front entrance garden for a home on the coast of New England (Figure 7.2), long, relatively narrow stones have been so artfully set and surrounded by perennials that while they certainly act as a path to the house, they have become a subtle part of the garden as well. The pillars of the overhanging roof act as entrance posts to the house and a clear destination for the paths. Their color is a variation on the theme established by the boulder and the stepping-stones. This is not a utilitarian entrance but an aesthetic one. After driving in traffic to arrive at this home, you park your car and begin to calm down. As you walk through this intimate garden, your pace is slowed further by the stepping-stones, which carry your attention to the ground so you notice details of the garden. But then you look up as you step onto the covered landing, and are drawn on by the promise of a view to the coastline that you can see through the plate glass windows. This is a most successful use of stepping-stones near the home.

Harland Hand, whose garden is described on pages 94 and 95, has used stepping-stones to help him knit together a garden, that slopes quite steeply in places, away from the back of his home. Standing on the deck (Figure 7.3), I looked down on Hand's garden to see pools, rock outcroppings, ledges and benches. All were knitted together with hand-formed concrete stepping-stones that enable Hand and his visitors to approach the myriad plants that make up this world within a world. From the deck, I felt invited to enter the garden by virtue of the many paths, knowing they would lead me in the right directions. The paths were of inestimable help in establishing the layout of this complex garden. When you are in the garden, and looking down at your feet (Figure 7.4), you realize how carefully detailed and highly textured it really is.

FIGURE 7.4: **Harland Hand's garden.** *Where plants flow up to and around each small stepping-stone, the path is completely integrated into the garden.*

CREATING A MOOD

In the Santa Barbara Hills, landscape architect Isabelle C. Greene used stepping-stones to create a rugged, desert feeling (Figure 7.5). Here Greene, unlike Chassé or the designer of the coastal New England garden, used bro-

FROM LAWN TO STEPPING-STONES

WHEN MY WIFE AND I first bought our neglected 200-year-old house with its equally neglected property, we knew we wanted gardens but we simply didn't have the money to put into anything but the house. I cleared brambles, junk, saplings and scrap metal, and then a local farmer harrowed, rolled and seeded most of our ground in return for the hay off our fields. Because we had a riding lawn mower, I could then maintain a good part of our 1½ acres on the seat of my pants.

In the areas the farmer couldn't reach with his equipment, such as under a copse of wild plums, I pulled up brambles and weeds and we planted the shade-tolerant perennials we had brought from our previous garden. To gain access through this area, and to give shape to the beds on either side of the path, I sowed some excess lawn seed to create a 3-foot-wide lawn path that curved through the copse and out the other side. It would hold the soil for a few years until we had the time to find, or the money to buy, a better paving material.

Two years passed. The house largely restored, we began to turn more of our attention to the garden. One of the first changes I made was to take up the lawn path through the wild plum copse and lay down stepping-stones. The lawn path had become a problem in several ways. When the soil was moist, especially in spring, we couldn't walk the path it was so squelchy. Mowing and edging what had become a somewhat sparse and mossy path in filtered shade was much too fussy, time-consuming and unsatisfying. Also, the spring garden had matured a great deal; astilbes, doronicum, Japanese painted ferns (*Athyrium goeringianum Pictum*), European ginger (*Asarum europeum*), *Anemone vitifolia* 'Robustissima' and *Epimedium rubrum* wanted to flop onto the path; grape hyacinth and forget-me-not wanted to self-seed in the pathway. The lawn had become an interruption in the natural growth of the garden, and no longer fit in, if it ever did. We were able to buy some fine stepping-stones so we took up the lawn path and laid them down. Drainage across the garden improved, and the stones kept us high and dry, even after heavy spring rains. I no longer had to maneuver a lawn mower along that narrow shaded path—I was forever scalping the edges, anyway. Candleabra primula (*Primula japonica*) has self-sown into the gaps between many stones, European ginger is slowly creeping in and transplanted moss now grows between other stones. The path is no longer separate, no longer interrupting the natural flow of the garden; in fact, it is an integral part of the whole. 🐝

FIGURE 7.5: An Isabelle C. Greene design for a dry garden in Santa Barbara, California. *Here, jagged stepping-stones, pulled first toward one boulder and then the other, are set irregularly in crushed stone to create a rugged, arid feeling that contrasts with that of the terrace where shapes are smooth, bouganvillea is bright and comfort is evident.*

ken, jagged-edged rocks. In all three cases however, the type of stone and its color are meant to reinforce the mood of the garden. In Greene's dry California garden, the jagged edges of the stones reflect the rugged conditions of the environment. Their placement, as they move the visitor along a circuitous path through the crushed stone base and between a few drought-tolerant plants and two rock outcroppings, is meant to alter one's perspective upon entering and make the garden look bigger than it is. At the outset of the path, she has placed a large stone which, much like Ryan Gainey's stone carpet (described in Chapter 4), is followed by much smaller stones that wander right and then turn left where they disappear around shrubs to an outdoor entertaining area. Thus a careful choice of stone size and placement creates the feeling of greater space. Notice, too, that the stepping-stones are a lighter color than the rock outcropping or the crushed stone, adding variety within an overall theme of reddish browns. Greene used the urns at the far end of the walk in much the same way Patrick Chassé used the Solderholtz vase at the end of his cut stone walk. The urns are a promise, a visible symbol of the respite at the end of the journey—the hospitable, man-made world in the form of a terrace around the corner to the left. (In fact, you will find that designing a path and thus garden around a metaphor like this helps focus your thoughts.) At the same time, the stepping-stone path defines the shape of the space as determined by the wall of the house and that of the outer garden. All are in proportion, and all are linked by the path.

Behind a home in Portland, Oregon, designer Hoichi Kurisa created a stroll garden (Figure 7.6). A stepping-stone path leads from the gate (visible at the top) just off the street to steps down through azaleas, pieris, pines and mossy boulders that cross a shallow stream. Neither children nor adults like to walk to the edge of a pond if it is mucky and murky, but they will go to the edge of a stream, because it is typically solid underfoot and the water is clean and moving. Stepping-stones across a shallow stream take advantage of this fact. A path that goes across the stream or nudges up to its edge encourages you to, at the very least, run your fingers through the water.

As you can see in the photo, a stepping-stone path on level ground can readily turn into steps down gentle or even steep slopes; the steeper the slope, the thicker and larger the stones should be for stability. Such a change in level will also change the perspective and can signal a new atmosphere. Coupled with a gate, as well as a change from sun to shade, stepping-stones as stairs can make you feel you are entering a new area.

CUT STONES

Rectangular or square cut stones approximately 18 inches wide can be used as stepping-stones through even the most woodsy of gardens, though cut stones are at their best when used in a straight line or a broad curve that respects the geometry of the material. Used either way, they introduce a note of formality into the garden not possible with randomly shaped fieldstone. For example, Michael VanValkenburgh, a landscape architect and head of Harvard's landscape architecture program in Cambridge, Massachusetts, designed a most unexpected woodland garden in a small urban site in Chestnut Hill (Figure 7.7). A simple cut stone path edged with dark brick runs through the garden. The contrast between woodland and the more formal paving creates a most unusual and pleasing atmosphere. The path is straight, the 2-foot squares of bluestone are set as diamonds rather than squares. Ferns, European ginger and myrtle form the ground covers under rhododendron, white birch, white pine and hemlock. Just off the end of the path is a 7½-foot gray granite monolith within which a trickle of water splashes down a series of 2-inch-wide stainless steel steps, introducing the soothing sound of running water.

FIGURE 7.6: Hoichi Kurisa's design for a stroll garden behind a home in Portland, Oregon. *In concert with* Pieris japonica *hybrids, a low* Sarcocca hookeriana *hedge, azaleas, pines and mosses, stepping-stones down a bank and across a shallow stream create a unified garden.*

USES FOR STEPPING-STONES

- Places where you want to slow people down and encourage them to stop, or at least, proceed slowly so they can regard what is around them.
- A meandering path through a woodland garden or in the midst of broad perennial gardens.
- A meandering path in a lawn, or as a way to make the transition from lawn path to stepping-stone path.
- A straight line a foot or two out from a perennial bed.
- A path across very shallow water, such as a stream or a reflecting pool, so set that they accept the natural gait.
- Steps set in sloping soil.
- As diamonds, squares or rectangles—use large rectangular or square concrete pavers—in straight or curved lines through shrub, perennial or even woodland gardens.
- As squares, rectangles or diamonds, in straight or curved lines through the lawn and on through beds.
- For boggy meadows or wild gardens, where wood rounds are useful.

FIGURE 7.7: Landscape architect Michael VanValkenburgh's design for a small city garden in Boston, Massachusetts. *Along with the granite monolith, cut stones used as stepping-stones add a touch of formality to this New England woodland garden.*

Two-by-three-foot rectangles of cut bluestone can also be used to mark a broad arc through a simple perennial or herb garden. With its strong geometric shape, the path clearly defines the area it passes through, while adding a touch of formality. Square stones can be set as diamonds (as in Van-Valkenburgh's design) or you could set every other one as a diamond, or every fifth or third one as in the Nanzenji Temple in Kyoto.

To make individual rectangular or square stepping-stones even more formal, set them in cleanly-edged gravel paths. They look especially good when set so as to scribe a broad curve. The concept of placing stones in gravel was first mentioned in Japanese texts. In the *Buke Myomokusho*, a record of Medieval warrior families, we read that Uesugi Kenshin (1530–1578), had a garden in the inner compound of his Kasygayama Castle spread with gravel in which cut stepping-stones were set.

WOOD ROUNDS

In the VanDusen Botanical Gardens in Vancouver, British Columbia (Figure 7.8), broad cross-sections of tree trunks have been set into the ground to lead visitors to and along the pond edge. The rounds are particularly apt here because they are similar in shape to the leaves growing along the edge of the path. One problem with wood rounds as stepping-stones, however, is that when wet or mossy, especially in shady spots, they can become very slippery. Care has to be taken when walking, but wood rounds offer a rustic look that is unlike that of any other material for linking woody shrubs and trees with the path.

WHETHER YOU CHOOSE FIELDSTONE, cut stone, concrete or wood rounds, remember that stepping-stones are far more insistent than any other form of paving. They determine where you will step, at what pace you will proceed, and that you and your guests must walk single file. If elderly people frequent a section of your garden, you shouldn't install stepping-stones in that area; stone placement demands an inflexible gait, one that may be difficult for a person with a shorter stride. But if you are able and aware, such a path will help you, step by step, slough off the cares of the day as you walk into the garden. 🐟

FIGURE 7.8: The VanDusen Botanical Gardens in Vancouver, British Columbia. *Wooden rounds, much the shape of nearby petasites leaves, lead through a pond-side garden of Japanese maples, primulas, Iris pseudoacorus and, across the pond, Siberian iris and gunnera, with its large leaves.*

TREASURED FRONT GARDENS

T HE LATE THOMAS CHURCH wrote in 1969, "There's a treasure in that small area between the house and the street, granted you can provide access and privacy." Green and Tyson, the designers of this intimate entrance garden in San Raphael, California, couldn't agree more (Figure 7.9). Notice the many stages you pass through when entering this garden. First, you step through the wooden gate from the public sidewalk to find yourself in a private garden. The aggregate concrete, a refined extension of the sidewalk, gently slopes up to a wooden landing, whose design derives from the unpainted fence and steps up to the front door. That concrete and wood path takes you through so many experiences—through the gate, under the trees, up the concrete slope, across the wooden landing, next to the dog, up the steps and between the railings, under the covered porch and across to and through the front door—that you feel you have been on a journey, yet you've walked only 15 or so steps. But that's the practical aspect.

Back there on that little wooden landing was the promise of so much more: two stepping-stone paths that lead into lushly planted front and side gardens. Give up the idea of the front lawn and foundation plantings, start thinking about privacy and access, and look at what you can do with that treasure between the street and the front door. ☙

FIGURE 7.9: **Green and Tyson's design for an entry garden near Santa Rosa, California.** *Stepping-stones of a color similar to the weathered wooden landing and by low ground covers lead past the topiary* Ligustrum japonicum *and off into other places, thus linking front to side and back gardens.*

Chapter Eight

WOOD: Boardwalks, Bridges and Stairs

ECAUSE WOOD CAN BE CUT SO easily, joined so readily, and can last so long on or in the ground, it can be used to construct any number of surfaces on which to walk: steps, stiles or stairs; boardwalks to take you over sand dunes, boggy areas or a forest floor you want to leave undisturbed; footbridges over streams, dry gullies, pools or ponds; a ramp from the driveway up to the house or around a pond or pool. Because wood can echo the texture and color of siding, decks and outdoor furniture, it is a paving material that can add the spine, and thus coherence to many parts of the garden.

Wood is generally used to create geometric shapes. It can introduce bold or simple, straight, angular or broadly curving lines that contrast with the natural forms of foliage, water, boulders or the undulating surface of the earth. While all other materials discussed in this book lie on or in the earth, wood alone can be easily raised above it with hidden supports and made to appear as if it were floating, so that water or air can flow under it. But unlike stone, wood will not last forever; it needs frequent maintenance and periodic replacement. In humid climates, even pressure-treated wood, typically certified for 40 years, needs replacement more often than that.

Wood has been used for steps, stairs or footbridges for centuries. But its use for decks, boardwalks or ramps is modern, and particularly American. Because wood has an informal look, it is inappropriate near a formal home, where cut stone is preferable, but it is appropriate near beach houses or unpainted rural homes in the woods. If you live in a brick, stone or painted wooden house, painted wood can be used to create a formal set of stairs and landing to the front door, while unpainted boardwalks or bridges are best used further away. But wherever wood is used, it has to appear functional, for its primary role as a paving material in the garden is to lift you above a surface you wouldn't want to or be able to walk on (water, sand, rough terrain) or to create steps and stairs.

BOARDWALKS

If you have a boggy area, this example from the Fairfax County Park near Mount Vernon, Virginia, might suggest a way to make it accessible. Visitors can take a boardwalk that acts like a nature trail through boggy wetlands of cattails, iris, reeds, and water-tolerant shrubs (Figure 8.1). It is a rare treat indeed to be able to walk dryshod and comfortably through a bog, and this walkway has curves that make you want to explore it. Were it drawn straight

> *The garden path leads to the mirror of the mind . . . . a place of life, a mystery of green moving to the pulse of the year.*
>
> HENRY BESTON
> *Herbs and the Earth*

FACING PAGE: A garden in East Hampton, Long Island designed by Thomas Reinhardt.

out into the bog, it would look too severe, imposing, uninviting and a bit like a dock.

Craig and John Eberhardt, designers and builders of summer homes on Fire Island, off the coast of Long Island, New York, have used the same principles when constructing many unpainted boardwalks that lead from their homes to twist and turn through the dunes. These boardwalks, which keep people well above the brambles, poison ivy and tidal vagaries that sometimes make beaches and dunes inaccessible, have a particular charm where the pie-shaped pieces in the curves set up variations of shapes and rhythms in the walking surface. The boardwalks also provide form and shape to the amorphous dunes, and visually tie them to the wooden architecture.

Landscape architect Dan Kiley had to make a path from his garage to his home in the woods of northern Vermont, where he and his wife Anne enjoy privacy and peace. The house is more than 100 feet from the garage, but Kiley didn't want to barge through the woods with a bulldozer to create a wide gravel or stone walkway. He wanted a gentle path that would be practical, in harmony with the woods, and that would not be eroded or turned to mud by heavy rains or the spring thaw running down the south-facing slope of the hill. Any paving material—brick, cut stone, gravel, pine needles—placed directly on or in the existing soil would collect runoff water that would freeze on the path from November until March. Only a complex drainage system and perhaps even a retaining wall could solve the problem, and those were costly and obtrusive solutions.

His solution was to design and install a simple boardwalk. It starts in a break in an arborvitae hedge that blocks a view of parked cars from the

FIGURE 8.1: **Fairfax County Park near Mount Vernon, Virginia.** *A wooden walk that appears to float on the water takes visitors between a willow on the left and a button brush* (Cephalathus occidentalis) *with its brown seed heads on the right and on through marshland.*

house. You step up 7 inches from the driveway into a metal-roofed, open shed where Kiley and his family keep rubbish cans, skis, snow shovels and the like. You then walk along a 2-foot-wide walkway about 50 feet to what he calls his halfway house, a small similarly roofed open shelter with a bench built into the back wall where you can sit enjoying the view through the woods or pause briefly during a rain storm to watch the rain. You then continue the final 50 feet or so to the house.

Because the walkway is so narrow, you feel you really are walking in the woods. It is a very gentle path that is just as wide as it has to be for one person, and no more. To enhance the feeling that the wooden path is gentle and respectful of the land, Kiley notched the edges of the walkway to accept the trunks of trees and even many saplings, a touch that links the boardwalk to the woods visually, and enables Kiley to feel he is walking among the trees. Because the walkway is 8 to 10 inches above the forest floor, woodland drainage down the slope was never disrupted, the roots of trees were not broken and Kiley can push the snow off the surface of the walkway rather than having to lift it off.

What Kiley has created is a respectful walkway that solves many problems, yet at the same time makes a direct visual link with the unpainted clapboard siding of the house. A gentle coherence results.

Wood can also be used to get people across small ponds or boggy areas. You might not like to walk to the edge of a pond or into the water there because it is often mucky, but simple bridges can get you over the water and the plants that grow within it. Perhaps inspired by the classic Japanese two-plank bridge, Anthony Paul, a landscape designer who lives in the English countryside south of London, designed a bridge over a boggy area on his own property (Figure 8.2). To make the bridge, he drove pairs of posts into the boggy soil and then connected them with crosspieces on which he laid stout, 12-foot-wide planks to create a zig-zag bridge that does not disturb the delicate ecology of the place. Unlike the Virginia boardwalk, which appears to float, Paul's design enables you to see how the planks are supported; it feels

FIGURE 8.3: **Designer Sydney Baum-gartner's wooden walkway to the beach in Santa Barbara, California.** *Baumgartner planted the salt-tolerant grass 'Excaliber' to stabilize the sandy soil. She then planted a westringia hedge, marked at the top right by* Eleagnus pungens. *On the left, you can see the low gray mounds of santolina and the larger* Atriplex lentiformis.

grounded and stable. Halfway along, the bridge moves around a partially submerged boulder in the pond, which becomes a place for a metal sculpture. The fact that the bridge makes this detour to one side and leads to and from trodden earth paths on either side of the pond, reinforces the logic of its placement and design, so the pond, boulder, bridge and land are all linked. The bridge also provides places for plants: at its beginning, the large ligularia; rushes at the ends of the planks; waterlilies on either side and moisture-tolerant ferns and the trees at the far end. Nothing appears out of place. Everything is in simple, natural harmony, related by the bridge.

Designer Sydney Baumgartner used a straight boardwalk to invite people, shod or barefoot, from a house in Santa Barbara, California out to the beach and the connected sitting area, seen on the left in the photo (Figure 8.3). Many of her design decisions were made to help stabilize the sandy soil against erosion. The salt-tolerant grass 'Excaliber,' used here to hold the sandy soil in place, comes right up to the edge of the boardwalk. As in so many examples in this book, plants, like the *Eleagnus pungens*, top right in the photograph, and the low westringia hedge, grow along the side of the steps to add interest and, in this case, to help stabilize the soil. Rocks, set tight against the ocean side of the boardwalk, also help. The boardwalk not only stabilizes the sandy soil, but also the whole design. Lawn, rocks, plants, sitting area and furniture, as well as the house, which inspired its color, design and material, are all tied together by it.

FOOTBRIDGES

In southern Vermont, a bridge over a dry gully is used in a similar way (Figure 8.4). On the west side of the home, within the woods, is a 15-foot-wide cleft in the bedrock and a raised foundation that prevents easy access from the driveway to the front door. The owners could have filled in the gully with gravel and installed a stone walkway, but that would have sacrificed the drama of the entrance over the gully and covered up the natural beauty of the mossy rock. Instead, they built a wooden footbridge, whose siding and color, like those of the Santa Barbara boardwalk, were suggested by those of the house.

When walking across this bridge, you pass under a canopy of mature pines, maples and white birches under which grow mountain laurel, *Vinca minor,* haircap moss and ferns. The woods on either side of the bridge have been cleared of undergrowth to allow you to see well into the woods. On the footbridge, there is one point on the left where you are given just a hint, between the hemlocks, of the expansive view across the meadow to New Hampshire. As you can see in the photo, a hinged glass door gives you another hint of the view: the further you walk toward the door, the more clearly you can

FIGURE 8.4: **A wooden footbridge in southern Vermont.** *Winter or summer, this bridge makes the home feel a world apart.*

FIGURE 8.5: Landscape architect Patrick Chassé's design for a bridge on an island off the coast of Maine.

Chassé created this Japanese-style bridge to match the style of the home to which it leads.

see down the hallway, across the living room and through plate glass windows to the view off to the east. At night, the experience is cozier. Lights from the hallway and nearby living room shine through the glass door to create a more intimate destination for this lit footbridge. The glass-panelled door, then, is an integral part of the whole experience; had the door been solid wood, a subtle link between footbridge and view would have been lost. It is the view, and the coziness at night, that draws you into the house. The wooden footbridge, then, forms the transition, the link between house and setting better than any other type of walkway could have done.

The design of the bridge also solves some practical problems. Because it is in Vermont, it is likely to be covered with snow four months of the year. A 4-inch-wide opening runs along both edges of the walkway so snow can simply be shovelled or swept through the gap rather than having to be lifted over the hand railing. The closed siding prevents children from falling the 10 feet or so into the gully. (If you don't have young children—or grandchildren, as in this case—you could create a lighter look to the footbridge by not filling in the sides as solidly.) Replaceable jute matting is stretched tight the length of the bridge to provide good traction year round. And finally, because the gully was not filled in but wood was used to span it, existing drainage patterns and the natural forest floor remain undisturbed.

This same idea could be applied to any gully or drop in your land. Rather than building up the soil with backfill and running the danger of creating a variety of drainage problems, you can build simple, even rustic bridges of two logs with boards nailed across them. Bridges give people the feeling of entering another space; bridging a gap.

In Chapter 7, I described a photograph (Figure 7.1) of a stepping-stone path that leads from the wooden deck of a Japanese-style summer house on an island off the coast of Maine. The bridge in Figure 8.5, which spans a drainage gully, is set within the gravel path we walked to that home. Designer Patrick Chassé, who created this bridge, nestled it into its surroundings so skillfully that it looks as though it has been there for decades. In fact, many of the rocks and boulders and all of the moss and birches were placed by Chassé to create this utterly natural look. This bridge and the next one I describe are Japanese in style, and their design is inspired by the Japanese architecture to which they lead, or the Japanese-style gardens through which they pass.

Designer Hoichi Kurisa set a wooden bridge into stone carpet paving that leads to the offices of the Oregon Dental Association in Portland (Figure 8.6). The design for the footbridge allows for the flow of water through a handsome entrance garden. The material from which it is constructed echoes that of the architecture, and therefore fits with its surroundings. In our Vermont garden, such a bridge would seem a conceit. We have a bridge of similar dimensions, but it is simple and rustic: two old beams across which I nail weathered wood. It has to be replaced periodically, but it fits the setting.

STAIRS

On a steeply sloping site, wood can be a great help in dealing with the slope and holding the garden together visually. In an Oakland, California garden, Henning Associates used wood to tie stairs, retaining walls, planters, trelliswork, benches and deck together to form the spine, the organizing principle of a steeply sloping garden (Figure 8.7). You get out of your car at the top of the slope and step in under the trelliswork, between the two large trees and onto the landing to walk down the wooden stairs through the garden. At the bottom, a wooden landing broadens out to form a bench and deck that leads to the front door of the house. Notice the subordinate path through the trelliswork is made of a different material—stepping-stones—to mark its different purpose; it leads to a utility shed. Coherence among all the wooden elements of the garden comes in part from the fact that the designers used wood of similar dimensions and the same color wherever possible: in the slat roofs of the two entrance gates; in the decking, bench and retaining walls. Wisteria flows over the lower entrance gate, and other lush plantings come right up to and flow over the wooden structures, to ensure this further link between garden and architecture. The stairs provide framework and also animate the garden; with every step down them, you are offered a new view of the garden.

The late Thomas Church also used wooden stairs in his San Francisco garden, but to take him up, not down, to his front door (Figure 8.8). Grace Hall, one of Church's last associates, told me, "Both he and Mrs. Church went to Fontainbleau in the early fifties and they saw that wonderful double staircase at the main entrance. He thought, 'Well, I'd like to have something like that.' He came back here and straightaway put in that double stairway you just came up. That was about 40 years ago."

FIGURE 8.6: **Designer Hoichi Kurisa's garden for the Oregon Dental Association in Portland.** *A Japanese garden of azaleas, moss, rhododendrons and carefully crafted stonework—along with the Japanese style footbridge—feels wholly appropriate near this spare architecture.*

A RAMP TO THE FRONT DOOR

THOMAS REINHARDT was faced with several problems when he was asked to design the gardens and entrance path to a property in the Hamptons on Long Island, New York. First, the modern house was built on a high foundation that made it look disconnected from the land. It was a very angular, wooden-sided house that bore no relationship to its surroundings. (See illustration on page 106.)

He used a wooden walkway from the drive to the front door to solve many of the problems, and took his inspiration from the shape of a tree itself. Looking down from the house, viewers see the outline of a tree. The wooden ramp starting at the driveway as a sweep of steps roughly suggests the broad trunk and upper-root system of the great tree. It then becomes narrow and curves toward the house like a tree trunk. The deck sweeps to either side of the front door, turning the house into the crown of the tree. To the left, the deck turns into a raised boardwalk through annually planted canna lilies and then becomes steps down to the swimming pool and the back gardens. Reinhardt's wooden structure gives form to the entire garden, at the front, sides and back of the house.

The problem of covering the obtrusive foundation is solved because the ramp slopes up gently from driveway to house, where it covers the entire foundation. Over the supports of the ramp, he nailed pressure-treated plywood to further define the sweep.

The shape of the entire garden then emanates from the shape of the path. Perennial beds run along sections of the ramp or are small islands in the lawn, and the shapes of those islands are reminiscent of the sweeps of the ramp. In this way the lawn becomes water-like, and the ramp becomes a bridge. Reinhardt used wood because it could be easily worked: he could easily create beautiful curves to work against the angularity of the house; he could provide a dry, easily-maintained surface year-round; he could cover the foundation without resorting to heavy stone and retaining walls; and he could visually link the house to the surroundings by using wood—the same material as the house.

Wooden steps and decking bring people close to Japanese maples, clivia (in blue-flowered bloom), ivy (Hedera helix), impatiens and a wisteria vine growing over a wooden trellis.

This set of steps takes people from the concrete ribbon path (described in Chapter 6) to the front door 10 feet above. While Church included details in balustrades and handrails to fit with the Victorian architecture, they were all painted the same color, so as not to draw too much attention to detail. By designing two sets of stairs (that change direction twice) along the sides of the space, rather than a single set of stairs up the middle, he was able to leave

FIGURE 8.8: The late Thomas Church's home in San Francisco. *In front of this Victorian home, Church designed this double staircase. To get to the steps, you pass through a calm and serene garden punctuated by the Japanese box topiaries underplanted with ivy (Hedera helix).*

the important central part of the space open. In *Gardens Are For People,* Church wrote that a "long flight of steps in a steep site can be more important than you intend: too much masonry, too many retaining walls, landings . . . . [can overpower] all other elements in the garden." By putting the staircases at the sides and then planting Japanese boxwood topiaries in large wooden planters at their base, he was able to lighten a set of steps that might otherwise have looked massive. He also sheared the boxwood in such a way that the plants became a kind of semi-transparent screen that enables you to see the steps. Furthermore, being of wood, the steps act as an extension of the clapboard-sided house, and so provide the transition between architecture and garden.

These steps, in conjunction with the path, lead you through a private, calm, welcoming garden. While this may not be exactly what you need or want, you can work with the spirit as well as the fact of such a design. Adapt it to your own needs.

ONE FINAL QUALITY OF WOOD, a quality possessed by no other material, is that it can be painted, thereby introducing color in traditional or nontraditional ways into the garden. Because the Epsteins (see Figure 1.7) felt guests might not see the footbridge near the pond, and not explore that part of the garden, they painted it white. Robert Dash, a painter and gardener who lives in Sagaponac, New York uses painted wood to bring striking colors into his garden—colors that he periodically changes. The last I knew, the English stile, which he installed to go up and over a section of hedge and among overhanging limbs just for the fun of it, was painted chartreuse. ☙

Chapter Nine

HARD LOOSE MATERIALS:
Gravel, Crushed Stone and Other Crunchy Surfaces

T HERE IS A MIDDLE GROUND between the hard surfaces of cut stone, brick and concrete and the soft surfaces of lawn. That middle ground is made up of loose materials. Some are hard—finely crushed gravel, peastone, pebbles, crushed stone or crushed seashells—and will be discussed in this chapter. Some are soft—pine needles, bark mulch, leaves and trodden earth—and will be discussed in Chapter 10.

Gravel has been used to create even the grandest of broad formal walkways, such as the 20-foot-wide paths in André La Notre's (1613–1700) Vaux-le-Vicomte just south of Paris, or the only slightly narrower ones at Blickling Hall in Norfolk, England, where Anne Boleyn lived. In fact, Samuel Pepys (1633–1703) wrote that English gravel walks were among the most well-designed paths in the world, but then, such broad straight paths have more to do with an expression of power over people and nature than they do with access into a garden.

Considerably narrower but equally straight gravel paths run throughout the formal French rose gardens at Bagatelle and the water gardens in Annevoie, Belgium. Gravel or crushed stone, often raked, is also associated with centuries-old Japanese gardens. Crushed seashell paths, *pietra compressa*, have been constructed in Italy for generations.

Much less formal, curving gravel paths are associated with areas where the climate is hot and the land dry. In the American Southwest, in the Mediterranean and in Central and South America, for example, gravel paths wander through gardens of indigenous or imported plants. John Brookes, who designs gardens in England today, has made particularly good use of freely formed gravel gardens through which implied or clearly delineated gravel paths run.

Because gravel, finely crushed stone and peastone are loose and easily managed, they add a degree of flexibility to garden paths, for they can be changed when you want your garden to change. Beyond flexibility, they offer distinctly different colors, textures, and sounds as well; gravels crunch when walked on; peastones click. This quality of sound can be used to underscore a change in mood as you move from one area of the garden to another. And because gravel comes in a wide variety of grades, different textures can be introduced into the garden to underscore different moods and purposes: fine gravels for fine gardens, rougher gravels for more utilitarian paths. Gravel or crushed stone usually comes from the area where you live, so there is a quality about the material that feels right.

> *Once paths are comfortable, all other elements of the garden fit together.*
>
> JEFF BLAKELY
> a Florida landscape architect.

FACING PAGE: Into the Hayward's herb garden.

FIGURE 9.1: Snowshill Manor near Broadway in Gloucestershire, England. *Behind a Cotswold stone wall, a simple cottage-style garden contains peonies, poppies, forget-me-nots and an espaliered fruit tree.*

Hard loose material paths don't require the time to lay or the initial expense, equipment or skilled labor that might be required for the heavier, more durable paving materials such as cut stone. And if properly laid, these paths require very little maintenance. Edging is necessary, however, with those materials that don't pack down, particularly peastone, and loose pebbles because they tend to spread.

DESIGNING PATHS NEAR THE HOUSE

To decide where to place the path, what its width and shape and surface material will be, try to come to a clear understanding of the relationship between existing or potential garden spaces and their adjacent structures, such as buildings, walls, fences and hedges. Such an understanding can help you determine what is the best line for a path, and thus the garden. For example, in the English garden shown in Figure 9.1, the lines of the fence and wall create a rectangle. Why fight it? Why create some niggling curve in the path? As the designer did here, run a simple gravel path right down the middle of the space to create two adjacent beds. Or what about putting the path directly against the fence and joining the two beds against the wall? That would have created a wider bed, which would demand a much stronger, large scale perennial border, clearly inappropriate behind a wall and next to a sheep pasture.

Once you have decided on the shape of the path, you have to decide what to pave it with, and that relates to the mood and feeling you want to create in any garden space. Again, consult the site. Close to a sheep pasture and behind a garden wall, with orchards and fields in the distance, the mood should be informal. Indigenous gravel or chipped stone, as is used here, helps create that mood. Lawn, cut stone, stone carpets or brick would have been too formal and self-important out there next to the sheep.

Designing the path, and thus the shape of the adjacent garden, is a little harder when existing features give less obvious clues. Take a close look at part of Monet's garden at Giverny (Figure 9.2). The main path, to which this one leads, is about 10 feet out from and parallel to the front of the house. This subordinate path and several others like it, run perpendicular to the main path across the entire width of the facade of Monet's home. Perennials and annuals, especially nasturtiums on other paths, flow onto the gravel softening the look of the crushed stone.

In both the Monet and the English garden, then, the straight lines of the paths come from the straight lines of the buildings. The choice of light-colored gravel underscores the relaxed mood the designers wanted at the edge of a pasture or near a country home: simple, predictable to walk on, easy to maintain, but still confident and firm in design.

The shapes of the buildings and doors within them can also give you the initial clues for your garden design, but you have to be willing to make some decisions out there in the open space, and that can be daunting. Here's what a professional did. In designer Lockwood deForest's garden in Santa Barbara, California, a straight path leads directly from a door and small patio off the kitchen (behind the shrubs on the right) out into this rectangular herb gar-

FIGURE 9.2: Claude Monet's home, Giverny, in Vernon, Normandy, France. *A crushed stone walkway edged with sweet alyssum and bearded iris leads between flowering trees to the main walk along the front of Monet's home.*

FIGURE 9.3: **Designer Lockwood deForest's garden in Santa Barbara, California.** *Boxwood spheres along the crushed stone walkway give form to the otherwise naturalistic garden that includes lavender, a vitex by the garage,* Clematis armandii *climbing the corner of the house and below it, a hedge of variegated pittosporum.*

den (Figure 9.3). All garden shapes as well as their proportions, colors and textures are suggested by the low, stucco house: the intimate patio off the kitchen; the relationship of the path to what is in fact a garage door; the proportions of the beds along that path edged in concrete (here wholly appropriate in relation to a stucco house); the color and texture of the gravel, both of which are similar to stucco. Straight gravel paths, not self-conscious curving lines, give deForest's garden a simplicity and firmness of design. The style of planting, where the repetition of the pairs of boxwood globes adds a note of formality while the casual planting of the rectangular beds adds a touch of informality, establishes the tension between straight architectural lines and a relaxed mood. Normally, gravel or crushed stone paths should not be used close to the house, especially since your shoes carry the grit into the house

USES FOR HARD LOOSE MATERIALS

- A straight path that is strictly edged with wood, brick or stone;
- A ribbon path winding through lawn that can provide interesting shapes in the lawn;
- A straight path that is simultaneously an edge for a perennial garden;
- An edging or surround for island beds within;
- Paths of indigenous material through gardens such as those in the American Southwest.

and onto wooden floors or carpets, but in this case, no material could have been better.

Where deForest's house and gardens demand geometric lines on a large scale, the more modest home calls for curving lines that will make this small entrance garden feel larger. In this garden designed by Ellen Reed in Albuquerque, New Mexico, drought-tolerant plants flow up to and sometimes over the rock edging to colonize the path itself (Figure 9.4). Again, the informal path suits the informality of the stucco house.

Gravel paths can also curve and wind through cottage gardens. In front of the writer Thomas Hardy's thatched cottage in Devon, England (Figure 9.5), the crushed stone path is edged with roofing tiles to contain the loose material, but also to provide a crisp edge. It creates a more formal feeling than the garden just described. To take advantage of the fluid nature of gravel and crushed stone, notice how the path through this cottage garden broadens as it approaches the house to form a generous area where visitors can linger before taking their leave. In the middle of that area, the designer has placed a stone trough garden. The line, then, from the front door to the sidewalk, garage or street need not be straight, but can curve and wind, depending on the mood you want to create. Just be certain the curves appear logical.

In a redwood grove in Woodside, California, landscape architect Jonathan Plant designed a winding woodland path that leads from the house, winds through the grove and, at the end, broadens into a shady sitting area well within the woods (Figure 9.6). At one point, the path divides to go around both sides of an especially large tree. To increase the light in the grove and create a more dappled effect, Plant removed around 15 redwoods. Then he put in the 30-inch-wide path that he edged with redwood for more definition. To link the path with its surroundings, he covered the existing soil with crushed beige stone from the hills in the Bay area. It has a color similar to that of the redwood bark. He then planted oxalis, woodland sorrel and ginger, which drift into the woods as well as over the redwood edging. As Plant pointed out to me, half the time the path is covered with redwood needles

FIGURE 9.4: Ellen Reed's design for a garden in Albuquerque, New Mexico. *This informal entrance garden, which takes its form from the walkway and steps, overflows with blooms from salvias, platycodon, santolina, hardy geraniums and other drought-tolerant plants.*

FIGURE 9.5: Thomas Hardy's cottage in Dorset, England. *A wandering gravel path leads through a cottage garden of lupins, meadowsweet (Filipendula ulmaria) in the middle right, the red Rhododendron catawbiense hybrids, a boxwood sphere and roses round the door.*

FIGURE 9.6: **Landscape architect Jonathan Plant's design for a walk through a redwood grove in California.** *To bring more light into the grove, Plant thinned out the grove and then installed the edged walkway before planting the shade-tolerant perennials.*

too, creating an even closer link between nature and the path. The result is a path that feels natural and comfortable to the foot and the eye, and invites one into the woods.

But are there alternatives to crushed stone? Why not stepping-stones, for example? The purpose of this walkway is to soothe, to relax visitors, and to provide them with a free and easy walk to the secluded sitting area. Stepping-stones require that you look at your feet too much; they should be used where you want people to look closely at plants on the ground, or to manipulate pace. Here, the points of interest are the patterns of tree trunks as you walk through the grove. The nature of this "garden" calls for people's attention to be directed out or even up, not down.

DESIGNING PATHS AWAY FROM THE HOUSE

Out in the garden, existing trees, shrub borders or views you want to frame can help you determine the placement of straight paths. All of these must have been considered when the path in the Lakewold Gardens in Tacoma, Washington, was designed (Figure 9.7). While the path might have been straight when first designed by the Olmsted Brothers in 1907 or by Thomas Church in 1954, over time the edges have softened through rhododendrons and azaleas, Solomon's seal and other plants. Notice how gentle the relationship is between the ground covers and the path: At one point, the ground cover creates a narrow passage while further along the path broadens out. This is part of the flexibility of gravel and crushed stone.

This dark crushed stone path gently slopes down to the lake, so the grade is barely apparent. (With cut stone, which demands to be set flat, steps are necessary and so the slope is defined.) The dark color of the crushed stone also plays a role here in reducing one's sense of the slope; had it been lighter, it would have drawn more attention to itself and been more visible in the moonlight. But being dark gray, it recedes from view, allowing your eye to focus on the flowering shrubs along the way and the distant view of the lake. And it is the bench, along with the promise of a wider view of the lake, that invites you along this path, which surely links with others. Had this path curved through its dense plantings, you couldn't have seen the bench; suspense would have resulted.

Major existing shrubs or trees can also help you locate paths, which in turn can help you design the whole garden. John and Margo Ratliff had recently built a home into the slope of Paradise Valley, just outside Phoenix, Arizona. The construction had proceeded carefully so that the native desert plants—mainly brittlebush (*Encelia farinosa*), creosote shrubs (*Larrea tridentata*), jojoba (*Simmondsia chinensis*) and foothill paloverdes (*Cercidium microphyllum*)—remained largely intact. The view from the living room window onto the 100-by-75-foot area screened from the road by citrus trees was a pleasing enough native desert landscape (notwithstanding the citrus) but it had very little variety and only looked truly inviting when the many brittlebushes were in bloom in late winter. Margo liked to walk in the desert, but here the plants were so close that she would not be tempted to wander among them, especially given her fear of snakes. So what to do?

She called Peter Curé, a Phoenix landscape architect, and his wife Jennie, a certified horticulturist, and asked for their help. Peter told me, "It was a bit of a dilemma as to whether we should do anything because it was a native desert spot, but what we ended up doing certainly has a hundred times more interest than before."

What the Curés did was to start by uprooting 90 percent of the brittlebush while leaving certain trees and shrubs that would echo the native desert behind the house. Then, paying attention to the natural contours of the land,

FIGURE 9.7: Lakewold Gardens, Tacoma, Washington. *A dark, crushed stone path leads to the lake through tightly planted azaleas, rhododendrons, polemonium, Solomon's seal, bergenia and ajuga.*

and where existing trees, shrubs and bedrock were, he simply raked the surface of this section of Sonoran Desert to create gravel paths. The paths would enable the Ratliffs and their guests to walk through what would become a small botanical garden containing existing and introduced desert plants from New Zealand, Australia and America in particular (Figure 9.8).

As Curé and his helpers raked, they collected the rocks to construct low retaining walls that were backfilled with fresh topsoil to create small terraces for new plants. The existing gravel, a honey-colored decomposed granite, made the best possible surface for the paths, because it made the whole garden feel natural.

The direction of the gravel paths was determined by existing foothill palo verde trees and shrubs such as the creosote bush, by the position of immovable bedrock or boulders, by natural slopes or levels, or by the need to keep the paths curving, thus inviting people to continue their exploration of the garden. Where the slope was too great, Curé used some of the existing rocks to build up simple, rustic steps to the next level. As Curé said,

> I kept the beds fairly similar in size, if not in shape, because we didn't want people to get too far away from the plants. And once we created the paths, we then knew what kind of microclimates we could plant, and that knowledge gave us clues as to what new plants to introduce that would provide color in flower and foliage throughout the year. Without the paths, we would have been limited to only plants that could be seen from the windows of the house. With the paths, which would bring people into the garden, we could introduce a wide range of plants such as Mexican evening primrose (*Oenothera berlandieri*), red yucca (*Hesperaloe parviflora*), purple lantana (*Lantana montevidensis*), bush dalea (*Dalea pulchra*), blackfoot daisy (*Melampodium leucanthum*), *Penstemon parryi* and barbatus.

FIGURE 9.8: Landscape architect Peter Curé's design for a garden for the Ratliffs near Phoenix, Arizona. *This late winter garden is stitched together by an indigenous decomposed granite path; all the walls and rockwork were accomplished with material from the site.*

Once the paths were in, Curé installed low voltage lighting along them so that the Ratliffs and their guests could wander in the garden even in the late evening, or see the form of the garden at night from the living room window above.

With the new annuals, perennials, shrubs and cacti within various microclimates of sun and shade, with two benches and lighting, and with the paths and steps giving shape and access throughout, the Ratliffs now have a garden as opposed to a rocky desert slope. Curé told me, "This was a little bit like diamond cutting. There was a nice, basic desert plant community here but it was in the rough; it needed form and shape, accessibility, and variety, and the paths provided all of that. The paths, in many ways, are the basic concept of this garden."

You can see the principle of curve-equals-suspense at work in a dark gravel path through the Bishop's Close Garden in Portland, Oregon (Figure 9.9). It was designed by John Olmsted around the turn of the century. You want to know what is around that corner. To invite people from across the garden to this path, Olmsted planted, on the left, an *Acer palmatum* whose autumn colors could be seen from a considerable distance. The boulder is there, too, to mark the entrance. Stones have been set along the edge to give

a clearer definition to this path than the previous example. But still, the feeling is relaxed, informal and welcoming.

This path suggests another subtle facet of gravel and crushed stone as a paving material. Because the width of hard loose material paths can be so easily manipulated, they lend themselves to the intriguing creation of the illusion of greater distance. Notice how this gravel path, just like Ryan Gainey's stone carpet, is wide at the outset and then narrows considerably as it curves out of sight behind dense shrubs. The same altering of perspective is possible with a straight gravel path whose width should diminish as it recedes into the garden from a terrace or patio. This illusion of depth and space can be increased if a proportionately small gate or statue is placed at the far end and on a slightly higher level. No other materials could enable you to achieve this illusion so easily; rectangular cut stone or brick, for example, would have to be stepped down in size, thus giving a clue as to the trick being played. But gravel, crushed stone or other hard loose materials, especially light-colored ones set into dark foliage plants and ground covers or lawn could help you achieve this illusion convincingly. A gravel walk can be made more formal with a strict edging of brick or cut stone, either of which can be laid flat or on edge.

THE PATH AS EDGING

As is true with paving stone or brick, a band between a lawn path and a perennial bed can be paved with several inches of gravel to form a pathway that doubles as edging. In an expansive private garden in Burghfield, Hamp-

FIGURE 9.9: John Olmsted's turn-of-the-century design for the Bishop's Close Garden in Portland, Oregon. *The bright red* Acer palmatum *marks the entrance to this gravel path bordered by witch hazel (*Hamamelis japonica*) on the right underplanted with epimedium, and on the left, a large rhododendron. A large enkianthus with yellowing leaves is underplanted with a fading hosta.*

shire, England, just such a path leads from the house and along a serpentine brick wall of the greenhouse and pool (Figure 9.10). Plants at the front of the border can flop onto the gravel surface without creating the problem of maintenance that results with a lawn path. This compacted surface will also ease maintenance because wheelbarrows can be pushed on it easily. Such a path could be installed by cutting a curving or straight edge 2 feet out from an existing perennial bed, laying ground cloth down and atop it, 3 inches of gravel or crushed stone. To reduce maintenance, the surface of the lawn could be flush with the surface of the gravel, unlike the raised lawn in the photograph.

The distinctly different color of gravel can be used to advantage when you want to create a strong visual path directly through lawn. Narrow bands of golden-colored gravel set lower than the adjacent lawn can lead you while simultaneously dividing the lawn into satisfying shapes.

It is possible to carve garden beds into a large gravelled area. John Brookes, a landscape designer in England, takes up about 3 inches of soil—more if clay is underneath, less if gravel is underneath—in a broad area, puts down 3 inches of gravel and then top dresses the area with a layer of uniformly sized crushed gravel. He then digs individual planting holes or broad sweeps in the surface (as Steve Martino does in his gardens in Phoenix, Arizona) and fills the holes with mixed topsoil and compost before planting them. The areas he does not plant become the paths. Because the gravel tends to have a dry, Mediterranean look and to increase drainage, plants associated with dry gardens are especially appropriate: lavender, rosemary, thyme, artemesias, santolina, poppies, *Alchemilla mollis* and euphorbias, for example. Brookes also uses gravel near water where the size of the stones can be gradually increased until small fist-sized or even slightly larger rocks are gathered right at the water's edge; such a treatment is a subtle way to fuse water with garden to create a low-maintenance edge to a pond. Gravel steps can be

FIGURE 9.10: Hampshire, England. *Here, the curves of the gravel path are made logical by the curving serpentine wall. The gravel is held in place by steel edging, which disappears in shadow.*

A SAN FRANCISCO COLLAGE

GRACE HALL, one of the late Thomas Church's last associates, told me about the Jean Wolff garden in San Francisco (Figure 9.11): "Jean called Tommy in the late fifties, I think it was, and asked if he would come take a look at a garden she wanted him to design. Well, he went up to take a look. The place where the garden would be was a gentle slope that had turned utterly to mud from all the rain we'd just had. That was all there was, except for the underground spring, which later turned into a real problem. The garden was to be behind the building, which was actually three apartments, and Jean wanted each to have a part of the garden but not be so divided that it spoiled the look of the whole.

FIGURE 9.11: Thomas Church's garden for Jean Wolff in San Francisco. *This is a typical Church garden of greens and whites within a firm structure of paths and shorn hedges.*

Jean asked him, 'Well, what about the landscaping?' and Tommy said, 'You tell me!' "

Thomas Church did come up with a solution. What Church created has all the elements of most city gardens he designed: walkways, stairs, retaining walls, sitting areas, clipped hedges held within a strong form and structure. And it is the diagonal paths along the clipped hedges on the middle level that break the space in such a way that it looks larger than it really is, creating a complex collage or even Cubist picture reminiscent of a Braque or Picasso. In unison with the hedges, potted plants and unpainted wood, the bluish pea gravel paths form one of the central themes to give this complex set of shapes coherence. ৵

---

combined with wooden beams acting as risers and then plants can be set in along the edges of the steps.

Where lawn paths demand a crisp edge and thus a more formal look, gravel paths as used by Brookes enable you to create a very natural, easy style in your garden; at any time you can dig planting holes directly into the gravel, fill them with topsoil and change the nature or direction of the path. In places where the sky is frequently overcast, light-colored gravel, far better than lawn, is brighter to look at on a cloudy day, and drier to walk on.

LOOK BACK THROUGH THIS CHAPTER and you will see references to Belgium and France, England and Japan, Italy and the Mediterranean region, Oregon, Arizona, New Mexico, Thomas Church, the Olmsted brothers, Monet's Giverny and Thomas Hardy's cottage. Gravel and crushed stone paths have a long history worldwide. They are associated with gardens of power and prestige, formality or informality, large scale or intimacy. Create a gravel or crushed stone path in your own garden, and the walkway through carefully considered planting will link it to one of many traditions. ৵

Chapter Ten

SOFT LOOSE MATERIALS: Bark Mulch, Pine Needles, Leaves and Earth

WOODLAND PATHS COVERED with redwood bark chips in California; cypress bark mulch paths wandering through areca palms, ficus trees and oleanders in Florida; fragrant, long-leaf pine needle paths through Georgia woodland; white pine needle paths inviting you through a pine grove in Massachusetts; a trodden earth path across a Wyoming meadow. Such paths, which are never straight, invite you out and into the furthest reaches of your property. These are the artless paths, the unschooled, unself-conscious meanderings that take you, step by step, from your consciously constructed garden into the beauties of the natural world. These are also the paths—especially the trodden earth paths—that echo back into our own childhood memories and the timeless paths of prehistory.

Patrick Taylor points out, in his book on the garden path (see bibliography), that the earliest known surfaced path is the Sweet Track to Glastonbury built about 4,000 B.C. by the lake-village people of Somerset, England; remnants of it are still intact in peat. Imagine how far back trodden earth paths go. Paleolithic and Cro-Magnon people surely walked such paths that linked their semi-permanent encampments in the Dordogne river valley of south central France to favored hunting grounds or their sacred caves Lascaux and Font de Gaume. The trodden earth path, then, that winds through planted or natural woods or across a sloping meadow, is as ancient as humanity and domesticated animals, and can be used today in the further reaches of your own garden. In fact, the main axis path in Michael Pollan's garden in northwestern Connecticut is based on the old cowpath from the barn to the meadow.

These simple paths through woodland and across meadows are the paths that seem to make themselves, and as such are always evocative: the shortcut your kids take through the woods and fields to school or their best friend's house; the path that leads along the stream where you fish every spring, or the one that leads along the fence or stone wall to the swimming hole, the beach or the lake. These might even be the paths your dog, sheep or cows made.

You might use a trodden earth path like any one of these as a jumping off point for other informal paths, all of which can link up to create a whole system of woodland paths that run from the lawn right on out into the woods. These are the paths along which to plant azaleas, rhododendrons or native American shade-tolerant shrubs and perennials and then naturalize with daffodils. Paths of this type might be simply of bare, trodden earth, or covered with soft natural materials such as leaves, pine needles or bark mulch. These

> *In writing of the woodland path: "Let it wind: but let it not take any deviation which is not well accounted for."*
>
> WILLIAM GILPIN
> *Remarks on Forest Scenery,*
> 1791

FACING PAGE: The woodland walk in the Hayward's garden.

are the paths furthest from the house; they are most appropriate in woodland or settings where the materials would be found naturally. But there can be exceptions.

BARK MULCH

In 1966, Charles F. Gillette of Richmond, Virginia designed a bark mulch path and gardens around a pond and gazebo for Wyatt and Dorothy Williams in nearby Orange (Figure 10.1). The bark mulch establishes a relaxed and natural link between the wooden tie steps, the mature trees in which the garden is set and the distant views out into cow pastures. To define the paths, Gillette used steel edging that had been allowed to rust almost to the color of the mulch. Any other paving material, with the possible exception of gravel or crushed stone, would have interjected the human hand much more forcefully into this natural setting.

Similarly, behind a mixed shrub and perennial border along the west boundary of her Portland, Oregon garden, the late Jane Platt put in a path through a deciduous woodland of native trees, azaleas, rhododendrons and dogwoods, paving it with chipped prunings from her own property (Figure 10.2). The result is a path that meanders comfortably through the woodland, curving and twisting as it comes upon trees, groups of shrubs or boulders. Such a simple path can easily be constructed by pruning branches and low limbs from existing plants and then adding plants along the path to give it more interest. It is always so much more interesting to walk within rather than simply look at, the wilder parts of your garden.

USES FOR SOFT LOOSE MATERIALS

- Through woods or a shady garden. Use pine needles in an evergreen forest, especially when pine trees are present. Bark mulch, leaves, trodden earth and the natural forest floor also make good woodland paths. 🌿

PINE NEEDLES

Pine needles as a paving material are especially appropriate in shady woodland gardens where white pines, or any evergreen trees, grow. The needles should be laid down so thickly that they have the same soft springiness associated with the floor of any evergreen forest. Needles don't make as much sense in sunny gardens because they don't appear to have fallen naturally onto the path. Also, in sun, they tend to gather and hold heat, become brittle and break down quickly underfoot. In shade, their color is deeper and they don't dry out as quickly, which means they are less brittle and last longer.

A pine needle path is best where you want a very light touch to the path, where you want to tread lightly in the woods, yet still have a clear direction and stylish surface. The color of pine needles adds a gentle, earthy color to the woodland, and their soft texture allows people to walk barefoot on them, especially after a few months of use, when the needles have broken down. Their fragrance, especially when first laid, or after a rain, adds yet another element to the walk. There is never anything to trip on, though pine needles should never be used on a steep slope because they can be slippery, especially when dry. On steep places, shift to bare earth.

At a summer home on the coast of Maine, Patrick Chassé used a pine needle path, in concert with other elements of design, to create an understated entrance garden. To fulfill his clients' desire to create a feeling of complete seclusion around their home, Chassé removed the circular driveway that lead to the front door. Where the driveway had been beyond the front door,

FIGURE 10.2: The late Jane Platt's garden near Portland, Oregon. *Well away from the house, this bark mulch path blends quietly with the naturalistic plantings of azaleas and rhododendrons underplanted with blue muscari, and the dark pink* Anemone pulsatilla.

FIGURE 10.3: Patrick Chassé's design for a garden near Acadia National Park on the coast of Maine. *Because this is a summer home only, the pine needle path functions well leading directly to the house.*

he backfilled with topsoil to re-create the natural contours, and recreated the natural woodland of young maple, birch, pine and spruce underplanted with bunchberry and haircap moss. The first half of what had been the driveway became the pine needle path from the garage and through the woods to the house (Figure 10.3).

One problem was that the kitchen door is the only door guests can see as they walk the path; the front door is tucked behind an ell at the end of a 15-foot wooden walkway further along the house.

THE WOODLAND DISCOVERED

A WOODLAND PATH, whether it leads through a small copse of trees or acres of forest and across meadow, has the power to create a mood that is unlike any other in the garden. It is relaxed, shaded, cool and contemplative and offers the potential for a remarkable range of beauty, from the smallest gatherings of lichens and moss on a rotting stump to vast views through the trunks of trees to distant mountains. One moment you might be in full shade and the next in a pool of light. A path offers seasonal changes as well. In spring, azaleas, rhododendrons and any number of shade-tolerant perennials planted or naturally existing along the path add drama and color. In the summer, the path is shaded and cool with foliage creating an interplay of greens and textures. In autumn, in the northern parts of America, brilliant red, orange and yellow leaves hang overhead for a week or two and then fall to the ground to cover the path with a new layer of color. And in winter, the woodland path leads walkers and cross-country skiers past evergreens and among gray and black trunks, their branches highlighted against the bright blue sky.

Paths covered by the naturally occurring leaf mold lead to an increased appreciation of the beauty and peace inherent in woodland. As an extension of this idea, the woodland path can link several adjoining properties. Neighbors living in rural areas can get together to design, clear and enjoy a path that winds for miles through woodland, sections of which can be added, or a bench situated, to create points of rest and interest.

Dan Kiley told me that, "I think of how I take a walk along a path in the woods, and how that is an inspiration for a garden path. First, each curve and corner in the woods draws me on, because I want to know what is around the next bend. Then I see an opening into a field and I plunge into the meadow and to the top of the hill and on and on I go. I am always lead by the mystery of the path." ✿

To pull guests to the correct door, Chassé used the path, architecture and lighting. First, he made the kitchen door path much narrower than the main path, and he angled it just slightly away from approaching guests so that where it met the main entry path, there would be no backflow.

His second answer to the problem was architectural. First, he simplified the trim detail around the kitchen door. Next, he extended the wooden walkway and its hand railing about four feet out from the side of the house into the landing so that visitors had another visual clue as to where the front door was. To make the area more intimate, he placed a curving stone bench on one side of the landing, and used a large piece of driftwood to catch the eye and draw guests into the area where the front door would become apparent. (If you look back to Chapter 2, you'll see how Chassé did much the same thing with a cut stone path and an antique vase at another Maine residence.)

To reinforce all these signals at night, Chassé used minimal lighting by the kitchen door, which could be switched off when guests were expected, with more, but not necessarily brighter, light around the main entrance. Through a combination of path design and surface, architecture, lighting and plant choice, Chassé was able to give visitors all the right signals. At the heart of the garden was a quiet pine needle path unifying the whole picture.

The pine needle path in the Hall garden on the coast of Maine (see Chapter 5) wanders through pine and birch woods at a distance from the house (Figure 10.4). The pairs of trunks—birch on the left, pine on the right—provide a feeling of entrance into this woodland. The fact that the path curves rather than goes straight hides the eventual destination, and that is what draws you on. As you walk, you animate the woods; tree trunks align and realign; branches overhead move and shift; views appear and disappear; a clump of ferns, a mossy boulder, the bark of a white birch appear at a distance, then you see them up close and finally they disappear as you go around a corner. Without the path, you might have sat motionless in a lawn chair on the edge of the still woods. It's the path that is the teacher. (Take a look at Chapter 17 of this book for help in designing a satisfying woodland path.)

LEAVES

In winter, Willem Wirtz and Cy Roossine live in Palm Beach, Florida, in a small home tucked in with a few other houses at the end of a cul-de-sac. The dominant feature of their garden and home is a massive *Ficus benjamina* that towers over a secluded pool garden that Wirtz and Roossine created a few years ago.

When making this intimate, private garden out of what was wholly visible space to passing motorists, Wirtz wanted to create a feeling that the 20-by-30-foot wooden decking at the center was the floor of an outdoor living room. The walls would be shrubs: scheffleras, oleanders, crotons, gardenia, areca palms, grapefruit, avocado and mango trees, and a 12-foot-high pencil cactus. The ceiling would be the huge ficus branches that arched 20 feet overhead.

Wirtz and Roossine were in their seventies when they created the hidden garden, so the path to the garden had to be easy and inexpensive to install and maintain. They solved the problem by working with rather than against nature. Wirtz designed a gently curving, 30-foot-long, 3-foot-wide path

FIGURE 10.4: In the late Thomas Hall's garden near Acadia National Park on the coast of Maine. *The lawn path through the lower section of the Hall garden turns into a pine needle path at the stand of firs, birches and interrupted ferns.*

so that no part of the wooden decking could be seen from the public concrete walkway, and then he covered the earth of the path with leaves from the ficus tree.

We were sitting on the deck one February noontime enjoying lunch when Wirtz pointed out the practicality of using the ficus leaves for the surface of the path. He noted that once the garden was planted, all he had to do was rake the leaves from under the tree onto the unplanted soil and he had a path and a surface material. If he had used cut stone, brick, gravel, anything other than those leaves that fall year round from the tree, he'd be forever sweeping leaves.

> And using those leaves for the surface of our path helps with housekeeping, too. Every afternoon, I sweep the leaves from the wooden deck right onto the path and every now and again rake them along it to renew the surface. So I really never have any maintenance chores to speak of to keep that path looking good. And weeds rarely appear because it is so shady.

The same would be true of a pine needle path in Maine, a redwood needle path in California, and a maple leaf path in Vermont.

He also pointed out the aesthetic appeal of the solution. From where we sat, we could see the leaves all around the trunk of the massive tree, under all the shrubs and trees that screened the garden and the leaves at the end of the path. As Wirtz said, "It all holds together quite nicely, doesn't it?"

One problem does arise from the color of the leaves, however. Because they are brown and thus absorb rather than reflect light at night, this path as a visual clue disappears after sunset, whereas a lighter colored material such as a pale gray or beige gravel would remain more visible. Wirtz came up with some solutions: In addition to a soft incandescent light that drifts down from lighting very high in the ficus, he currently has 4-to-5-foot white poinsettias flanking the entrance that will make an opening statement for several months. Along the length of the path, he used potted white impatiens to help identify the path in the evening. Splashy spathophyllums—or any white flowering plants—along the path retain their visibility at night and help guide evening visitors on their way into the garden.

TRODDEN EARTH

Another example of a woodland path is on the Bloedel Reserve on Bainbridge Island near Seattle, Washington (Figure 10.5). On what is now public land but was once owned by the Bloedel family, a path leads from the driveway to a formal pool area, but both are obscured at the path entrance by dense plantings. Your attention is drawn, therefore, to the mosses and ferns growing up the trunks of the alders and red cedars left from earlier logging and along this irresistible walkway.

The trodden earth path is the one that is the most ancient, the most natural of all. It is also the one least used in the garden proper, the one that is at the bottom of the hierarchy of paving materials. It is the alternative to the pine needle path when you want to go down or across a slope, because, unless it has just rained, it is rarely slippery. It is the path just over the fence into the woods. It is the path into the mystery of the natural world. The trodden earth path may well have been first etched out by cows, horses or sheep that wandered across a meadow, under an old apple tree and on into woodland (Figure 10.6).

THIS TRODDEN EARTH PATH wandering across a meadow at the Winkworth Arboretum in England, like all the others in this chapter, draws little attention to itself, or the hand of the designer. Whether covered with bark mulch, pine needles, leaves, or made from the bare earth, these are natural, anonymous paths far from the house. They are the least insistent and perhaps the most irresistible, in part because they are timeless. ஃ

FIGURE 10.6: At Winkworth Arboretum in Sussex, England. *This trodden earth path could well have been made by sheep or cows. It wanders under the flowering apple tree and across the sloping field of English bluebells and is as natural as the landscape through which it passes.*

PART III

Making the Path

Introduction

Wᴴɪʟᴇ Pᴀʀᴛs I ᴀɴᴅ II of this book were written to inspire your thoughts about design, this section is more practical. Part III tells you how to determine where paths might go, what materials you should use for the surface, and how you can install those materials yourself. Chapter 18 gives you specifics for planting between the paving materials, along the sides of your paths or along or within steps. Before getting into the specifics of how to lay various paths, however, be certain to read the following background information. It takes you through the sequence of questions you need to answer and the steps you need to follow to determine what materials to use where.

INITIAL QUESTIONS TO ANSWER

In considering which material or materials to use on a new path, there are a number of questions you should ask yourself about your existing property:

1. What clues are provided by the materials or style of your house, out-buildings, existing pathways or steps already within the garden that can help you choose the materials and proportions of the new paths?
2. What clues does the purpose of the path offer regarding the material you should choose for the walking surface? Do you want to move purposefully along the path to get from A to B, or is it a path where the pace should be slow, circuitous or contemplative?
3. How does the mood in one part of the garden differ from another? What impact does that have on the materials you should choose and the way you will make the transition between the materials? Might a gate or some other form of entrance help?
4. What impact will your choice of paving materials in one path have on your choice elsewhere in the garden, so that you don't end up with paths that feel unrelated to one another?
5. What are you prepared to invest, both in time and money, for installation and maintenance? How confident do you feel to do part or all of the work yourself?
6. What special skills do you or workmen in your area have? Are there especially skilled stonemasons, bricklayers or people who work well with cement?
7. What indigenous and relatively inexpensive materials are readily available?
8. What impact does weather or climate in your area have on your choice of paving, and the base on which the paving will be laid? (Where snowfall is

a consideration, keep in mind that some surfaces are easier to shovel than others.)

9. How can you use the properties of different materials to help you make smooth transitions from one garden area to another?

A CASE STUDY

Here is an example of a sequence of thought that will determine where a path will go, what material it will be made of, and how plantings can be used to make the path lead you through a satisfying space. Let's say that you have a 15-foot-long path that's now made of individual concrete pavers acting as stepping-stones that runs between the kitchen door and the side door of the garage. The gaps between them are trodden lawn, and you've always felt they looked awfully pedestrian, awfully practical. There's an inexplicable curve in the path that no one in the family pays any attention to, so the lawn across the curve is worn to a frazzle. The house and the garage are white clapboard. When you are half way along that concrete paver path you can look down a trodden lawn path between the house and garage to see just a corner of the cut bluestone terrace and the lawn at the back of the house.

Here are the options for paving materials, in the order of the listing in Part II.

- Cut stone, particularly bluestone is a possibility, especially since some already exists in the back, and once it's down it's easily maintained.
- Small stones built up to a paved surface are a possibility, too, but weeding between the cracks might require a good deal of time, and the surface might make it tough to shovel snow.
- Brick is a possibility, but the gaps between bricks can get weedy, and in shade they might become mossy and slippery. But still, brick is so warm-looking, easy to walk on, and simple to lay tight to reduce weeding.
- Lawn would be worn away in no time; the area is too shady.
- Concrete is too plain, but very practical. Embedded with pebbles? Who would take time to look at it there? Concrete pavers are a possibility, though.
- Stepping-stones are possible only if they're very large and you don't have to think about where to put your feet.
- Wood is a possibility, but only if sunken to ground level because you have to get the lawn tractor through the area weekly so you can mow the back lawn.
- Gravel would track into the house and ruin the floors, and although you don't mind weeding, you don't want to do it in a practical path like this one.
- Crushed stone or peastone is impossible to shovel, and anyway, it would break up and be tracked into the house. Outside, the little pieces would get scuffed around; only edging, which you don't want here, would hold the material in place.
- Wood chips, pine needles or any soft loose materials would never work, for all kinds of reasons.

So here are the possibilities: bluestone; brick; fieldstones built up to a stone carpet; wood, but only if sunken to ground level so the lawn tractor can get over it; concrete pavers, but organized differently than what's there now. But there's one last question to ask. Could these materials be mixed in some way to create a path that would be practical and pleasing to the eye?

As you begin narrowing the list of possibilities—the beauty of brick would be lost in this practical site, you don't really want concrete pavers there, large stepping-stones would require professional help and be costly—other thoughts surface, and one of them turns out to open up your way of thinking, and it has to do with getting the lawn tractor out to the back another way. All you have to do is move the compost pile behind the garage to make room for a simple gravel service path so you could get the lawn tractor to the back lawn that way.

With that in mind, your imagination takes off. A slightly raised wooden walkway—maybe even covered—might look great between the house and garage. It would be largely maintenance-free, would provide cover from rain and snow, would literally and visually link the two wooden buildings, and the uprights would be fine supports for the five-leaved akebia vines you've wanted for years. You and your spouse are both good with woodworking tools, and you don't argue too much when working together.

Then bluestone could be used as a cross path from the driveway up to the wooden walkway, and from the other side and around back to the bluestone sitting area, thus visually tying the two areas together. And then, you thought, all that scraggly lawn could be taken up on either side of the new path between the garage and house and planted with *Vinca minor* and fern or even taller shrubs and maybe even a white birch or two so that you couldn't even see out back, and the new bluestone path would beckon you and your visitors. You'd be walking through a garden instead of on beaten lawn. And then you start thinking about how you could make the transition from that bluestone path and terrace out into the new beds you've planned for the back lawn, and pretty soon you're getting graph paper out to redesign your whole property. And that *is* the way a path, any path, ripples out to affect what you thought were unrelated elements of the garden.

So, after consultation with the family, it's decided. You'll all construct a raised and covered wooden walkway between the house and garage. The uprights will be painted white to echo the color of the two existing buildings, and will frame views of the new garden between the garage and house. The roof will be cedar shakes, the decking will be western unpainted cedar, and the handrails will also be unpainted cedar. You'll set large rectangular cut bluestone pieces down as stepping-stones from the driveway to the raised wooden walkway and the same material will be used to construct steps up to and down from the wooden decking. The bluestone steps will then continue out back. You'll take all the lawn up between the house and garage and plant shade-loving shrubs, maybe even a couple of trees and a variety of ground covers on either side of the path.

Now comes the question of how to lay the bluestone pieces. Like any paving materials in the next chapter, they will need good drainage so they don't heave in those areas where winter frosts are prevalent and so they don't get soggy or slippery or shift when stepped on. Following is a formula for the ideal foundation for all the paths, including the bluestone path mentioned above. You will have to decide, given the nature of your soil, your climate, and how fussy you are, which variation on this theme you will choose to properly support your path.

THE BASIC FOUNDATION

Preparing the base is one of the most important parts of creating a path. It is never seen, but it is what will assure a long lasting trouble-free path. If the base is carefully established with such inert materials as crushed stone, gravel and sand, fewer weeds intrude, drainage is assured and paving materials aren't wallowing in mud. Thus year-to-year maintenance is needed to reset paving heaved by frost.

If you live in an area where the ground freezes in the winter, such as New England, or areas where soils expand during the wet season and contract during the dry season, such as parts of California, you will need to be especially careful about the base you create. Dig down a foot or more to see how freely the soil drains. Heavy topsoil or clay will drain slowly and require deeper base preparation with crushed rock and gravel; sand or gravel will drain quickly and won't require much if any amending. You also have to consider how frequently you and others will walk on the path, what kind of equipment, if any, the path will have to support, and what kind of a person you are. If you are happy to make adjustments to a path periodically in order to save on a lot of difficult up-front work, then don't worry about deep excavation and backfilling. If you're the kind of person who wants everything just right, then make the best job of it. In any event, here is the theme; you choose the variation on it, and that variation may well be different for every path you lay.

First, excavate to a depth of 10 to 12 inches and a little more than the desired width of the path. Shovel the soil right into a wheelbarrow, so you can use it elsewhere in the garden: to fill low spots in the lawn, to build up the compost pile or to store under plastic for later use in transplanting.

Backfill with gravel or, if the drainage is poor, 4 to 6 inches of 1½-inch crushed stone. If the drainage is particularly poor, first lay PVC perforated pipe at the bottom and along the center of the trench with the holes down and the blue line of print up, aligning section to section. The end of the drain can come out to daylight somewhere along the side of the path with a 45- or 90-degree angle section; a grating piece should be put on the open end of the pipe to prevent small animals from crawling inside.

If you laid gravel, wet, tamp and lay over it whatever thickness of sand will be necessary so that the surface of your paving material will be flush with adjacent soil. If you put large crushed stone down, lay porous ground cloth over the stone, and then spread 2 inches of gravel on top of the cloth, wet and tamp. Then spread a bed of sand to whatever depth will be necessary to bring the surface level of the paving material flush with, or just slightly above, existing ground levels.

This is a generic foundation for all paths. If there are any differences that arise because of particular paving materials, those differences will be made clear in the individual chapters. Once you have laid the foundation, you need to decide on whether or not you need to lay edging.

EDGING

Certain materials, particularly small-scale ones such as brick, cobble, granite setts, concrete paving bricks or loose materials like peastone and gravel, may well require edging to keep the material in place. If you raise the edging a few inches above the surface of the path, it will keep soil in adjacent beds from being eroded onto the surface of the path, whether by hoeing or the action of rain or sprinklers.

If you want a simple, unadorned look, use the same material for the surface and the edging: Bricks on end create a handsome edge for a brick path; bluestone on edge along either side of a bluestone path makes a fine, clean line and if raised as much as 6 or 8 inches, or even more, can simultaneously form low retaining walls for adjoining beds.

But consider also that paths and edging of different materials can be very interesting. Blue-gray, rounded river stones edging a path of cut bluestone would offer an interesting contrast of form; large, irregularly shaped flat stones can be used to edge gravel or lawn; brick can be used to edge cut bluestone; redwood can be used to edge bark mulch. The best way to decide whether to mix materials or not is to obtain samples of the materials you're considering, and lay them out right in your garden, paying attention to nearby materials such as brick walls, wooden or stone outbuildings, or fieldstone walls.

STEPS

Steps should also be considered before you begin to lay the path. In general, outdoor steps should have wider treads (the part you step on) and shorter risers (the vertical distance between treads) than indoor steps. Thomas Church wrote in his *Gardens Are for People,* "There are few rules that can't be broken with delightful results, but this is one to respect: twice the riser plus the tread must equal 26 inches. So, if you want a 4-inch riser you need an 18-inch tread, and all steps should have a ⅛-to-¼-inch pitch included in the riser dimension to shed water."

Willem Wirtz, a garden and lighting designer in his early 80s, concurs: "You cannot trifle with steps, especially when it comes to the elderly. You *have* to be careful. Body rhythms demand certain things that you cannot tamper with. You cannot be free just to do what's pretty."

WITH THE WIDELY ACCEPTED RULES as expressed by Church in mind, you can create steps from cut or irregularly edged stones, stepping-stones, brick, wood and practically any of the hard materials discussed in Part II. While it is usually best to use the same materials for paths and steps because of the coherence that results, that is not always feasible or desirable. For example, a brick pathway with thyme between the joints will not look good leading up to brick steps that have to be mortared. The steps will look rigid in comparison to the more relaxed planted path. It is best, then, to change the material altogether; you might construct the risers from large stones or wooden ties, which in turn retain brick treads. Some of the bricks can then be left out and soil pockets can be created in which plants can be set, so the mood of the steps relates to the mood of the pathway. ❧

Chapter Eleven

The Cut Stone Path and Stone Carpet

T YPICALLY, SQUARE OR RECTANGULAR cut bluestone or sandstone walk-ways are associated with the geometry of houses or buildings, and are more often than not straight rather than curved, though softer cut stones such as limestones, sandstones or bluestones can be shaped to make a curve with a mason's scribe.

There are several types of cut stone available across America. In the North-east, Pennsylvania bluestone is readily available. It is dark gray, though it can sometimes have a rusty red wash or streaking from iron deposits within it. Bluestone, and the various sandstones available in the West, have a texture that assures a good grip by the sole of your shoe. Slate and marble cut stones are also available, but while both make handsome walkways, they are so smooth they can become slippery when wet or mossy. Slate should be avoided altogether as a paving material; it is slick wet or dry, it sloughs off at the edges, or even on the surface over time.

Be aware that cut stones can reflect or retain heat more efficiently than rougher fieldstones. White marble, for example, stays cool because it reflects the sun's rays; bluestone, being darker, absorbs the heat and makes an area hotter and a little less comfortable for bare feet during the midday sun.

FACING PAGE: **Part of a New Hampshire garden.**

TOOLS AND MATERIALS

Wooden stakes, string and two hoses

Straight-nosed spade to cut the edge

A round-pointed shovel for excavating and spreading material

A wheelbarrow

A metal tamper or a piece of 2x4 at least 4 feet long

A rubber mallet for tamping each stone in place

A 4-foot level or a smaller level and a truly straight 8-foot 2x4

If you need to cut stone:

A Skil-saw or circular saw with a diamond or masonry blade

A masonry bit and a spare

A 2x4x8 piece of lumber

A dust mask, and eye and ear protection

A carbide steel mason's scribe

A cement trowel, if you'll be setting any stone in concrete, along with

A cement mixing trough and a shovel

Sand, purchased by the cubic yard, for cement mixing or underlaying

Gravel, with no stones larger than 1-inch diameter, purchased by the cubic yard

Flat stone, quarried or cut, purchased for between two and three dollars a square foot and typically between 1 and 2 inches thick

Optional: (if using concrete as a base or as grouting) pigment for mortar used in the joints between the bricks

Wire reinforcing mesh and concrete mix if creating a concrete base

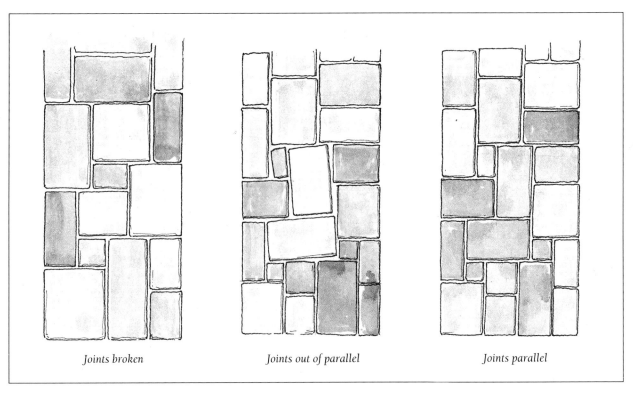

Cut Stones of similar size

DESIGN

Determine the direction and width of the path and, if on a slope, the position and width of steps

To help you visualize how such a path will look, lay it out initially with stakes and cord. Try to have the shapes relate to nearby lines of the house or outbuildings. Consider a 4- or even 5-foot-wide path that might, at some appropriate point, widen to form a patio, terrace or entrance court. Where steps might go, use sections of 2x6 lumber to help you visualize them.

Refine the design on paper

Once you have decided on the exact layout, measure it and make a scaled drawing of the pathway. Because bluestone, for example, is manufactured in 6-inch modules, use graph paper with ⅛-inch squares, each square representing 3-or-6-square inches of stone, depending on the size of the walkway and paper you're working with.

Before deciding on a final design, consider the whole range of possibilities, from using only two or three sizes of stones set in a repeating pattern the length of the walkway, to using any number of sizes to form a more complex patterned or random surface. But whatever you do, don't set small stones on the edge because they more easily dislodge underfoot than do large stones. If you need small stones to fill in the design, set them in the interior.

It is important that no stones are laid so that their joints form a cross because the design will appear to "break" at that point. Lay stones so that their joints form a 'T' or an 'L' and the design will remain coherent. The first and last stones, or any stones that mark a juncture to a secondary or side path, should be the largest stones in the walkway. These threshold stones are important cues in a design, and they are the first to set on your paper layout.

Joints broken	Joints out of parallel	Joints parallel

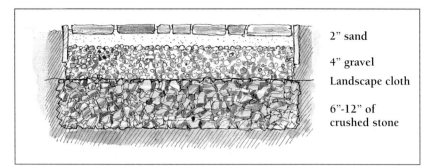

2" sand

4" gravel

Landscape cloth

6"-12" of
crushed stone

Once you know the number and dimensions of the stones you'll need, you can place an order with your supplier. It's a lot easier to design beforehand with paper than it is to try to create a walkway on the spot with randomly chosen stones.

MAKING A CUT STONE WALKWAY
Preparing the Base

The standard base for a walkway as outlined on page 142 would certainly suffice for the construction of a major cut stone walkway. There is a heftier alternative. The base could be set in a 2-foot-deep trench. Place 14 inches of 1½-inch crushed stone in the bottom of the trench; then 3 inches of 1-inch crushed stone; then 3 inches of ⅜-inch crushed stone over which you lay landscape cloth. Over that go 2 inches of sand on which the 2-inch-thick stone is laid. A variation on this theme is to dig an 18-inch trench, lay a foot of 1½-inch crushed stone in the trench, and then put down a layer of hefty woven plastic weed barrier fabric covered in turn with 4 inches of sand or stone dust. The cut stone is then set on top of that (Figure 11.1).

It's easy to read a sentence such as "Excavate to a depth of 2 feet and then lay 16 inches of 1½-inch crushed stone the length of the walkway," but it's another thing to do it. That's a lot of trench, and crushed stone is very difficult to shovel. If you want to create such a sound base for your walkway, hire a contractor with a small backhoe and dump truck to do the trenching and backfilling with the crushed stone, drainage fabric and sand. Then you can lay the stone; the easier, fun part of the job.

Cutting the Stone

If you are using relatively soft bluestone, sandstone or limestone, you may discover as you proceed that some of the stones purchased aren't shaped right. You can make straight cuts easily; curves are another matter and are best left to professionals. Use a circular saw equipped with a masonry cut-off wheel or a diamond blade and a board as a cutting guide. You don't have to cut all the way through the stone unless you are just cutting off an inch or so. Simply score the stone with the blade to a depth of about half an inch. Then lay the stone atop the board so that the cut is uppermost and parallel to the edge of the board. Push on the center of the section you want to remove and it will snap clean along the score line. You will find that the masonry blade does wear down as you make cuts, so you will have to adjust the depth of the blade after each cut. When cutting, be certain to wear a dust mask and eye and ear protection.

Cut Stones of similar size set parallel

Rectangular stones set across the path

Another way to cut relatively soft stones is to use a mason's scribe. This is a light, sharp, carbide-tipped, two-bladed instrument. Scribe a line three or four times across the stone and then rap the piece you want to break off with a blunt cold chisel along the score line and it will snap.

Laying the Stone

If a path of cut stone is leading to or from a building, start work next to the building and work toward the other end. If the path is between two buildings, start the path at one end and work toward the other. If steps along the way are required because of too steep a grade, start at the bottom and work toward the top.

Start by choosing one of the largest stones to form the threshold stone, one that will promise sound footing. (Don't step on the stones until they are completely supported underneath; many kinds of 2-inch thick stones will readily snap underfoot if not properly supported.) Roughly place the large stone first and then try out a few other stones near it to get the feel of how they will look together and how far apart they should be. If you want a tightly set feeling, they can be butted one to the next, but given that the cutting of the stones in the manufacturing process is rarely perfect, it might be best to leave ¼ to ½ inch between stones to assure room for adjustment and drainage.

Once you have roughly set five or six stones in place, twist them down into the sand until they are level and in the correct position. Then tap each stone several times with the rubber mallet to set it firmly in place and check with a spirit level to be certain they are level. As you progress, continually use your level atop a 5- or 6-foot perfectly straight 2x4 laid across several stones. In this way, any inaccuracy in levelling one or two stones won't be compounded when you use them as reference points for adjoining stones. When you are finished, spread sand over the whole walkway, sweep it into the joints, and then set a sprinkler on the path and let it run for half an hour

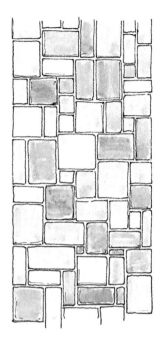

Cut stones set in random rectangular way

FIGURE 11.2: Cut stone paving and edging.

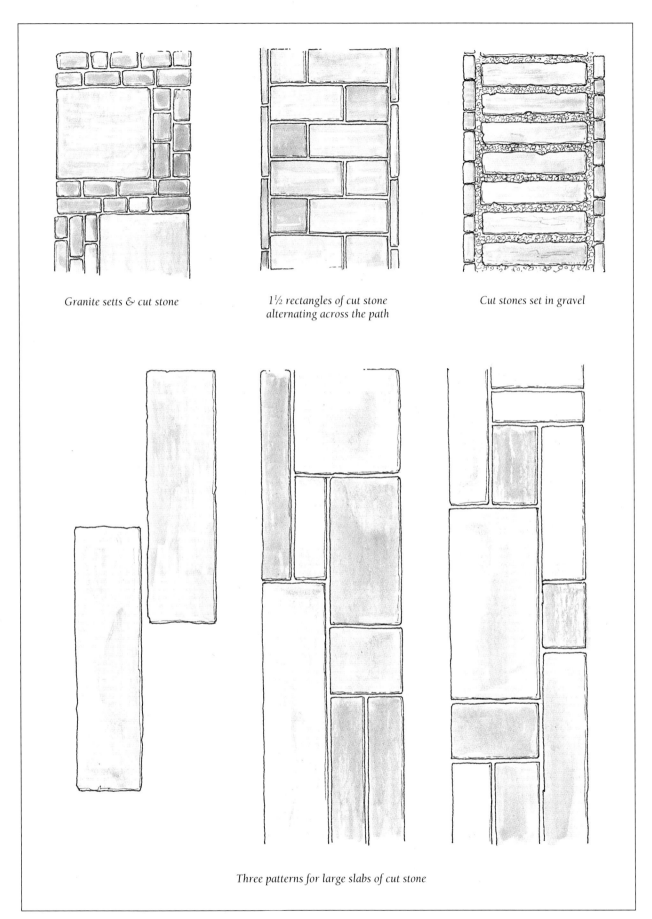

Granite setts & cut stone

*1½ rectangles of cut stone
alternating across the path*

Cut stones set in gravel

Three patterns for large slabs of cut stone

to settle the sand. You may have to backfill the gaps a few times before everything is finally settled. Leave about a half-inch gap between the top of the stone and the sand, so the sand won't scatter onto the surface of the stone, end up on the soles of people's shoes and thus on your floors and carpets.

Edging Cut Stone Walkways

If the cut stone path runs along the edge of a perennial bed, it might be a good idea to use the same stone set on edge to create a low retaining border that will separate soil from paving surface. In this way soil cannot leach out onto the surface when you weed, or during heavy rains. Set foot-wide stones on edge, so they are 3 or 4 inches above finish grade. That edging will not only hold soil in place but also create a neat edge to the path (Figure 11.2).

Steps

Start with the bottom step. Build up risers and treads with the same stone used for paving the walkway, or use other complementary stone or brick being certain to follow the dictum: twice the riser plus the tread must equal 26 inches. Lay sections of stone to form the face and sides of the riser. Then backfill the resultant space with either crushed stone or stone dust, not sand—rain water will wash it out—and tamp it down to form a solid base for the tread stone. Use your level to be sure the step slopes ever so slightly forward

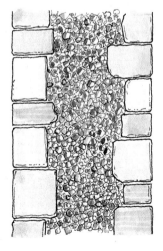

Cut stone & gravel

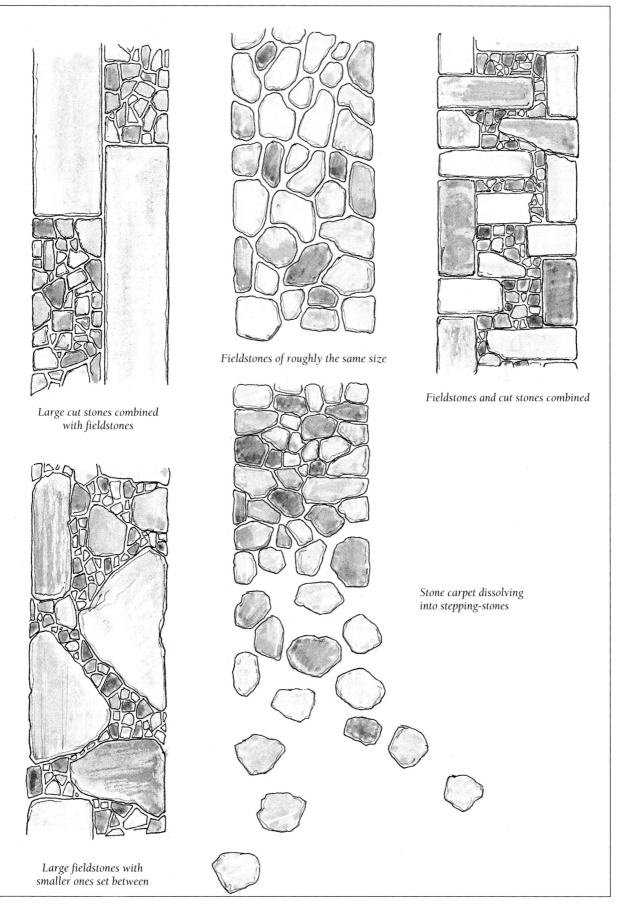

*Large cut stones combined
with fieldstones*

Fieldstones of roughly the same size

Fieldstones and cut stones combined

*Stone carpet dissolving
into stepping-stones*

*Large fieldstones with
smaller ones set between*

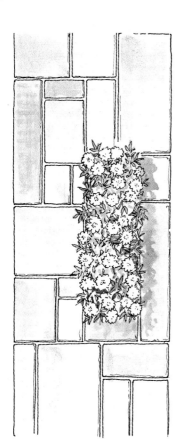

Planting bed in path

so that drainage is certain. Cut stone steps should have a slight overhang or nosing where riser meets tread so that a shadow forms just under the edge of the step. This shadow tends to emphasize the horizontal and mark the steps. Cut stone steps can also have green or planted risers, as in the case of the steps up to the twin gazebos at the Hidcote Manor Gardens in England, where the risers are covered with *Cotoneaster congestus,* kept clipped throughout the season.

Setting Cut Stone on a Concrete Base

If cut stones are to be laid with concrete joints, which are appropriate for a very soft, brittle stone like Crab Orchard stone from Tennessee, then

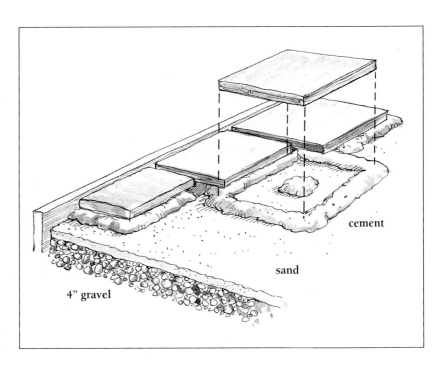

cement

sand

4" gravel

FIGURE 11.3: Stone set in concrete using mortar spotting.

the base of the walkway should be concrete. Excavate the soil to at least 10 inches, and put in a 6-inch layer of crushed stone or quickly draining gravel. Cover with a wire mesh for reinforcing and then a 3-inch layer of concrete; a good proportion for such a foundation would be 1 part cement, 3 parts sand and 5 parts gravel. After the concrete has set overnight, a thin coat of concrete should be spread over it and the cut stones set in the thin layer. When the stones are set, the joints can be mortared. When laying a colored stone such as bluestone, Arizona sandstone or a reddish Colorado sandstone, tint the concretized grout with a coloring agent to blend the color of the grout and the stone. That way the gaps will not be in stark contrast.

Another technique for laying cut stone is called mortar spotting (Figure 11.3). A large dab of concrete is laid where the center and four sides of the stone will be. The stone is set atop the concrete and pressed down.

One way to ensure stability and drainage and prevent monotony is to mortar the inner third of the walkway but leave the outer thirds set in sand or gravel. The water from the mortared section can drain to either side and disappear.

STONE CARPETS OF FIELDSTONE

Stone carpets are made from randomly sized and shaped stones that are gathered from fields, walls or quarries. They can be either formal or informal depending on how linear their edges are. The best material for such walkways is flat—mica schists from the Northeast, randomly shaped bluestone from Pennsylvania or sandstones from Arizona or Colorado. The size of the pieces you lay for the walkway can vary anywhere from only a few inches across to three, four or even five feet, if you can find and handle such large pieces. The smaller the pieces are, the firmer the base on which you lay them has to be.

Designing the Path

Stone carpets can vary from 18 inches, that is, a ribbon path snaking through beds, lawn or woodland, to a 4-to-5-foot-wide walkway broad enough for two people to walk side by side, perhaps between formal perennial beds.

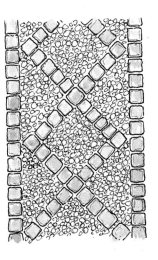

½ setts (cobbles) in gravel

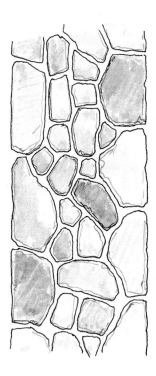

Stone carpet with large and small fieldstones

Because stone carpets can be laid on flat or gently sloping land, consider a wide variety of places in your garden; looking back at Chapter 4 will help you see where they will make most sense. Once you have decided where the path should go, define the path by pounding stakes into the ground and tying strings between them to determine the exact width and length of the path. If you want to create broad curves, use hoses to suggest the outer edges of the path and then set stakes every 5 or 6 feet to record the edges. Consider, too, that the edges need not be perfectly straight or curved. You can set the edges of some stones a foot or more into adjacent beds to create an irregular, informal edge.

Laying the Stones

Base preparation, as described on page 147, is the same for this stone as for cut stone.

The most important element of designing and laying a satisfying stone carpet is to be sure the shapes of the stones speak to one another: The convex of one should fit into the concave of the next. Lay out all your stones on the nearby lawn or on tarps so you can see all their shapes. Then start trying out various combinations. Take your time. See it as a jigsaw puzzle, or as Zen and the Art of Stone Carpets. At the path site, start by laying the edge stones along the strings to create a pair of clean, straight or curved lines; at first, simply set the stones on top of the sand so you can easily change your mind. Once you've got 5 or 6 feet of edges done, fill in between them to create interesting and complementary shapes. And don't be afraid to shape stones with your mason's hammer to make them work well together.

Once you have a few feet just the way you want it, set the stones permanently into the sand an inch or so above the grade of adjacent soil for good drainage, and then tap with a rubber mallet to settle the stones in place. If you are using flat stone, consult your spirit level frequently; if it's a rougher fieldstone, eyeballing usually suffices .

Gaps Between the Stones

The gaps between individual stones can be determined on site, but the general guideline for a stone carpet is to join them within ½ to ¾ inch of one another. Suffice it to say that the larger the stone, the greater the gap can be. As you proceed, fill the gaps with gravel and then water so as to settle the material around the stones. That will have to be done periodically for a few weeks because rain and people walking on the path will further settle the backfilling. If the color of the joint material in the gaps is similar to that of the stones, the visual emphasis will be on the shape of the whole walkway; if they contrast, the emphasis will be on the shapes and patterns of the walkway stones. If you want to plant thyme or moss between them, backfill with a mixture that is equal parts topsoil and peat. This will give plants organic matter for their roots. Vertical edging is rarely put in place with a stone carpet walkway because the strict edging would conflict with this informal style of paving.

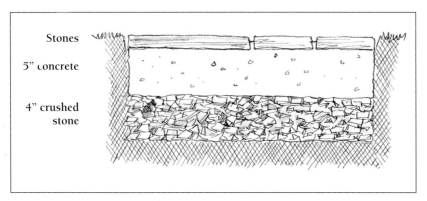

Stones

5" concrete

4" crushed
stone

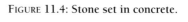

Laying Stone Carpets in Concrete

Because smaller stones can mean an unstable edge, walkways built up with many small stones should be set in concrete or crusher dust. Depending on the ability of your soil to drain, excavate to a depth of around 1 foot and lay down 6 inches of 1½-inch crushed stone. Then set thin edging wood in place, held by stakes pounded into the outside of the wood. Pour a 3-to-4-inch concrete slab. Let it set, leaving the uppermost surface rough. When it has set, you are ready to lay down ¾ inch of wet concrete on which you lay the stones that will make the finished surface of your walkway (Figure 11.4).

The joints could be filled with mortar that has been colored with a pigment that will blend with the color of the stone. The grout surface should be at least half an inch below the surface of the stone to create well-defined shadows.

In areas of the country where no frost stays in the soil, you can lay the stones directly on the soil, without preparing a base, but to be certain the stones will hold in place, set them in a bed of concrete poured right onto the soil; then pack the concrete in under the stone and around the edges. Grout the stones with the same concrete mix, wait 20 minutes or so, and then sponge the excess off the surface of the stones.

If you want plants between the stones, leave a gap at least 2 inches deep and wide between the stones, wait until the next day when the concrete under and around the stones has hardened, and then backfill the gaps with a loamy sand. Chapter 18 will give you lots of ideas for plant choice.

THE MAINTENANCE OF THESE two styles of paving are quite different, and you may want to take this into consideration when deciding which of the two to install. Tightly fitting cut stones leave little room for weeds to get established, whereas the soil-filled gaps between stones in a stone carpet can quickly give rise to unsightly weeds. ꙮ

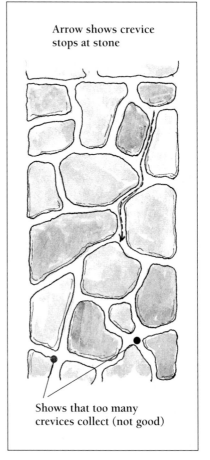

Arrow shows crevice
stops at stone

Shows that too many
crevices collect (not good)

Chapter Twelve
The Brick Path

BRICK WALKWAYS ARE OFTEN associated with brick homes or brick walls that might be near or well away from the house. Their width is often determined by their placement. A brick walk to the front door might be 4 or even 5 feet wide whereas a path along the side of the house might be only 2 or 3 feet wide. Paths that meander through the garden can be narrow or broad, straight or curved, depending on the mood you want to create. The mood created by the path is also determined by the type of brick you choose.

DESIGN
Choosing Brick

Bricks are divided into two categories: facing and paving. Facing bricks are typically for interior use or the outside walls of buildings and should not be used in the garden. They are made of softer, less dense clay than pavers, were fired at lower temperatures for shorter periods of time, and thus more readily absorb water and crack in those parts of the country where winter temperatures regularly go below freezing.

Paving bricks are usually manufactured in modules; that is, they are measured in full inches, typically 2 inches thick, 4 inches wide and 8 inches long. They are considerably less absorbent than facing bricks because they have been fired at much higher temperatures, and the clay from which they are made is denser.

When choosing the individual paver, consider the following: whether you will use uniformly colored brick or colors that are slightly different brick to brick; whether you will use old or new ones; what color and texture you want, and whether the brick should have a sand coating or not; whether you will lay them on edge or flat; what their pattern will be in the path; what the width and depth of the joints, and the material in the joints will be; whether or not you will use the same brick as edging.

Texture is an especially important consideration. Some bricks are finished with a smooth surface, while others have been sand-coated. Sometimes only the sides are smooth; sometimes, the tops and bottoms are. If you are making a brick walkway in shade, be sure to get sand-coated or highly textured brick. With time, mosses and algae invariably form on all brick, so the grainier and rougher the surface at the outset, the better.

Color is important, too. Bricks come in a wide range of earth tones: reds, browns, tans and grays. If you are laying a patio or walkway, consider the

FACING PAGE: A potager in the Cotswold Hills of England designed by Rosemary Verey.

TOOLS AND MATERIALS

A pair of strong leather gloves
A mason's brick hammer
A level
A rubber mallet
String and stakes for straight edges
Hoses for curved edges
A cutting chisel or cold chisel for rough cuts OR
A rented brick cutter if you want finely cut unusual shapes
A kneeling pad (a piece of pink board or blue board insulation will do)
A broom
A wheelbarrow
A round-nosed spade for excavating
A straight-nosed spade for cutting the edge of the trench
Paving brick, chosen at the suppliers from the variety on hand. (A path typically takes 4½ bricks per square foot, but it will take more if you want fancy cuts that increase waste)
Gravel, sand or stone dust ordered in cubic yards
Optional: (if using concrete as a base or as grouting) pigment for mortar used in the joints between the bricks
Wire reinforcing mesh and concrete mix if creating a concrete base

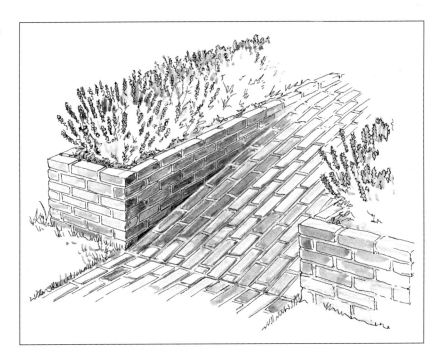

Running bond aligned with path

Offset running bond with bricks on edge

colors of nearby buildings and their shingling, nearby brick walls, or the dominant colors of the plants and their foliage in adjoining gardens. It is best to go to a supplier who has many varieties to offer. Ask for a sample of each color brick you would consider and take them back to your garden and hold them against the building, plants and shingles to see which is the most pleasing. Or, if you have brick left over from the construction of nearby walls or buildings, take some along to get a match or a complementary color.

Sometimes brick has been coated on one or more sides with an impervious ceramic glaze. Don't purchase these for outdoor use. The problem that arises in all climates is called spalling. Being impervious, the glaze will not allow moisture absorbed on unglazed sides to escape. In colder climates, the trapped water freezes, expands, and separates the glaze from the brick. This exposes the softer interior of the brick to weathering and further erosion. In warmer climates, spalling can occur as a result of salt buildup after evaporation; as the salt dries, it crystallizes and expands, again separating the glaze from the body of the brick. Because of this problem of spalling in all climates, it's best not to use glazed brick outdoors or apply any moisture barrier such as paints, sealants or waxes to brick.

Old bricks with patches of old mortar add a rustic, established and charming look to a garden. And once laid, the walkway looks as though it has been there for years. When purchasing old brick, be certain that it is dense and hard and thus suitable for outdoor use. Many old bricks come from the interior walls of demolished buildings and were never intended for exterior use. If you do put soft brick in a garden where winter freezing occurs, the bricks will be in hundreds of flakes in a year. If you do find a good supply of hard, old brick, be sure to order more than you will need because replacement can't always be guaranteed; stockpile a hundred or so in the garage or shed for later use or replacement.

Do It Yourself

Brick is a highly flexible material you can lay yourself. You can vary patterns, using a herringbone or basket-weave pattern for a straight walk and then shifting to running bond to form a juncture in the path. You can change patterns readily to mark the transition in a path, or use a different pattern (or a different material such as cut stone) as you move through a gateway into a different garden space. To further mark transitions, you can combine brick with cobble, bluestone, tile or wood, or use these materials to visually and physically separate the two brick patterns. Brick can also be used to edge an existing perennial border; if enough courses are laid, the edging doubles as a path. Another attribute of brick's flexibility comes from the fact that they can be taken up easily, and different patterns or materials can be added later. Where bricks have been removed, plants can be set in the spaces, breaking the monotony and cooling that part of the surface if it is in full sun. Bricks can even be used to pave small slopes (see below) where you do not want the expense or trouble of installing a retaining wall.

Being small, however, they must be set firmly into place to ensure that they do not shift underfoot. Some material—cut stone, wood, terra-cotta edgers or brick itself on edge or on end—has to contain the edges so the bricks do not move when stepped on.

The Bond or Pattern

The way bricks are arranged in a walkway (or wall) is called the bond, and when it comes to walkways, the decision is primarily aesthetic, as opposed to walls, where the varying strength of bonds is a consideration. When deciding on the pattern, remember that the more intricate the bond, the more cutting the bricks will require, so be certain to keep in mind your will-

Diagonal running bond

Running bond over slopes

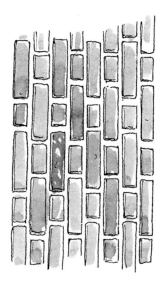

Flemish bond (whole and half bricks)

Whole and half bricks alternately

ingness and ability to cut brick. When paving a large area such as a terrace or patio, keep the pattern simple; the smaller the area, the more appropriate an intricate design. Having said that, I will add that a panel with an intricate pattern within a surround of a simpler pattern is very appealing. To choose a pattern, look at the drawings in this section and read the captions carefully; they will steer you right.

Edgings

The method of edging a brick walkway should also be carefully considered so that when walked on, the edging bricks do not give way. The nature of your soil or backfill will help you decide how strong the edge should be.

Several options are available:

1. Set the length of the edging bricks into the ground so only the end shows and is either flush with the top of the walkway or an inch or so above it. If the bricks are set tightly together in a row, this method will form a strong edge.
2. Set a tightly fitting row of edging bricks flat or on edge but perpendicular to and flush with the surface of the path.
3. Use wooden, pressure-treated ties to edge a straight path. Drive wooden stakes into the ground on the outside of the timber and secure the stake to the timber with galvanized nails. Using standard lumber that is not pressure-treated or naturally long-lasting is a very short-term solution, since the wood will rot in a few years and have to be replaced.
4. Lay the entire path atop a concrete base so no edging is necessary, or at least is optional.

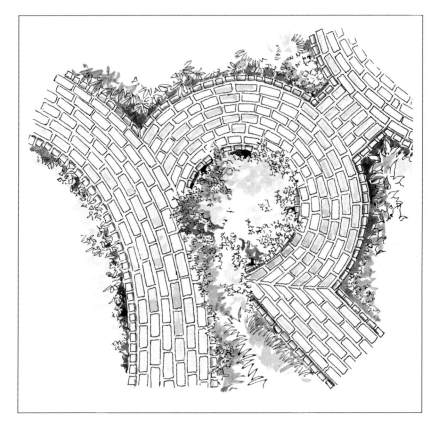

Curves

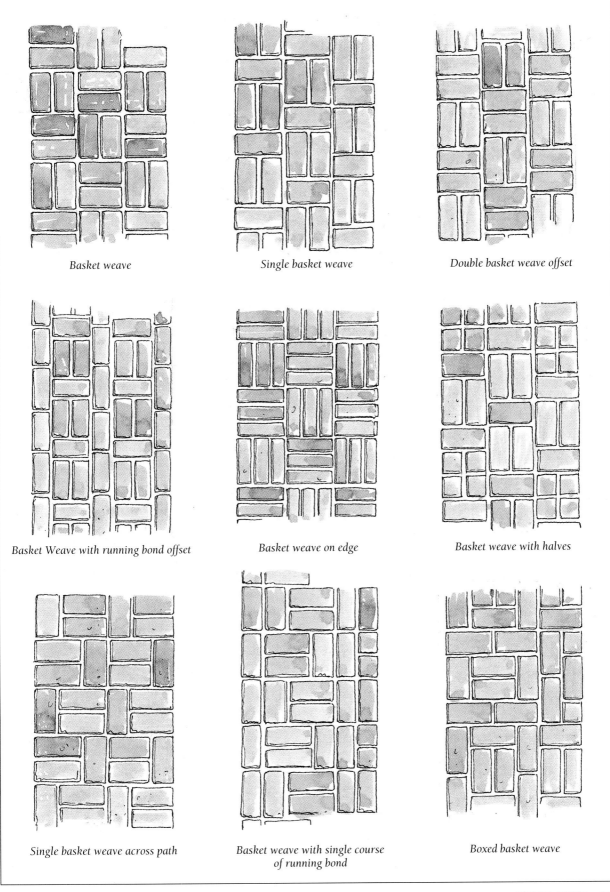

Basket weave

Single basket weave

Double basket weave offset

Basket Weave with running bond offset

Basket weave on edge

Basket weave with halves

Single basket weave across path

Basket weave with single course of running bond

Boxed basket weave

*Running bond across
path with edges flat*

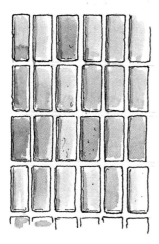

*Stack bond running
with direction of path*

5. Granite setts as an edging material set flat or on edge, parallel or perpendicular to the run of the path.

The Gaps Between the Bricks

Joints with almost no material between them create a tight finish that is most appropriate for a patio or a small garden where formal lines are important. Joints that are ½-inch wide and are filled with sand look more relaxed and are more appropriate for sunny pathways or paving through gardens. Joints as wide as 1 inch are even more relaxed and would be appropriate in naturalized areas of the garden, or on casual paths.

Wide gaps can be filled with a loamy sand and will then support plants to further enhance the relaxed, natural look. Once the path is laid, you can plant moss or any number of thymes. (See Chapter 18 for more ideas.) In England, favorite plants for planting between the gaps of brick (or stone) are lady's mantle (*Alchemilla mollis*) and English daisies (*Erigeron perennis*).

A tighter gap between the bricks can be filled with stone dust and an even smaller gap can be filled with a commercial product called Drypac, which is a sand/cement mix that, once laid down, can be sprinkled with a hose to set the material. Never backfill with dry concrete mix and then water it down because the concrete will splatter or even run onto the brick, dry, and you'll be weeks chipping it off. A mix of cement and a generous amount of sand will suffice, however. Rather than sprinkle with water, let ground moisture work in over time.

Concrete with Brick

In France, the combination of brick and concrete is much more frequently used for paving than it is in America. To create the combination, lay the concrete base (see Chapter 14) and then lay the bricks in a pattern that crisscrosses, or creates a rectangular or diamond-shaped pattern along the path. Once all the brick is in place, go back and fill in the spaces with premixed concrete. A small quantity of reddish pigment might be added to blend the color of brick and concrete together. Terra-cotta tiles can also be laid combined with the brick and cement. Or brick could be laid, the concrete backfilling could be done and then brick dust could be swept over the entire wet concrete surface to blend the two materials.

MAKING A BRICK PATH
Preparing the Base

With brick, the amount of preparation is determined by several variables: Will the path be wide enough for one, two or more people at once? Will small or large equipment have to pass over it? To what degree does the soil under the path freeze and thus heave? How quickly draining is the soil through which the path passes? Have answers to these questions in mind before proceeding.

Professionals in the northern two-thirds of the country, where heavy, slowly-draining soil freezes in the winter, excavate the area for a walkway to a depth of around 12 inches. They then backfill with 8 inches of compacted gravel to ensure good drainage, and cover the compacted gravel with 2 inches of builder's sand and lay the bricks onto that (Figure 12.1). You can certainly

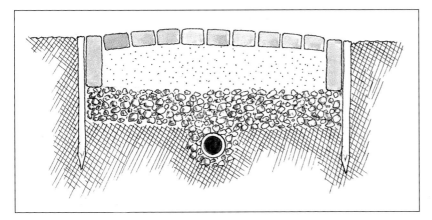

FIGURE 12.1: Cross section brick walk.

be less ambitious and excavate 4 to 6 inches down with a straight-nosed spade and then put down 2 to 4 inches of sand on which the bricks will sit. Just understand that the deeper the gravel/sand foundation, the better the drainage and the less heaving will result where winter freezing is a possibility.

Mike Norris is a stonemason who does much of Ryan Gainey's stone and brickwork in the Atlanta, Georgia, area, where the soil rarely, if ever, freezes. Norris told me that he excavates quickly-draining soil to a depth of only 5 or 6 inches and backfills with 3 inches of sand. He then lays the brick directly onto that base. In more slowly-draining soil such as the red Georgia clay, he lays a 3-or-4-inch mortar pad with reinforcing wire mesh and then returns the next day after the pad has hardened. He pours a thin, 1/2-to-3/4-inch layer atop the pad and then lays the brick on that.

If the soil through which your brick path will run drains slowly, you should build the base so that the surface of the walkway is at least half an inch above the existing grade to assure adequate drainage. Use PVC drainage pipe in poorly drained sites (Figure 12.1.). If you set a brick walkway lower than the adjacent grade, you run the risk of having puddles form every time it rains. In the winter, those puddles will turn to ice in a large part of the country.

Laying the Bricks

If you are going to lay brick in a pattern that will require straight lines of any kind, be sure to pound stakes accurately in the ground along either side of the path, and stretch mason's line between them to establish the edges. Also, set two stakes and line across the path so that you have a guide to laying the brick crossways, too; while bricks are generally the same size, they do differ slightly, and that difference can throw a design off quickly. Reset that pair of stakes and string after every course or repetition of pattern.

Before actually laying the brick, wet the sand or stone dust with a hose, tamp it well and check for level. Then you are ready to lay the brick. Set your knee pad on the wet sand and then set out several bricks to see that the pattern you have in mind will work. Once you have laid a foot or so of the pattern and you feel comfortable with the look and the work the pattern involves, set to it with a will, starting with the edging bricks and then laying the path bricks within them. (See Figure 12.2 for help with a screed.)

Once you have laid a brick, tap it sharply with the rubber mallet to settle it in. Continually use the straight edge of the level to check the alignment

Spanish

of the brick across the path, use the bubble to check the level of the path as it develops.

Once you have completed a section, spread a shovelful of sand, stone dust or a loamy peat/sand mix atop the bricks you've laid, sweep it into the cracks and sprinkle it with a hose to settle it. You may have to repeat this process several times before the cracks are full. As with other paving materials, leave at least half an inch gap between the top of the brick and the surface of the backfilling material, so you won't pick up the sand or stone dust on your shoes and track it into the house.

One alternative you might consider to the perfectly flat path is suggested by the way Ragna Tischler Goddard of Higganum, Connecticut laid her brick paths, and she should know. She set 18,000 bricks herself to form an intricate paving pattern that knits her herb gardens together. The paths are not flat; they arch an inch or so at the center, not only to improve drainage, but also to lift the visitor just that little bit above the adjoining surface.

If you want to create a brick walkway laid in sand, use a different material for steps. Consider using large stones or wooden ties to act as the step, and pave the treads with a row or two of bricks. You could then leave one or two bricks out and backfill the resulting space with soil and plant the space to further soften the step.

Brick on Concrete

If you want to use concrete between the bricks, you should lay a concrete base for the entire path. Excavate to a depth of a foot below finish grade. Lay down 3 inches of crushed stone or freely-draining gravel, depending on how much drainage your soil will require. If you used gravel, wet it and tamp. Lay another 3 inches of gravel and again wet and tamp. Then place wire mesh atop the tamped gravel to prevent the walkway from breaking up over time. It may well do that anyway, but the mesh will slow the process. Then a 3-inch layer of concrete should be laid using a mixture of 1 part cement, 3 parts sand and 5 parts gravel. Once this has set for 24 hours, lay a thin coat of con-

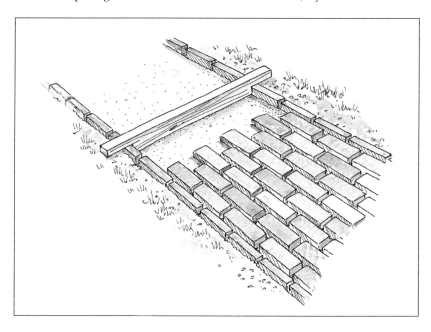

Figure 12.2: Using a screed.

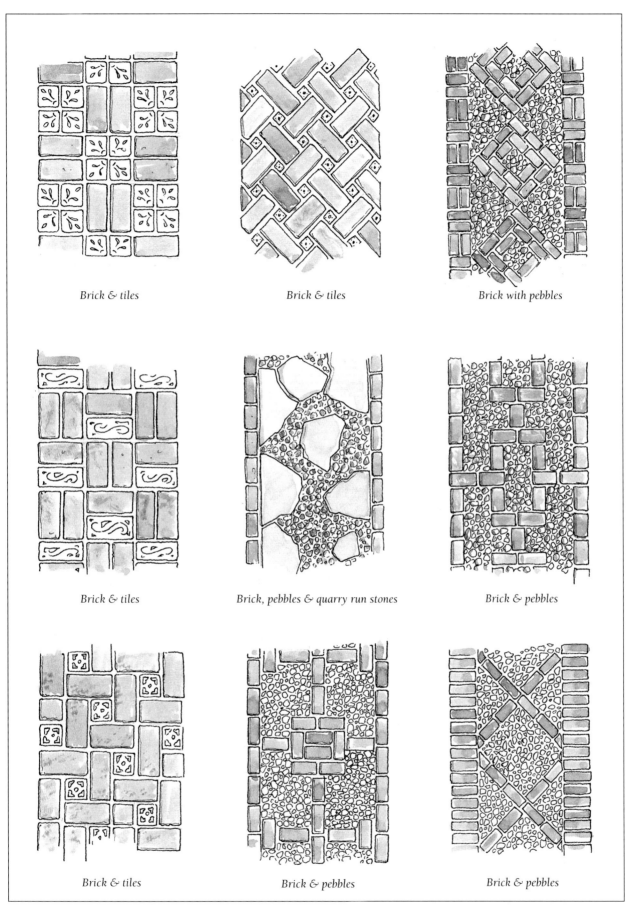

Brick & tiles

Brick & tiles

Brick with pebbles

Brick & tiles

Brick, pebbles & quarry run stones

Brick & pebbles

Brick & tiles

Brick & pebbles

Brick & pebbles

Herringbone

Diagonal herringbone

crete (Thin Set is one commercial product) as a base on which to lay the bricks. If the resulting joints are ¼-inch or less, lay the bricks but don't backfill. Once the whole path has been laid, sweep a mix of 1 part cement and 2 parts sand and then water very gently so that no splatter results. The mix will set in place. If the joints are larger, lay them with the same concrete mix you are using for the base.

When joints between brick are mortared, the recess or depth of the joint is a consideration. The narrower the joint between the bricks, the tighter and more formal is the look. The deeper the joint or recess, the more pronounced is the shadow and therefore the more pronounced is the pattern. The color of the mortar is also important in this regard; the lighter the mortar, the more pronounced it is and therefore the more attention it calls to itself. Pigments can be added to ensure that the color of the brick and mortar are nearly the same or highly-contrasting.

One point to consider is that when you use mortar, you are creating a fixed path that can only be changed with a good deal of effort. By not using concrete, you are keeping many options open, and you will be glad you did if you find that an electrical or plumbing line has to go under your path, or you want to plant within the path or run another material across it.

Cutting Brick

If you have an intricate pattern, or a complex panel in a simpler surrounding pattern, you may want to cut the bricks. One easy method is to use the sharp end of a mason's hammer. Rap the brick several times along the

Brick, cut stone & ground cover

line where you want it to break; then hold the brick sideways in your hand and give it a sharp rap on that same line. Another approach is to use a brick-cutting chisel called a brick set that is as wide as the brick (Figure 12.3). Set the brick on a bed of sand and gently score the brick on all sides where you want it to snap. Then with the brick set's bevelled edge away from you, hit the handle of the chisel sharply with the mason's hammer. If you have many bricks to cut in many different ways, it might make sense to rent a brick cutter or brick saw from a local rental outlet. When cutting brick, be certain to wear gloves, goggles, and ear protection.

FIGURE 12.3: Breaking a brick in half.

Cleaning Old Brick

You may also find you have a lot of old bricks to which plaster is still adhering. If you soak them for a few moments in a tub of water, the mortar will come off more easily and with less dust. Use gentle to moderate blows with the sharp end of a mason's hammer at an oblique angle. (Try not to hit the brick directly on; that is, at a 90-degree angle, because being brittle, the brick may well break.) Use a wire brush to complete the job and then stack them carefully; throw bricks one atop another and many will break.

MAINTENANCE

Before you know it, crabgrass, weeds and Johnny-jump-ups will appear as if by magic even in stone dust. Uproot them immediately by hand, or use a flame gun to burn the seedlings out. There are also specific weeding tools made for maintaining the gaps between bricks. You should accept the fact that plants will end up growing in the gaps. If the path runs through lawn anyway, why not preempt weeds by sowing grass seed, and in that way you can maintain the walkway with a lawn mower (see Figure 3.9).

Once a year you will likely have to sweep more stone dust or sand into the gaps to keep up the look and the solidity of the path. If a section of the walk settles more than another with time, simply lift all the brick in that section, backfill and reset.

OVER TWO OR THREE YEARS, new brick walkways settle into the landscape. Mosses might form in the gaps between them; plants set along the edge flop over onto the bricks, softening the edges. The bricks settle a bit and lose the perfectly flat look they had when first laid. Yellow autumn leaves that fall onto red brick walkways look especially handsome, as do fallen petals from crab apples in the spring. Time works especially well with brick. 🥀

Chapter Thirteen
The Lawn Path

For many years, the American lawn has been a sacrosanct institution, but with a growing ecological awareness, we are beginning to realize that lawns do not have to be part of everyone's garden. If you live in a drought-prone area where lawn only grows if given intense irrigation and maintenance, consider carefully the many alternatives before choosing a lawn path. From southern Florida to Texas, New Mexico, Arizona and a good part of southern California, lawn paths may not be feasible, given the growing concern about water supplies in these areas. In climates more benign for lawns, there are three ways to create a lawn path: laying sod, sowing seed, and cutting a grass path and beds from existing lawn.

Sod gives you instant coverage (and satisfaction). It can be installed almost anytime when the ground is not frozen, though midsummer installations do demand a lot of water. It establishes itself quickly and can be placed on slopes, where it won't wash away as seeded soil might. Being carpet-like, it smothers potential weeds that would sprout if you seeded the path. There are also more and more professionals who have experience laying sod; it certainly was the way of the eighties. At the same time, it is much more costly in terms of initial layout, about 20 to 30 cents per square foot, and there is a limited choice of grasses available from any one supplier.

Seeding a lawn path means that you have an almost unlimited variety of seeds to match soil, site conditions and your own preference. Seed is less expensive to purchase and establish, and it can be sown quickly over a large area. On the other hand, kids can't run on it for at least two or three weeks while you water it daily and intermittently thereafter. Weed and other grass seeds already in the soil also benefit from all your soil preparation and watering and will sprout too. Seeding is more difficult on slopes because of the danger of erosion from rain or overwatering during the time it takes to get established. You are limited to spring and autumn for successful seeding times, and you will usually need to spot-seed areas that don't fill in.

Weighing these pros and cons, you can make your choice. For a path, I use sod. If you are going to lay sod, have all the soil preparation done well ahead of time so that when the sod arrives stacked on pallets, it can be laid immediately. Leave it on the pallets for as little as 36 hours and it will begin to yellow.

> **TOOLS COMMON TO LAYING A LAWN PATH WITH SOD OR SEED**
> A straight-nosed spade
> A round-pointed shovel
> A wheelbarrow
> An iron rake
> A lawn roller that can be filled with water
> Stakes, string and two hoses for laying out the edges of the path
> A spading fork or a Rototiller if you have one
> Hoses and sprinkler for watering
>
> For maintenance:
> A half-moon edging knife on a short or long handle
> Vertical action edging shears

FACING PAGE: **In a Vermont garden designed by Gordon Hayward.**

DESIGN
Choosing a Site

While there are many successful lawn paths in filtered shade or semi-shade, lawn prefers sun. Lawn paths in our own garden tell the story: those in full sun flourish; those in filtered shade, as under our heavily pruned apple tree, are becoming thinner by the year. Those in dense shade, like the one under the wild plums, turned almost completely to moss before we took it up two years ago and installed stepping-stones.

The problem of thinning can develop over time. Where you have filtered shade now for just a few hours a day might be dense shade in a few years when the limbs of nearby trees have grown out over the path. Many people just cut the trees down or change the garden altogether. I take a middle ground and prune the trees high to allow more light in; that way, the trees and the garden can remain intact. But if you are in the early stages of making a path, keep in mind that while there are shade-tolerant grasses, the most luxuriant lawn paths are in sun.

Shape and Width

If you want a lawn path between sunny perennial beds, you need to consider how wide the path will be in relation to the beds. By setting out stakes and bright surveyor's tape, you can develop a sense of the width of beds and lawn. Naturally, the wider the path, the grander the scale. If a path is too wide between beds, the path will read more like lawn than path, so be careful to keep the width of beds and path in scale with one another. One general rule of thumb is that the path between beds should be no wider than half the width of the widest adjacent bed. Visiting gardens where lawn paths run between perennial beds, such as those at Old Westbury Gardens on Long Island, or those of friends, will give you ideas regarding scale and proportion.

SOIL PREPARATION FOR SOD AND SEED

Plan ahead. Send a soil sample to your nearest testing lab to learn how to treat the soil for a lush lawn. All weeds, rocks, debris and/or previously existing sod has to be removed from the ground on which you'll be planting

FIGURE 13.1: Straight sown path #1.

FIGURE **13.2**: Straight sown path #2.

the lawn or setting the sod. A straight-nosed spade, a sod cutter or even a round-pointed shovel will enable you to remove the old sod or weeds. All of what you gather can be put on the compost pile, unless it has gone to seed. Place sods upside down on the compost pile and they will decompose; place them upright and they'll grow.

If the area to be sodded or seeded is covered with 4 to 6 inches of top-soil, rototill to a depth of at least 4 inches (Figure 13.1). Spread lime, if necessary, according to the pH needs of your soil, and use a starter fertilizer that is high in phosphorus (the middle number of the analysis 13-25-12, for example) and thus promotes root growth. Be careful not to use too strong a fertilizer or it will burn the tender rootlets. If you have large amounts of compost, spread 2 inches or so on top of the soil, or use an equivalent amount of moistened peat moss, and rototill that in with the lime and fertilizer. Peat moss, which holds moisture in sandy soil, also serves to keep clay soils porous; in very sandy or heavy clay soils, add approximately 30 cubic feet per 1,000 square feet of area to be seeded. Then smooth the surface with an iron rake, roll it with a heavy roller and rake it lightly again to smooth out your footprints (Figure 13.2). You may have to roll again, or use a heavier roller, if your heel forms an indentation in the soil that is deeper than ¾-inch. This is particularly important on a lawn path as opposed to open lawn.

Before laying the sod or sowing the seed, crown or raise the soil near the center of the path an inch or so above adjacent sides to assure good drainage and to accommodate the inevitable compacting that will result over time as people walk on it.

THE SOD PATH
Selecting Sod

Sod is sold in strips with root systems ½ to ¾ inch thick and 1-to-2-inch-high grass. The sods are 18 inches to 2 feet wide and anywhere from 2 to 5 feet long. Even the largest rolls don't weigh more than 20 pounds, so they are manageable. Thickly cut sod with root systems as thick as 2 inches is a specialty turf for instant use on athletic fields. Don't buy it. It's cumbersome to work with, will be unnecessarily expensive, and the thinner sods root more rapidly anyway. These pregrown rolls of mown grass are purchased in square feet, so once you have the area you want in lawn staked out, multiply the length times the width to get the square footage; that's what you want to buy or order for delivery.

Purchased directly at the sod grower's farm, a square foot would normally cost between 15 and 25 cents. You might pay more at a garden center because it will have to cover its costs to transport the sod from the farm. While garden centers might be able to order sod, you may want to look first in the yellow pages for sod producers or contact a professional gardener in the area and ask for a source of sod; buying it yourself will be less expensive.

In the Northeast, and in similar moist and cool climates across the country, Virginia bluegrass sod is the finest-bladed and most readily available sod. In Georgia and similar climates generally considered zones 7 and 8 according to the new USDA climatic zone map, zoysia and fescue sods are frequently used. But there are tradeoffs with both. Zoysia is a refined, thin-bladed, thickly-growing grass that is lush green from late spring until late autumn, when people are most often in their gardens. Zoysia grass paths are brown throughout the basically snowless winters in the South.

Fescue grasses in that part of the country do not form the same dense mat that zoysia forms. But unlike zoysia, they do remain green throughout the winter and are not at their best during the hot weather months when people are out walking in their gardens. Fescue is not a good lawn sod for high-traffic areas, as it wears thin much more readily than zoysia. To solve that problem, many gardeners in the South overseed with annual or perennial rye to carry the dense greenness through the hottest summer months. For lawn paths in shade in the South, fescue is the only choice. Even in the fleeting shade thrown by a low retaining wall, zoysia fades while fescue flourishes.

In the far South, as in the area around Palm Beach, the typical grass is St. Augustine, and more specifically the new cultivar 'Floritam.' At the Church of Bathesda-by-the-Sea in Palm Beach, where there are several lawn paths, Keith Risely, grounds manager, used St. Augustine grass sods into which he set several sods of the new 'Floritam' as a stay against cinch bugs and weeds. St. Augustine is a coarse, aggressively stoloniferous grass—that is, it sends runners along the surface, which send roots down and grass blades up. It can't be cut much closer than 2½ or 3 inches from the ground; cut closer and the rhizomes become exposed to direct sunlight and die, which seems to happen anyway when the grass is planted in shade. People from the north, Risely told me, have the initial impression that it is a crabgrass because it is so coarse, but it is the grass most used in that area of the country today. Being coarse, it does not make a particularly pleasant path to walk on, so other hard paving materials are generally used in such warm, even hot climates. The grass, however, does absorb heat and keeps an area cooler than stone, which would collect and reflect the heat.

While in Palm Beach I did see one superior zoysia grass lawn path, but I learned that it kept its green, lush look only with great maintenance: almost monthly spraying for fungus and cinch bugs; frequent liquid fertilizer applications; mowing only with reel, not rotary, mowers and frequent insecticide applications. Richard Roberts, a professional maintenance gardener in Palm Beach, told me that zoysia grass is susceptible to sod webworms and army worms, both of which can be controlled with monthly applications of diazinon or the biological control, *Bacillus thuringiensis*. Look into sod lawn paths closely wherever you live before making a final order. You'll be glad you did.

Laying Sod

In hot weather, sod should be laid within 12 hours of being harvested at the sod farm; in cool weather, 36 hours is the maximum. Otherwise it begins to deteriorate on the pallets.

Where you lay the first sod determines where every other piece of sod goes, so choose your starting point carefully. If it is along an existing border, stretch string tightly between two stakes and set your first sod at the corner. If you're laying sod on a slope, be sure to lay the length across the slope so as to prevent erosion. Just before beginning to lay the sod, water the area lightly so the dried soil does not pull moisture from already-stressed rootlets.

Roll out the sod and be careful when pulling at the ends; it does tear. While it is important to keep the sods moist, don't water deeply until the whole job is done or you'll be working in a mudbath.

Once you have the first sod in place, set a small board or piece of plywood on it to take your weight as you set the next piece, so your knees won't leave indentations as you work down the path. Be sure to lay each piece snugly against the adjoining one along the sides and ends, for it is at the outer edges that the sod can dry out. When you start the second row of sod, be sure to

FIGURE 13.3: **Straight sod path.**

alternate the joints, just as you would when laying brick in a running bond (Figure 13.3).

Once the sods have all been laid, go over the entire area with a full roller to get rid of all air pockets so as to be sure the undersides of the sods are in contact with the underlying soil. If you find gaps between any sods, sprinkle a mixture of moistened peat moss and topsoil into the gaps. The sod will fill in the space quickly. Go over the grass with a bamboo or plastic rake to lift the blades so that they aren't matted. Once the path is raked, set up an oscillating sprinkler and water thoroughly. Water as needed, but at least once a week, or even daily if where you live is hot and dry, keeping an eye on the edges where drying is most likely to take place.

Bermuda grass sod may root sufficiently in as little as 3 to 5 days whereas Kentucky bluegrass may require careful irrigation for 2 or 3 weeks to become established during summer heat. Mow when the grass has increased in height by 50 percent; that is, if the grass in the sods is 2 inches high upon delivery, mow it when it has grown to 3 inches.

While it is best to stay off the newly laid sod for a few weeks, you will be surprised at how resilient it is; if need be, you can walk on the sod almost immediately, but walk more on the balls than heels of your feet.

THE LAWN PATH
Selecting Seed

In zones 2 to 6, a good grass seed mix for lawn paths in full sun should include at least 50 percent Kentucky bluegrass (*Poa pratensis*); pratensis means "of the meadow." The mix should also include 30 to 40 percent red fescue (*Festuca rubra* or *Festuca rubra* var. *cummutata*), which adds durability as well as a greater degree of tolerance to shade and drought than the finer-bladed bluegrass. Finally, 10 to 20 percent of the mix should be the quickly germinating annual ryegrass (*Lolium multiflorum*), which gives the lawn a quick green cover as well as a degree of stability against erosion during the period of vulnerability while the slower-germinating bluegrass and fescues are developing their root systems.

Be aware of the clover content in any seed mix. Clover will overrun grass if the nitrogen level in your soil is low; grass will overrun the clover if the nitrogen level is high. Clover flowers are a plus because they look good, but a minus because they attract bees. A recent introduction called O'Connor's legume, or strawberry clover (*Trifolium fragiferum*) has smaller flowers and is thus less attractive to bees. Keep in mind that clover, when wet, is very slippery and that's a problem in a lawn path, where people will frequently walk.

In zones 6 to 10, grass seeds commonly used include perennial ryegrass (*Lolium perenne*), Bermuda grass (*Cynodon dactylon*), Colonial bent grass (*Agrostis tenuis*), creeping bent grass (*Agrostis palustris*) and zoysia grass (*Zoysia japonica*).

Dryland Grasses

All lawns in America are measured against the lush green Kentucky bluegrass lawn we associate with the East. If you live in the drylands of the

---

TOOLS AND MATERIALS
FOR THE LAWN PATH

All those mentioned above plus a drop-seeder; that is, a wheeled and geared seeder

Grass seed purchased in pounds per 1,000 square feet

Salt marsh hay or straw as a mulch

A three-tined fork for spreading mulch

west, you should consider the many alternatives because while bluegrass will grow, it will require extensive irrigation. Dryland grasses need less water and are also slower growing, and thus require less frequent mowing and less fertilizer. Research shows that they require only half the amount of nitrogen bluegrass demands to stay healthy.

There are two dryland options. The first are native grasses. In Colorado, for example, they include buffalograss (*Buchloe dactyloides*), blue grama (*Bouteloua gracilis*) and western wheatgrass (*Agropyron smithii*). The second are introduced grasses: fairway wheatgrass (*Agropyron cristatum*), smooth bromegrass (*Bromis inermis*), tall fescue (*Festuca arundinacea*) and Bermuda grass (*Cynodon dactylon*).

These grasses are further classified by their season of growth. Cooler season grasses show peak growth in the spring and fall. These include bluegrass, tall fescue, perennial ryegrass and fairway wheatgrass. Warm season grasses show peak growth in the summer, and may be dormant or even brown in the spring and fall. These include buffalograss, blue grama and Bermuda grass. Warm season grasses usually take three weeks longer than cool season grasses to green up after the winter browning of both. In the warmest parts of the Rocky Mountain West, Bermuda grass seems to be the best, while buffalograss may well be the best overall dryland turf. It has excellent heat and drought tolerance, though, being a warm season grass, it does brown significantly with the first heavy frosts.

Bermuda grass is the most widely used seed in the southern states and the Southwest. It creates a very dense sod, and has excellent heat and drought tolerance. Keeping this grass green in the fall, winter and early spring is possible, especially in the warmer parts of the Southwest, with a fall fertilization with iron and nitrogen. In Tucson, Arizona, for example, grass can be kept green a month longer in the fall and can be encouraged to green up a month earlier in the spring by close mowing and spraying ½ pound of soluble iron per 1,000 square feet in late September. Because the soils in the Southwest are primarily alkaline, iron chlorosis can cause yellowing in lawns; spraying iron in the form of ferrous sulfate can remedy the situation. If you have a shady path in the Southwest, you might be more likely to use St. Augustine grass, but it is particularly subject to yellowing in such limited sunlight.

Another drought-tolerant grass for the drier parts of the United States is *Festuca elatior*, one of the tall fescues. It is sold under such names as 'Alta,' 'Goars,' or 'Fawn.' These clump-forming grasses are coarser than most fine lawn grasses and don't create a dense turf. But they are extremely tough and wear-resistant, and thus particularly well suited for paths. In recent years, turf-forming tall fescues have been developed. They are nearly as drought tolerant as those mentioned above, and can be obtained as seed or sod: 'Olympic,' 'Mustang' and 'Falcon' are three cultivars. Because these tall fescues send roots down several feet, they can withstand longer periods of drought and thus need less irrigation.

Be aware, too, that overwatering a dryland grass can cause any bluegrass or other cool season grasses and weeds in the lawn or seed mixture to gradually dominate, which means you will have to irrigate more often.

The Time to Sow

In climatic zones 2 to 6, the ideal time for sowing lawn paths is within a very short range of time, from late August to mid- or late September. In these zones, such timing will ensure that the seedlings have the cool weather of autumn and early spring to become established while annual weeds and crabgrass seeds are dormant.

The only other time that is good is in early spring, before the lilacs leaf out. Be sure to sow the seed, however, only when the soil is moist, not soggy. If you can form a ball of soil in your hand that holds together, it is too wet for seeding. If you have to bring in topsoil, it is far better to seed in the fall. Crabgrass, all too common in topsoil that has been stored in a contractor's yard, will not germinate until the warm, early summer months. Then, in May in zones 2 to 6, a pre-emergent spray or pellets can be applied to the soil to kill the crabgrass seeds.

The problem with seeding from late May through early August is that excessive watering is necessary. Furthermore, that same watering and the heat at that time of year causes crabgrass seeds and other weed seeds to germinate, in many cases before the slower lawn seed, thus creating a most inhospitable situation for the lawn seedlings and a major problem for you.

Seeding, Mulching and Mowing

A wheeled and geared drop-seeder is the best for paths (see Figure 13.2); a cyclone seeder that hangs around your neck will spread seed too far afield, with seeds invariably ending up in adjoining beds. Wheeled seeders can usually be rented from a rental shop or borrowed from a friend. An alternative is hand seeding, which can result in irregular distribution but can be accomplished successfully if you are careful.

A typical distribution rate is about 4 or 5 pounds per 1,000 square feet, but you should consult distribution rates on the seed box. Once the seed has been spread, drag an iron rake or bamboo leaf rake over the whole area and then roll with a roller filled with water. This rolling will give good contact between seed and soil, thus assuring germination.

Mulch is necessary to help retain moisture in the soil and to slow erosion by breaking up raindrops. The ideal mulch is marsh hay or straw, neither of which carry weed or grass seeds. If you mulch lightly enough so that you can see the soil through the mulch, the marsh hay can be left to decompose. Straw will have to be taken up carefully with a rake once the seedlings are 2 to 3 inches high since straw takes too long to decompose. If the lawn path is not too extensive, cheesecloth or jute matting can also be used and then taken up or left to decompose.

The first seeds to germinate will be the annual ryegrasses, which might need mowing as early as two weeks after seeding; bluegrasses and fescues can take as long as 3 or 4 weeks to need mowing. Wait until the grass blades are 2 to 3 inches high. And it is best to have sharp blades when mowing a newly seeded path because the seedlings have not had sufficient time to set down their roots; a dull blade will tend to uproot 2-to-3-week-old seedlings. Mow only when the soil is fairly dry; the wheels of mowers, not to mention your feet, are going to disrupt the seedlings on muddy soil. Once you begin mowing, continue weekly, just as you would any lawn.

After 6 weeks or so, stretch a line along the edge of the path and cut a deep, clean edge. Take up the seedlings and hoe the adjoining beds to kill any seedlings that you inadvertently sowed there. Be careful when walking on newly seeded paths; until the root systems become well established, the edge can be easily broken down as you step on it.

CUTTING PATHS AND BEDS FROM EXISTING LAWN

Lawn paths can be cut out of existing lawns with ease (Figure 13.4). You just need to look at your existing lawn and adjacent beds with a new eye. You may have two beds out in the lawn now that are separated by 10 feet or more, and don't relate to one another at all. Consider enlarging the two beds by removing all but 5 feet of the lawn between them. In so doing, the beds can be reshaped so they are similar. Plants can then be reorganized within them so there is a degree of similarity of style and content. What results is a 5-foot-wide path between two beds that are related to one another by the path, their shapes and the plants within them.

Design

If you have a lawn that comes up to the edge of an existing perennial bed and you have been trying to decide where to add an additional perennial

<table>
<tr><td>TOOLS</td></tr>
</table>

All those mentioned earlier
 plus a sod cutter
A half-moon edging knife or
 straight-nosed spade
A spading fork
A straight board as a guide
A wheelbarrow

FIGURE 13.4: Cutting curving path in existing lawn.

Area to be planted

Area to be planted

A LAWN PATH IN TREE SHADE

GEORGE SCHENK, author of *The Complete Shade Gardener,* notes that there are certain trees that are better companions for lawns than others. Among deciduous trees, some of the better ones are oak, hackberry (*Celtis occidentalis*), European ash (*Fraxinus exelsior*), jacaranda, flowering crabapple, orchard apple, pear and lemon tree, and the Japanese pagoda tree (*Sophora japonica*). Of the evergreens, palms are the best, and Douglas fir, especially if limbed high to allow light to penetrate to the grass. Some of the worst are hemlock, spruce, maple, beech and other shallow-rooted trees.

One of the best seed recipes for deciduous shade under hospitable trees, according to Schenk, is 44 percent creeping red fescue, 30 percent chewing's fescue, 15 percent Kentucky bluegrass and 11 percent High-land colonial bentgrass. Such a lawn needs to be mowed every 3 or 4 days in the spring, once a week in the summer and fall and kept about an inch high, which is considerably shorter than is suggested by lawn seed companies. Schenck's theory is that a thick carpet of short grass (apparently) presents more leaf surface than a thinner stand of longer blades. Such a lawn needs to be fortified with a liquid fertilizer once in the spring and fall; 5 percent of the mix should be ferrous sulfate, which kills moss and thus encourages a thicker lawn. You should also spread dolomitic lime on the lawn once a year in the fall if moss has begun to appear, showing that the soil is becoming too acidic. During the summer, you should water the shady lawn once a week if the top 2 inches of soil dry out. Follow these tips and your lawn path will flourish.

bed, the lawn path might be a help. Clean up the edge of the lawn where it meets the perennial bed so that you have a clear line to work with. Then, with stakes, mark out a 3-or-4-foot-wide path by measuring out from the existing edge along its entire length. At the beginning and end of what will be your new path, set more stakes so that you come round to the beginning again, thus establishing the limits of your new bed.

If you find the resultant lawn path to have a curve that is too fussy, consider changing the edge of the existing perennial bed. You can even use the sod you have removed from one area to fill in another to alter the shape of the existing bed immediately. Or you can fill in an area with topsoil and seed.

Straight edges are even easier. Using stakes, bright string or tape and a tape measure, try making straight lines for existing or proposed beds. When you have the right lines established, pin the string to the ground every 15 feet or so with 4-inch metal staples you can make from old coat hangers.

Cutting the Edge

When working in crumbly loam, set your half-moon edging knife slightly toward you to give the edge more support, and don't dig the edge more than 2 inches deep. When working in heavier soil that can support more weight, make a right-angle cut about 3 or 4 inches deep, usually the full depth of the blade.

Also, pay attention to the nature of the soil on the day you cut the edge. If it is wet or soggy, or so dry that it will crumble, find an 8-to-10-foot-long 1x4 board to stand on as you work. Put the board down next to the string and use the edge of the board as the guide, running the half-moon edger along it.

Once you have the edge cut, go back to the beginning and, with the straight-nosed spade, take up the severed sods, place them in a wheelbarrow, and either place them upside down on the compost pile to decompose, or use them to fill in blank spots in the lawn. Once the sod has been removed, tidy up the edge by setting the straight-nosed spade at the desired depth and giving it a swift kick, you will send excess soil into the beds.

This type of edge not only helps improve the bed's health and appearance, but it also brings adjoining beds into relationship with one another, thus bringing two elements of the gardens into a coherent picture. Clean edges make grass paths and gardens look well cared for. A crisp edge has practical benefits too: it discourages weeds, clover, and the lawn itself from sneaking into the garden. And a lawn with clean edges is easier to mow than one that flows in and out of the garden. Paved edges, whether of brick, cut stone or fieldstone make the lawn path even easier to maintain.

Maintenance

Once established, lawn edges must be clipped regularly lest they become shaggy and lose their sharpness. A pair of vertical action edging shears is the tool for this job; the half-moon edger is not. The former is designed to cut blades of grass, the latter to slice through turf. If you use the edger to cut grass, you invariably have to cut some turf to get a purchase, and that means that over time the paths get narrower and narrower, and a blank and weedy space gradually opens up at the front of any adjoining beds.

The vertical action edging shear is an unlikely, oddly angled tool you may have seen in catalogues. It enables you to work standing up, though one-handed, short-handled shears are available if you don't mind working on your knees.

Gasoline or electrically powered string trimmers only work to a point; because their string turns horizontally, they cut well parallel to the ground but not at a 90-degree angle. And if you have hundreds of feet of edges, there are gasoline-powered edging tools with blades that can be set at the angle of your choice.

If you want to be a purist, edges should be clipped every time you mow the lawn, but every other time can suffice, particularly in the dry summer months or if you do not have a quickly growing lawn. Once an edge has been clipped, use a hoe to gather up the clippings for the compost pile.

BY FOLLOWING THE DIRECTIONS in this chapter carefully, you can create lawn paths yourself with a minimum of cost. Cut stone is considerably more costly to purchase, and requires strength and skill to lay; brick paths require careful base preparation and a lot of time on your knees; and stone carpets require a good eye and a good deal of time to get right. Lawn paths are straightforward and relatively easy to get established. ✿

Chapter Fourteen

The Concrete Path

BEING A LIQUID, CONCRETE'S uses are infinite. But unlike all the other materials discussed in this book, once the material is poured and hardened, there is nothing you can do to change your mind short of hammering the path to pieces and starting over again. And being a liquid, and a heavy one at that, concrete can squelch out from under or push over forms not properly set. Take your time preparing for what masons call "the pour." And here are a few precautions: wear gloves and plenty of clothes—don't let your skin come in contact with concrete; be sure to wash off tools and equipment you are using as soon as you are finished working with them—hardened concrete on a shovel is tough to remove.

DESIGN

Concrete walkways that have an aesthetic value to them are either plain and curved, or straight and embedded. Without detail, a straight concrete walkway will conjure up images of the walkway to the dentist's office. To help you visualize what the path will look like, lay down a pair of hoses or ropes in a variety of ways to give you a sense of the shape and width of the walkway.

Consider subordinate paths too. You might want to create concrete ones, or you might want to leave a space in the edge of the path for stones or bricks. Look closely at the illustration for the Palo Alto garden in Chapter 1, where brick and concrete are mixed to create a link between the concrete driveway and the brick walk. Think ahead; consider all the options, because once you pour the concrete and it hardens, changing your mind is no easy matter.

PREPARING THE AREA

First excavate to a depth of 10 inches. Lay down a 4-inch bed of crushed stone and cover it with landscape cloth. On top of this, lay a 2-inch bed of sand on which you in turn lay strong reinforcing wire mesh. Four-by-one-inch wooden battens nailed to stakes should then be put on edge along the sides of the path to retain the wet concrete and provide crisp edges to the finished walkway. (Pressure-treated battens can be left in place or prised out, whereas soft wood battens, which will quickly rot anyway, should be removed.)

You can also put battens across the path to create 3-, 4- or even 5-foot-wide panels (Figure 14.1). The wood, left in place or removed between concrete sections, creates important expansion joints that prevent concrete from breaking up as it expands and contracts with the changes in temperature

TOOLS AND MATERIALS

A cement mixing bin
An old hoe for mixing
A mason's float
A trowel
A hammer for making forms
A round-pointed shovel for removing soil (if setting concrete in place)
A wheelbarrow to remove the soil

Bagged concrete
Sand purchased in cubic yards
Wooden retaining pieces 4x8x1 inch
Stakes and nails
A 2x4 for leveling across the walkway

FACING PAGE: **Precast concrete pavers in a Florida garden.**

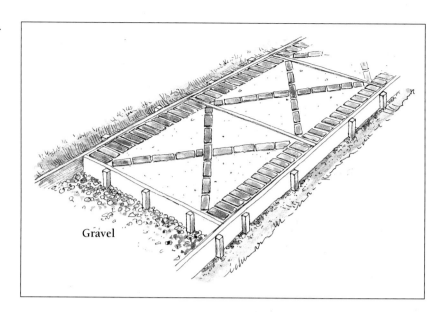

Gravel

throughout the year. You can oil the wood used for joints to keep it intact and handsome, but you have to oil it carefully or it will stain the concrete.

THE BEST MIX

Care must be taken in the way you mix concrete. For example, if the mix is too wet, the materials will tend to separate, resulting in cracking and uneven color. If the mix is not wet enough, the areas around patterns or corners will be difficult to finish properly. If too stiff, air can get trapped; only when the retaining boards are removed will the resulting gaps be exposed. A reasonable guide for the mix would be 1 part cement, 2½ parts sand and 4 parts gravel mixed with an amount of water sufficient to make it workable and easily finished. If you want a smooth finish into which you can set tiles, pebbles or other decorative elements, don't add any gravel. Two commercial products you can use for the surface of a cement walkway are labelled Cold Top and Marble-crete. The latter contains marble dust to increase the whiteness of the surface color.

Coloring Concrete

White or colored pigments or aggregates can be added to concrete to give you a wide range of colors and textures. Pigments can be purchased from building supply outlets as a powder in 5-, 25- or 50-pound bags. Mix the pigment according to directions on the bag. Pigments can be purchased by color: brick red, black, brown, natural red, medium red, cement black, brownstone brown, green, yellow, orange and gold are all available and can be combined to form any number of variations.

Add tinting agents to the concrete mix before pouring it; the color is permanent because it is in rather than on the concrete. If you want to color existing cement, you can use paints designed for outdoor concrete work, but the paint will not penetrate the cement the way a concrete pigment will. Even these tend to bleach out in hot sunlight, but they do hold better in shady parts of the garden. Gravel or colored sands can also be scattered onto wet concrete or into the concrete mix in order to color the finished surface.

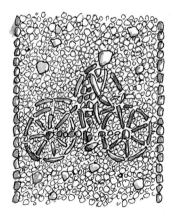

Colored rocks & pieces of brick in cement

EMBEDDING

Before mixing and pouring the concrete into a section of the path not much longer than 4 or 5 feet, lay all the tiles, pebbles or whatever you want to embed nearby so you are ready. Then mix the concrete, perhaps using a retardant to slow the hardening process, and pour it into a section of path until it is up to the appropriate level. Then, wearing rubber gloves to prevent your fingers from coming in contact with the concrete, push in pebbles or whatever materials you are using. It is very easy to do, but you should be careful not to prepare too large an area; depending on the mix, you'll have around an hour before the concrete becomes so hard that you can't press materials in any longer. That might mean that you would want to pour concrete and press pebbles into an area not much larger than 10 to 15 square feet at a time, depending, of course, on the complexity of the design and the size of the embedding materials.

Colored rocks & pieces of brick in cement

Brick or concrete pavers

2" sand

Landscape fabric

1½" crushed stone

Once the materials are pressed into the concrete, a board can be laid across the path from one batten to the next and can be used, on edge, to tamp the pebbles or tiles uniformly into the concrete. As the concrete begins to harden, brush with a stiff broom to expose the surface of the pebbles and gently wash the pebbles clean.

PRECAST PAVERS

During the last 20 years or so, paving systems have been developed that are primarily for commercial use: beach promenades, pedestrian malls, driveways, plazas or entrances to office buildings. While many of the interlocking systems are busy-looking, elements of the systems, which can be purchased separately, have some potential when it comes to creating walkways, paths and terraces. The individual pavers come in colors similar to the range available in brick: Reds and browns predominate, though grays are also available. They also come in a variety of shapes, all with rounded edges and from 2½ to 3½ inches thick. Large rectangles are around 4½ to 6½ inches wide, and as long as 9½ inches while smaller ones are 2½ by 4½. Squares are available in 4½-inch pavers and there are also pavers that are shaped so that 30 or 40 of them will form a circle or fan.

One problem with this kind of paving is that the resulting path can look rigid and unnatural when laid. That is particularly a problem with the interlocking bricks. You can set the rectangular pavers with ½- to ¾-inch gaps between them and then fill the joints with a loamy sand for plants that will soften the effect. Furthermore, whole bricks can be left out of the pattern, enabling you to plant larger perennials such as Lady's mantle (*Alchemilla mollis*).

Laying the Base for Precast Pavers

The nature of your soil will determine how deeply you should excavate when laying such material. If the soil is clayey or holds moisture, you should excavate down at least 10 inches and lay 4 to 6 inches of 1½-inch crushed stone (Figure 14.2). Lay ground cloth on top of it to prevent the next layer, sand, from filtering down over time. Enough sand should be laid in the trench so that when the pavers are laid on top of it, the surface of the path will be about ¾ inch above the existing grade on either side of the walkway. With the sand in place, water and tamp with a hand tamper or a rented tamping machine. Backfill to the necessary level. The material on how to lay brick in Chapter 12 will give you the necessary details for laying these pavers. If

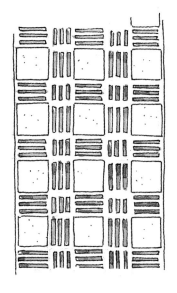

Roofing tiles set on edge in cement

you want to abut larger rectangular, circular or square pavers to make a continuous path, consult Chapter 12. If you want to set these larger pavers as individual stepping-stones, look at Chapter 15. Various edging systems are available with the paving systems; talk with your supplier about them and choose the system that suits you. The edging might simply be longer pavers of the same color set on end or edge.

One problem with concrete pavers is that their proportions—typically square—or their finish may not be very elegant, or the size you want may not be available. It is possible to create your own pavers that can be individually laid on sand so they can shift independently if frost heaving is a problem in your area.

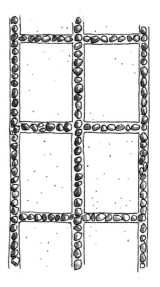

2-3" Pebbles in concrete

False Coquina Stones

Coquina is a southern Florida coral reef stone that was once quarried off the Keys. Because of increasing concern about the offshore ecology, sophisticated methods have been developed for creating a concrete copy of coquina stone called Buff Keystone. Henry Herpel and a company called Manyon Precast in West Palm Beach have both developed these systems. You can purchase the "faux coquina" from them. In some cases, they imprint the faux coquina with real stones.

Rather than buy the stones, John and Craig Eberhardt, who live in Palm Beach, make their own. They excavate down 6 or 7 inches and then lay 2 inches of sand atop which they place a reinforcing wire mesh. Over that they pour a 3-to-4-inch-thick slab of cement and let it harden so that it is about half an inch or less below the desired finish grade. They mix a fresh batch of cement, dip a broad mason's brush into it and splatter it onto the cured slab. This hardens for half an hour and then with a wooden mason's float, they flatten the little peaks left by the splattering. This results in a look that is very similar to that of natural coquina stone.

Eberhardt told me that an even simpler method is to pour the wet concrete slab up to finish grade and then immediately scatter baking soda on the surface. This method pits and mars the surface. When the surface is dry, it is hosed off, revealing pitting that is very similar to the natural coquina. Score marks to mimic the cut panels of the coquina can also be drawn directly onto the drying cement with a screwdriver.

WORKING WITH CONCRETE is not for everyone. If you feel confident enough to proceed on your own, then by all means do. But if you have any doubts, develop an initial design and then call in a professional mason who can help you refine the design in light of the material, and then install the walkway. Of all the paving materials, concrete perhaps requires the most expertise. As you can see in Chapter 6, when carefully conceived and laid, concrete can be used to create a handsome path. ☙

Chapter Fifteen

The Stepping-stone Path

WHEN YOU THINK of stepping-stones, you most likely think of flat fieldstones. But, as described in Chapter 7, there are other materials that broaden the range considerably. One is concrete, whether in the form of precast square, rectangular or circular pavers from 1 to 3 feet across, or concrete stepping-stones like those Harland Hand made (described in Chapter 6). A second is cut stone, such as square or rectangular bluestone, limestone or sandstone. Still other forms of stepping-stones are flat boulders, which can be positioned in shallow water, or wood rounds.

The site will determine the material and its scale. For example, for a stepping-stone path from the garage to the front door, you might want to use oversized stones for ease in walking. They might even be as large as 10 to 15 square feet each, whereas stones through an intimate shaded garden should be not much bigger than 2 or 3 square feet. Fieldstones that are slightly convex drain readily and provide a slightly rounded shape that rises to accept the foot; they should have some texture and roughness to ensure a good grip. River stones are too smooth to act as secure stepping-stones because they get too slippery, especially when wet from rain or even dew.

DESIGN

The size and proportions of the garden the steps pass through will suggest the size and position of the stepping-stones. To give you a rough idea of where the steps should go, lay out cardboard templates or, if the stones are light enough, lay them out. One thing to keep in mind is that stepping-stones are meant for one person at a time, so to make them much bigger than necessary for the passage of one person might be a waste of material and create a path that is out of scale with its purpose. Nevertheless, over-scale paths can be very appealing. Generally, stones in the range between 18 inches and 3 feet wide, square or rectangular, are appropriate.

Once you have a rough idea, the best way to determine exactly where to set the stones is to rake the area where the path will be and then walk the space yourself, moving at a comfortable pace for that site. Where each footprint remains is where the center of a stone should go. Of course, be aware that your pace isn't everyone's, but since you may be the most frequent walker, your pace is one of the most relevant.

The distance between individual stepping-stones determines the pace at which the walker moves. If you want people to slow down to observe plants,

FACING PAGE: A New Hampshire garden designed by Gordon Hayward.

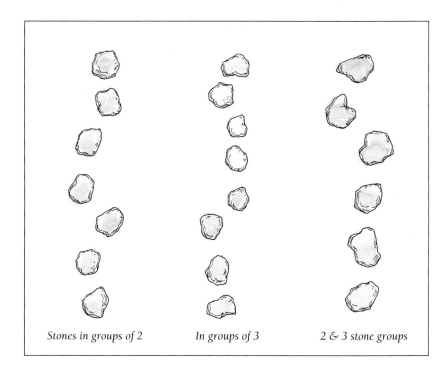

Stones in groups of 2 *In groups of 3* *2 & 3 stone groups*

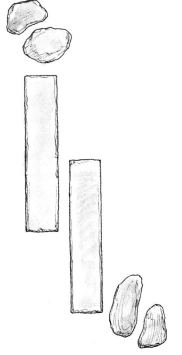

Cut stone & fieldstone

views or garden sculptures, create a curve in the path, but also place the stones so that there is no gap greater than 6 inches between them. If you want to increase the pace at which people move—say, from the house to the garage or out toward the swimming pool—place them so the gap between them is close to a foot. The faster people move, the surer the footing required, and thus the larger the stones should be.

The stones at the beginning and end of a path (threshold stones) and those at a juncture where a secondary path begins should be larger than all the other stones (Figure 15.1). Where a quarried stepping-stone might be around 18 inches in diameter, and shaped something like an ellipse, the threshold or juncture stones might be 2 feet across or even larger. There are few fixed rules, but there is one: The dimensions of the stones should always

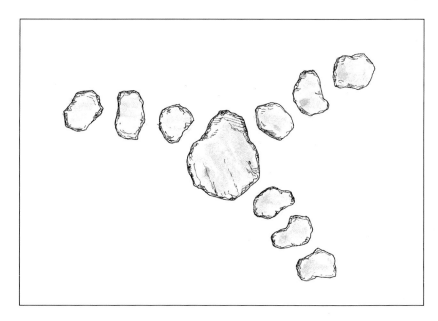

FIGURE 15.1: Path-dividing stone.

FIGURE 15.2

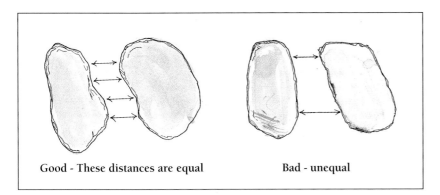

Good - These distances are equal   Bad - unequal

be bigger than the spaces between them. That ensures that the individual steps will read as a group rather than as isolated stones. For example, if you have a 10-or-12-inch gap between steps, the stones should be at least 14 to 16 inches in diameter; if the gaps between stones are 6 inches, then the stepping-stones should be at least 10 or 12 inches across. If you place the stones any further than a foot apart, you are running the risk of causing people shorter than you to have to stretch, perhaps beyond a comfortable gait, to reach the next stone. This can be a problem when the stones are wet and slippery.

Before laying any stones permanently into the ground, arrange all the stones where they will go. The threshold and juncture stones, which should have a shape that relates to their role of inviting people onto the main or subordinate paths, should be laid first. When positioning the smaller stepping-stones along the path, pay attention to their shapes, and try to create relationships between stones, so that they "read" together. For example, where one stone has an indentation, the next might have a shape that roughly fits that indentation (Figure 15.2). In laying out stepping-stones, then, pay heed to the give and take, the projection and indentation, the convex and concave, and the stones will relate to one another to form a coherent whole. The length of stepping-stones are generally laid across the path rather than parallel to the direction of it.

LAYING THE STONES
In Soil

Before laying the stones, be sure that you have considered how you want to set them in relation to the adjacent grade. Stepping-stones through a perennial garden or through woods should be set 1 or even 2 inches above grade so that they drain; this is most easily accomplished with 3-or-4-inch-thick fieldstones.

When setting stepping-stones into lawn, you have to decide whether or not you want them flush with the lawn so you can run the lawn mower right over them, or if you want to create more of a relief and set them an inch or so above grade, knowing that you will have to hand trim around the stones. The usual height in a cultivated garden is about 2 inches above grade. This allows a shadow to form around the edges, and allows moss and other ground covers to creep up to and perhaps even a bit over the stone.

Once you have the stones laid out, and you decided on their height relative to the existing ground, you are ready to start setting them. With a

Cut stone pavers

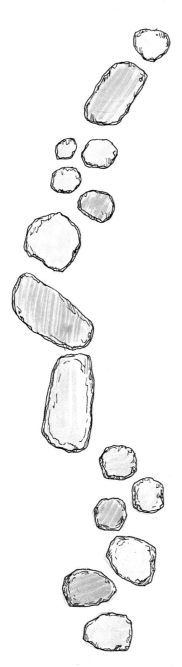

*Highly varied settings
& walking patterns*

trowel or straight-nosed spade, mark the outline of the stone, and then lift it and place it to the side of the position in which it will lay in the path; in that way you won't forget where to set it.

Most stepping-stones, if they are thick and heavy enough to stay in place when stepped on, can be laid directly on the earth, with no preparation underneath. However, if you live in the colder climates, you will find that frost action will heave the stones around somewhat. If frost is a problem in your area, consult the information in the introduction to this section regarding the base for any pathway. If frost isn't a problem for you, go right ahead and lay the stones in the existing soil.

In Established Turf

Lay out stepping-stones roughly across the lawn and then make fine adjustments regarding their shapes and exact distances apart. Once the final layout is satisfying, use a straight-nosed spade to cut around the perimeter of the stone. Take up the sod and excavate deep enough to allow 2 inches of sand to be laid in the bottom to ease the levelling of the stone. This is particularly important if the bottom of the stepping-stone is uneven. Lay the stone atop the sand, making whatever adjustments are necessary to make it level with the adjacent lawn. (If the drainage in the soil is very poor, you should excavate much more deeply and lay 4 to 6 inches of gravel or crushed stone before setting the sand in place.) By keeping the top of the stone flush with the lawn, you will be able to mow over it with ease rather than having to hand clip around each stone.

However, if you have the time and inclination to hand trim, each quarried stone can be an inch or two above the surface of the adjacent lawn. This

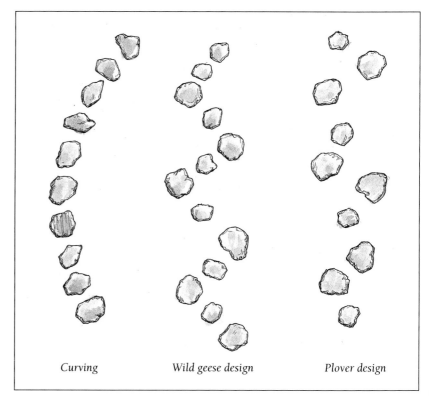

Curving   Wild geese design   Plover design

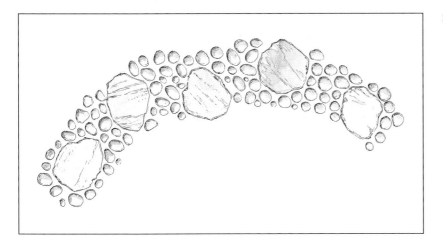

has a great deal of appeal, particularly if the shape of the stone is slightly rounded on top so that it appears to settle into the lawn around the edges.

STEPPING-STONE STEPS

In a rock garden, on the path to a summer cabin, or up through a woodland slope, fieldstones can also act as steps. Where the slope gets too steep to accommodate stepping-stones, larger stones can be used to create a flight of steps for just those few feet or yards that can't be served by individual stones set into the soil of the bank. The flight of steps should be constructed so that they look rough and rustic as they are in Figure 1.9. They can even lead over bedrock at some point, so as to remain consistent with the natural feeling of quarried or indigenous stepping-stones.

WOOD ROUNDS

An inexpensive form of stepping-stones can be created by cutting 8- to 10-inch-thick cross sections of trees. If they are cut with a very sharp chainsaw, the surface will be relatively smooth and the cross grain will show. Once they are well dried, they should be soaked in a nontoxic wood preservative that won't harm plants once set into the ground. (See Appendix A for a source of nontoxic wood preservatives.) Be sure to use wood rounds that are at least 18 inches across or they will look inconsequential in the woods or in a small woodland garden. Don't lay them in wet or even moist soils; moss will form on them over time and they will become very slippery.

Large pavers set in pebbles, edged with cobble

STEPPING-STONE PATHS INTEGRATE easily into the garden. Whenever possible, we use old fieldstones that have an age and patina to them. We set them in the ground, concave answering convex and then plant moss, ajuga, myrtle or any number of low ground-hugging plants between them. Instantly the path looks as though it has been there for years. 🌿

Chapter Sixteen
The Wood Path

THERE ARE MANY MORE SKILLS and expensive tools than I list for the construction of wooden boardwalks, steps, stairs and walkways. It might be best to hire an experienced carpenter to work with on the design and construction. What follows are a few notes that will help you approach the project with some background, and thus confidence during your conversations with the carpenter.

DESIGN

The beginning of the walkway needs to be located where it makes sense: off a wooden deck or from a doorway; between two trees on your way from lawn out to a beach, or at the edge of a pond or boggy area. Let your land and your architecture give you the clues.

Once you have the beginning established, walk a variety of routes to determine which is best. Keep in mind that a boardwalk, for example, can determine where people walk and what they see along the way. Look at Chapter 8 for ideas.

Keep in mind that 5 feet is the minimum width for a feeling of well-being when walking along any boardwalk or bridge raised 18 inches or more above ground and without a handrail. If narrower than that, you should consider adding a handrail.

Defer to local carpenters or building suppliers, for they will know the types of wood that are most suitable and available from local or far-flung sources. However, you should be aware that there are a number of woods that can be used for boardwalks, bridges or walkways. One rule of thumb is to use only phenolic woods; that is, woods that naturally produce phenol, which resists termites and decay: Redwood, western red or Alaskan white cedar are examples. Furthermore, these woods rarely splinter, they weather gracefully and have a natural feel. Softwoods such as pine are initially inexpensive but will break down quickly unless treated with wood preservatives. Even then, they will crack, twist and split and never look really good.

Pressure-treated wood is also suitable, and less expensive than the phenolic woods, but it does have a green cast to it for a year or more, and is produced with environmentally harmful chemicals; scraps or partially rotted pieces cannot be burned.

FACING PAGE: A simple wooden bridge in the Hayward's spring garden.

Flat footbridge

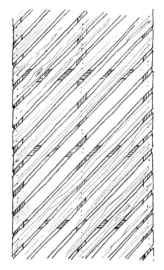

Decking

BOARDWALKS
Support

In order to secure the walking surface, support posts have to be sunk into the ground and/or concrete footings have to be set for the posts. Support posts can be made from pressure-treated lumber, certified for ground contact (as opposed to above-ground certification), or from hardwood trees taken from the area where the path leads, thus establishing a clear link between site and materials. For example, posts made of black locust, one of the hardest and longest-lasting woods, not only blend well in a New England garden, but the wood is so hard that preservatives are unnecessary. In a refined garden, sawn lumber would be more appropriate.

John and Craig Eberhardt, who have built many houses with connected boardwalks on Fire Island off Long Island, New York, dig 3-or-4-foot holes in the sand with posthole diggers and then pound in pressure-treated 4x6 or 6x 6 posts with flat, not pointed, ends so they won't sink further into the sand.

Jeff Blakely, who designs gardens in Palm Beach, Florida, uses another system, but it would work only in those areas the sea never reaches. He sets a 3-inch-thick, precast 18-inch-square concrete paver on level sand and then with a J-bolt affixed to a post hanger, he sets in and nails on an upright 4x4 pressure-treated post. He then nails 2x6 boards from one such hanger system to the next and then nails the surface boards across the 2x6s. In this way he doesn't have to dig any holes in the sand. This system would work well in boggy areas, too.

Boardwalk turning into a bridge

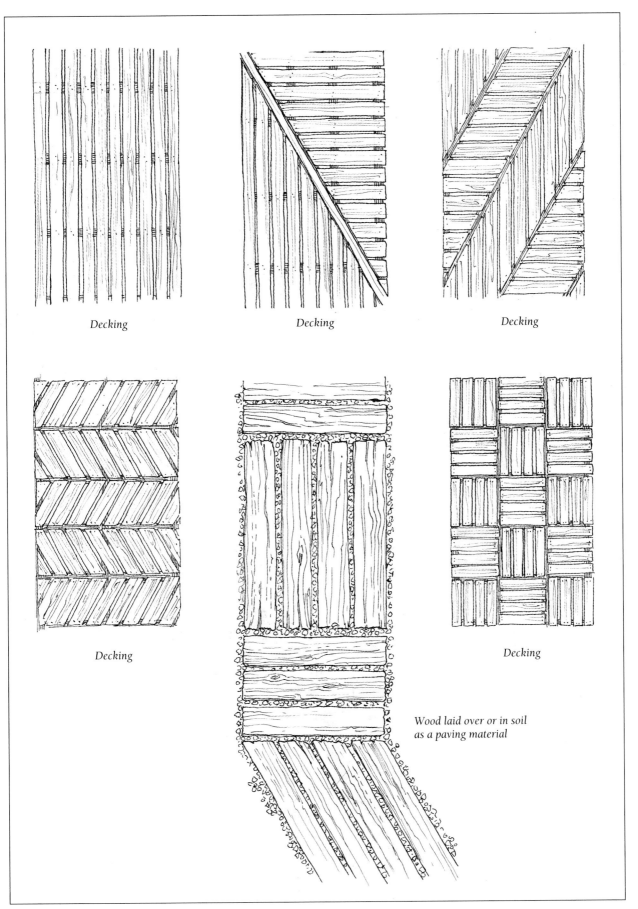

Decking

Decking

Decking

Decking

Wood laid over or in soil
as a paving material

Decking

Angled footbridge

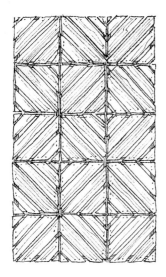

Decking

Creating Curves

Snaking and curving a boardwalk around drifts of dune grasses or scrub pines can make it more interesting than running it out for long straight stretches. Curves can be made by cutting 6-to-8-inch-wide boards with a Skilsaw along a diagonal, or near-diagonal line running the length of the board to provide wedge-shaped pieces. It is important to set the boards of any boardwalk as close together as you can right from the outset; as the sun dries them out, they will shrink, creating the necessary gaps for drainage between them.

WOODEN BLOCKS AS STEPPING-STONES

Wood can be used in smaller units much the same way bricks or concrete pavers are used. It's best to use them in sunny, dry areas. When wet, they can be slippery, and in cool shady places, moss and algae can colonize on them and make them slippery. Wooden blocks 4-or-6-inches square or larger are now available for paving, or you can make them any size by cutting wood into various modules yourself. Made of cypress, redwood or pres-

English stile

Wooden walkways over shallow water,
through boggy areas, or across slopes

sure-treated wood of many kinds, these natural-looking paving blocks can be used to create quite handsome pathways. Because they are light, and thus easy to work with, you can lay them yourself. Look at Chapter 12 on laying brick for information on how to prepare a bed for laying the wooden blocks. Be sure to purchase 8-inch-long edging blocks, which should be set on end down into the soil to hold the smaller interior blocks from shifting. Once the blocks are laid, sweep sand into the cracks.

Logs & gravel steps

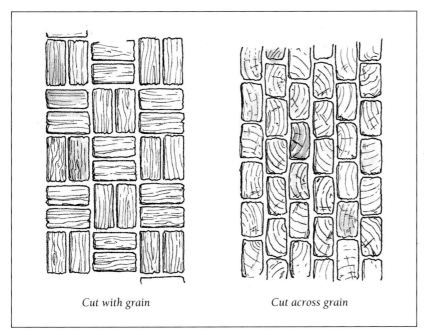

Cut with grain   *Cut across grain*

WOOD IN THE GARDEN ALWAYS blends well with the surroundings, especially when large trees are present. However, it is best not to use boardwalks or footbridges too close to the house unless they are made of materials that underpin a mood and style consistent with that of the architecture. Existing outbuildings, arbors and other features made from wood might well give you a cue as to the nature of the materials and design for any wooden walkways you might consider. ✿

Chapter Seventeen

The Loose Material Path

LAYING HARD LOOSE MATERIAL PATHS

P ATHS MADE FROM CRUSHED STONE, gravel and peastone can add ribbons of color through a garden. They can lead you through formal or informal areas, and can be narrow or wide as they flow in and around different parts or elements of the garden. They can also introduce sound; as you walk, the materials crunch underfoot.

DESIGN

Given that these paths can flow through a garden, consider any and all possibilities. Look for cues, such as a narrow passageway between two tree trunks or along the edge of an existing bed, where the path can double as edging. Have the path flow around an existing boulder, up through the rock garden and out to the woodland edge where the path can change to the soft loose materials considered later in this chapter.

Having decided where the path will go, you need to decide if you want a material whose color will blend or contrast with existing soils, plants and materials. Colored gravels or crushed stones from your local area, or similar ones from a distance, will blend in and not show the hand of the designer. While white or light gravels or marble chips will contrast with surrounding soils as strong visual statements, even at night when they reflect the moonlight. The problem with white gravels can be that they contrast too much and feel unnatural, especially on a wide path.

Texture, another consideration, has an impact on the look of the path, as well as the sound produced when you walk on it. Fine-textured quarter-inch minus crushed stone or decomposed granite is made up of tiny angular bits that will gradually settle underfoot into the gravel foundation and stay put so they don't need edging materials to keep them in place. This look, then, can be more natural, with the edges of such a path blending into adjacent beds. Such materials create a crunching sound when you walk on them. Because ⅜-inch peastones and small river stones are rounded, they don't settle into the soil in the same way as crushed stone, but roll around; without edging they easily scuff into adjoining lawn or beds and can look messy. They click when walked on.

TOOLS AND MATERIALS

A straight-edged spade
A round-pointed shovel
An iron rake
A saw for cutting plastic
   drainage pipe
Scissors to cut the cloth

¼-inch-minus crushed stone
   purchased by the ton or cubic
   yard
⅜-inch peastone purchased by
   the ton or cubic yard
Landscape cloth – 4-by-50-feet
4-inch perforated drainage pipe
Caps and grates for the pipe

FACING PAGE: **In Ted Child's garden in northwestern Connecticut.**

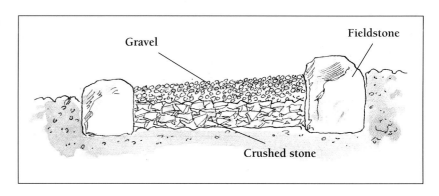

FIGURE 17.1: Hard loose material.

Gravel

Fieldstone

Crushed stone

LAYING GRAVEL OR CRUSHED STONE

When walking on a gravel path, you want to feel solidity underfoot, so a gravel path should be constructed on a foundation of coarser gravel or crushed stone to assure good drainage and thus solidity. If you want to create a path made of crushed stone over an area that is topsoil, excavate a trench 8 to 10 inches deep the length of the path (Figure 17.1). If the soil is wet or holds moisture in spring and fall, lay 1 to 2 inches of 1½-inch crushed stone, then a 4-inch PVC perforated drainage pipe along or across the path (with the holes down) to carry excess water off the downhill side of the path. The highest end of the pipe should be capped to prevent soil from clogging the pipe over time, whereas a grate should be placed at the lowest end to prevent small animals from crawling up the pipe. Then lay 4 inches of 1½-inch crushed rock or freely draining bank run gravel on top of the pipe.

Drainage fabric or landscape cloth should be laid on top of the crushed rock to keep the top layer of finer gravel from leaching over time into the crushed stone, causing the surface to drop and the drainage pipe to clog with the fine gravel. A permeable weed barrier ground or landscape cloth will do the job. You should be certain that the fabric is sufficiently porous so as not to trap water in the upper 2 inches of the pathway, yet at the same time not so openly woven that fine gravel can leach through.

Over this, spread 2 inches of screened gravel, water and tamp, and finally place ½ inch of fine crushed stone on top of the gravel to complete the path. The final grade should be about 1 inch below that of the adjoining surface, so the gravel will not migrate into the lawn or beds as people walk along. Because the gravel, drainage cloth and crushed stone base are all so porous, there is little chance that water can build up in the path even though it is slightly lower than the adjoining surface.

If the soil is not wet, or is already freely draining, excavate to a depth of 4 or 5 inches and lay in screened gravel to a depth of 4 inches, wet, tamp, and then lay 1 inch of top dressing quarter-inch minus stone and tamp.

Gravel is purchased in cubic yards, so to determine what needs to be ordered, multiply the length of the proposed path times the width (both in terms of feet) times the depth (as expressed in a fraction of a foot). That calculation will give you the cubic feet. Then divide the resulting number by 27, the number of cubic feet in a cubic yard, and you'll have the cubic yard figure to give the supplier when you call in the order. For example, if you have a 20-foot-long path 4 feet wide and you'll backfill with 6 inches of gravel, 20x4x.5=40 divided by 27 =1.48. Order 1½ cubic yards.

If the gravel path is going to adjoin a perennial bed, thus doubling as its edging, excavate 8 inches deep. Lay 4 to 5 inches of readily draining gravel or 1½-inch crushed stone and over it, a cloth, being sure to leave a 4-or-5-inch lip that will serve to separate the top layer of gravel from the topsoil in the adjoining bed. That cloth will also keep the perennials from gradually migrating into the path. Then backfill the remaining trench with the surface gravel to bring the grade of the path flush with the grade of the adjoining lawn and perennial bed. Wet and tamp to pack it down and then add another inch or so of gravel to bring it up to your final grade.

The Gravel Ramp

Often, we think that the only way to get down a slope is to create a series of steps. Consider, when using gravel, that it can be packed, that it allows for some water runoff, and so can be used as a ramp. There might be areas in your garden where a ramp would serve far better than steps: for handicap accessibility, for instance, or wheelbarrows or garden maintenance equipment. A wooden ramp set into a gravel ramp can help you up steeper inclines, and could even serve as a temporary access to get equipment over steps.

Gravel can also be combined with stone risers in steps, and the gravel sections can act as ramps, sloping slightly upward to the next stone riser. In this way, steps can be made to appear less arduous. The gravel can also be filled in with pebbles or river rocks, with cut stone acting as the risers.

Edging

Brick, stone or pinned-steel strips can be used, or the surface can be kept lower than adjoining surfaces to contain the material (Figure 17.2). This establishes a softer edge, though if you do set the surface below grade, you have to be certain excellent drainage is assured or the path, after a rain, will be one long shallow puddle. The edging might even be set in concrete to hold it permanently.

Pebbles Embedded

Pebbles can be set into soil or crusher dust to create any number of effects. They can be set on end at least half their length into crusher dust somewhat the way eggs are laid in a carton to create a rough surface that, to some degree, discourages walking. When laid this way they need to be edged with some material that will hold them in place: bricks on edge, granite blocks or concrete. They can, of course, also be laid in concrete for an even more sturdy set.

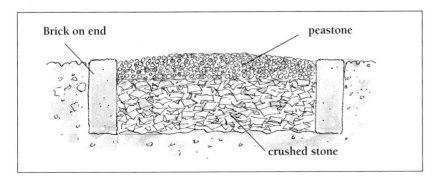

FIGURE 17.2: Hard loose material.

DRAINAGE

To avoid erosion of a gently or steeply sloping gravel path, you may need to create a swale to carry the water off on one or both sides of the walkway. You might also have to set drainage ditches across the pathway to carry off surface water when especially heavy rains fall.

One method is to construct a two-sided ditch that runs at a definite but gentle slope across the pathway (Figure 17.3). Dig a trench 8 inches deep by 8 inches wide at a slight angle across the path. Then set pressure-treated 2x8-inch boards the width of the path that are held about 3 inches apart with galvanized pipe spacers set into holes drilled partway into each board. Close off the upper end of this wooden trench with a nailed piece of 2x8 but leave the lower space open for the water to run out onto a stone placed at the end of the trench. The bottom of the trench can be lined with the same gravel as that on the path to a depth of 4 to 5 inches.

MAINTENANCE

One problem with gravel or crushed stone is that it can accumulate decomposing leaves from trees overhead; periodically a surface layer might have to be taken up and replaced. If your path isn't very long, the surface material can be taken up and stored under cover until the leaves have fallen (or the winter is over). In the spring, the path can then be raked clean of the winter's debris and the gravel that was stored can be spread again.

Another problem with maintenance is that when dry, gravel can be very difficult to weed. Wait until after a heavy rain or after adjacent beds have been heavily watered, and you'll find that the weeds are more easily pulled.

FIGURE 17.3: Drainage on a
sloping gravel path.

LAYING SOFT LOOSE MATERIAL PATHS

PATHS MADE FROM bark mulch, pine needles or trodden earth are surely the most natural of all paths. Although pine needle and bark mulch paths require a certain amount of maintenance because the materials break down over time, they are inexpensive, easy to install and simple to maintain. In fact, general garden maintenance is reduced by these paths. We put a bark mulch path through our woodland garden this past year and it reduced our maintenance considerably; what was previously open soil and sometimes weedy ground is now covered with 5 inches of dark brown mulch.

DESIGN

Because the materials in this chapter are so informal, the design of the path should be natural and simple too. In woodland, or within the shrubs and trees at the edges of your garden, there are places where you walk, or would like to walk for maintenance or pleasure. Lay out a path where you would naturally walk in those areas. Or perhaps there is a stream you like to walk along or a trodden earth path that you could design by simply removing a few saplings from just within the edge of the woods that run along a meadow. If you have an acre or more of woodland, perhaps you'd like to design a walk through the woods; the last section of this chapter will show you how. But first, let's take a look at three different types of paths, all of which can be linked to existing ones.

BARK MULCH

If there are lumber mills in your area, they are the place to look for large and inexpensive amounts of bark mulch. In southern Vermont, for example, a pickup truck load (2 cubic yards) costs between $20 and $30 at the mill, where for that price, they will also load it. This is a much better price than at a garden center, where you can typically purchase only bagged mulch. However, the trade-off is that you get what you're given at a mill; bagged material is inevitably uniform, often finer-textured, and easily handled in the back of the family automobile, while milled bark mulch can sometimes be very rough.

In the Northeast, hemlock is one of the more refined barks. It has a pleasant fragrance as well as a handsome rust-red color that holds for a good while. Oak from the debarker is typically shot through with long, broad, unattractive strips. White birch is good, though it, too, has long strips of papery bark that have to be sorted out as you lay the pathway. Sometimes mills separate their bark into various piles; it's worth the time to look over the piles and ask the loader operator to give you what you think is the best mulch available.

To lay a bark mulch path properly through heavy or slowly draining soils, excavate a trench 6 to 8 inches deep and pour in 4 inches of quickly draining gravel. If you don't lay the gravel down, the soil under a 3-or-4-inch layer of bark mulch can become muddy.

If the soil is already freely draining, excavating 3 or 4 inches will suffice, but before filling with the bark mulch, lay down a sheet of ground cloth to prevent weeds from coming up through the path. Or, you can spread the bark mulch directly onto freely draining soils to create a walkway raised about

---

TOOLS AND MATERIALS

A five-tined pitchfork for moving bark mulch and pine needles

A three-tined pitchfork for moving salt marsh hay

A round-pointed shovel for excavating

A straight-nosed spade for getting a clean edge on the excavated soil

Pine needles, in bales or collected from the woods

Bark mulch, purchased by the cubic yard

Peanut shells, purchased by the bag

Salt marsh hay, purchased by the bale

Trodden earth

Leaves from trees overhead

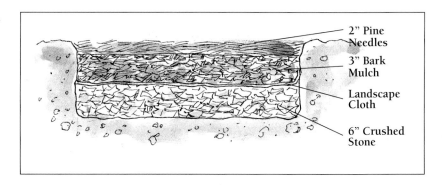

2" Pine Needles

3" Bark Mulch

Landscape Cloth

6" Crushed Stone

4 inches; when the mulch breaks down in a year or two, simply fork the decomposed material into the soil in adjoining beds and replace with fresh bark mulch.

Pamela Harper, who gardens in Seaford, Virginia, excavates paths through her gardens, sometimes to a depth of 2 feet. She mixes the soil with peat and digs it into adjoining vegetable gardens or beds. She then fills the paths with sawdust to within 3 or 4 inches of the surface, lays down layers of old newspapers and then covers the newspapers with 2 or 3 inches of bark mulch. Two years later, she peels back the layer of slowly decomposing newspapers and bark mulch, digs the decomposed sawdust out and forks it into adjoining beds. She tears up the not-quite-decomposed newspapers, mixes them with new sawdust, adds another layer of newspaper, relays the bark mulch and returns in two years to dig nearly everything but the recent layer of newspapers into adjoining beds before starting another cycle.

A simpler variation on this theme is to simply lay bark mulch directly onto the soil between rows or areas of vegetables in the vegetable garden, and every two years or so fork the decomposed mulch into the beds and replenish the path material. This approach will look attractive, build up the soil, and reduce maintenance in the paths. Salt marsh hay, straw or even baled hay from fields will serve the same purpose, though with the baled hay, you have to be sure to put at least 6 or 8 inches down to stop seeds in the hay from taking root.

PINE NEEDLES

To be sure drainage is adequate under the path, excavate to a depth of 8 inches and then lay down 5 inches of gravel on top of which goes 2 inches of bark mulch and finally, a covering of 1 or 2 inches of pine needles (Figure 17.4). (The top layer could also be salt marsh hay or even processed peanut shells.) The layer of bark mulch is there to provide the springiness you associate with pine needles underfoot in the forest; it also retains moisture and thereby keeps the needles flexible longer. Also, when the pine needles do break up or decompose, they expose another organic substance, the bark mulch, rather than gravel. In that way the illusion of the forest floor is kept intact. If the needles were laid directly on gravel, in a short time they would dry out, break up more easily, and the lighter gravel would be exposed, making the path look unsightly. You can rake pine needles off roadsides or driveways in late September when they are naturally falling from white pines. In North Carolina and Georgia, longleaf or slash pine needles are so plentiful that they are baled for sale.

If drainage is necessary across the path, dig a 2-or-3-foot trench across either side of, as well as under, the path and backfill with the same freely draining gravel you have under the path. Water can then cross the path rather that be dammed by it.

Every autumn, when the pine needles fall, scatter a new dressing of needles over the top. Depending on the nature of the moisture in your area, the bark mulch may need to be removed periodically and a new 2-inch layer put down. The decomposed bark and pine needle layer can either be scattered in the woods or used as compost around acid-loving shrubs such as rhododendrons.

TRODDEN EARTH

Trodden earth paths add to the natural feeling of a garden, and can be made in two ways. The first, the sunken path, has an aged look and brings the stroller closer to the plants so that they can be touched, smelled and seen at closer range (Figure 17.5). The sunken path in turn creates raised beds, which make maintenance easier and re-creates the childhood experience of seeing plants above eye level. The sunken path is a natural form, one reminiscent of paths trodden over years through woods or across back yards, or made by animals over time, the way cows or sheep create paths in a pasture or hillside. The second type of trodden earth path is raised to ensure adequate drainage. Mix gravel into the existing topsoil to elevate the path and at the same time increase the porosity of the soil.

PLANNING THE WOODLAND WALK

A woodland walk is best designed among the trees, not on paper, because points of interest in the woods—natural contours, rocks, trees and water—provide clues to the direction the path should take. The first clues to consider are existing plants and rocks. In some woodland, you will find huge lichen- and moss-covered rocks, vast rock outcroppings or smaller boulders with ferns growing here and there in crevices. Or you might find several closely growing trees that form a copse or pairs of trees that form entrances. There might be rotted stumps of trees that have given rise to miniature gardens of mosses, ferns and spleenworts.

Other points of interest include views through the woods to nearby meadows, mountain ranges or valleys, or pockets of soil that might later be easily and successfully planted. If you're lucky, you might find a variety of soil conditions among those areas, for with variety of soil type comes the potential for a broad range of plants.

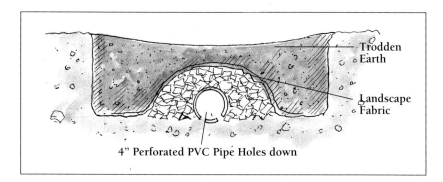

Trodden Earth

Landscape Fabric

4" Perforated PVC Pipe Holes down

FIGURE 17.5

As you walk through woodlands looking for those points of interest, carry a roll of bright orange forester's tape to mark them. Once you have explored the entire area, go back to the outside of the woods to consider the starting and ending points of the path. The starting point can be suggested by a door in the house, an existing pathway, an area of lawn or a break that exists or can be made in a wall or fence. A path should end near where it began, so that the house, for example, becomes both the setting-off point and the destination.

Once you know where the landmarks are in the woods and where the path will begin and end, you can begin to determine the exact layout of the path. Be careful not to be slavish in following the perimeter of the property, for you can end up with too many long, straight stretches. Curves and turns are what add suspense to a path and draw the walker on. Changes in direction are one way to vary the nature of a path. Changes in dimension are another. The trunks or branches of trees and shrubs on either side of the path can funnel closer and closer and then gradually or suddenly widen; tree branches above can also be left as is or pruned to create different effects. Pruning the lower limbs of several close-growing trees can create a cathedral-like canopy 20 or 30 feet above the forest floor, or the branches can be kept as low as 7 feet, to create a more intimate feeling.

Changing the distance between the viewer and a point of interest is yet another source of variety. After passing within 2 or 3 feet of a rock outcropping, you could come around a corner in the path and find yourself in a wide clearing, at the end of which is a dramatic view through the woods.

Once a path is roughly laid out, you can begin clearing. Divide the work into three phases. First work the length, removing saplings that can be uprooted by hand and shovel or cut with a handsaw. Next, if necessary, work the length of the path with a chain saw, removing dead trees and taking out larger ones that either impede the smooth running of the path, block views or confuse the image of more satisfying trees. Finally, make a third pass with pruning shears and a handsaw to fine-tune the path. Cut saplings to expose the trunk of a magnificent tree just off the path. Cut a "window" in saplings to open a view of a distant mountaintop. Consider where you might put a bench.

On low wet areas, you can take a cue from the old corduroy road. Tightly lay 15 or 20 3-to-6-inch-wide trunks of trees across or parallel to the line of the path in the wet soil to provide a solid walking surface. The trunks can be covered with bark mulch to provide a more uniform surface. Alternatively, cover 1-or-2-inch-thick wood with wood chips. Over a broader or deeper wet spot, you can lay 2 limbless tree trunks, and then nail planks across the trunks to form a rustic bridge. All of these solutions will make a graceful transition in the woods to carry you over wet, low places.

If you feel the path does not have enough inherent qualities, you might want to consider planting shrubs and woodsy perennials to create points of interest along the way. The next step, then, is to determine where to introduce additional plants to provide areas of surprise or intimacy, screening or drama. New plantings need to look as natural as possible, so place them, for example, near existing boulders and rock outcroppings.

A NEW PRODUCT FOR STABILIZING GRAVEL

In 1983, Jonathan Hubbs of Phoenix, Arizona, developed a nontoxic, organic soil binder that is just coming onto the national and international markets. Called "Stabilizer," this natural glue comes from a widely available desert plant that he dries and reduces to a powder. It is spread on the surface of gravels, decomposed granite, or small sandy aggregate materials at the rate of 10 pounds per 100 square feet, tilled into the top 2 to 3 inches and watered. Once dry, it binds particles ¼-inch or smaller together to the point at which erosion is stopped and people can walk or drive small machines over the surface, and not break it up. At the same time, it stays porous to water and air, and with a shovel you can dig through the stabilized surface to plant trees or shrubs. If at a later date the path needs to be taken up, you simply have to till it to break the binding action of the stabilizer. Because it is a new product, the jury is still out on its longevity, but it has been in use in Canada and Europe for at least three years and, even where the ground freezes, it remains intact. As Hubbs told me,"This is a very forgiving material. Landscape architects and homeowners can make use of more natural landscape materials like existing gravels and sands for paving paths rather than relying on less aesthetic and more costly materials like asphalt and concrete."

The soil is another consideration when siting new plants. In many cases, you will find woodland soil has been exhausted by ferocious competition for water and nutrients among existing trees and shrubs. In such cases, look for areas where the ground is not too rooty in relatively open spaces, in places near large boulders or rock outcroppings where roots have not yet penetrated, and in places where tree trunks have decomposed. Excavate the soil a foot deep or more and then replace it with a mixture of equal parts topsoil, compost and peat.

For relatively root-free areas where the soil is not wholly depleted but needs enrichment, I fork the soil and then amend it. In clay soil, use equal parts sand and topsoil; in sandy soil, use equal parts topsoil and compost.

You might want to plant on rather than in rooty woodland soil by spreading a 10-inch layer of a soil-compost-peat mixture on top of the woodland floor and planting directly in that, mulching heavily with leaf mold from the forest floor and then watering heavily. Tough woodland plants native to your area will then stand a good chance of getting established before the tree roots invade the low mound. Plants introduced along the woodland path should complement the beauty of the natural woodland, and your choices should be dictated by what native plants are available in your area.

The paths in this chapter run the gamut from the formal to informal, from the broad gravel paths of European manor houses to the simple trodden earth paths that might well have been created by sheep or cows. No other category of materials offers such a broad variety of possibilities as do loose materials. By using them in skillful ways, you can introduce any number of sounds, textures and colors into your paths and thus your whole garden.

Chapter Eighteen
Planting in the Gaps

PLANTS GROWING IN THE GAPS between bricks or stones not only look good against the paving material, but also soften the hard look of the surfaces. Having plants within the paving also underscores the visual link between paving and adjacent perennial beds or other plantings. Fragrance is another contribution plants within paving can make; when one walks on herbs such as thyme or chamomile, fragrant oils are released. In fact, the edges of any path should be considered for such plants. Interesting contrasts develop, too: the difference in texture and color between plants and paving materials; the impermanent feeling of the plant and the permanence of stone or brick.

If you have brick walkways, consider plants that will complement the color of the brick. For example, the blooms of *Geranium sanguineum* 'Ballerina' have brick-red striations that would blend the two colors together nicely. Another combination near brick might be the red-leaved barberry underplanted with *Polygonum affine* and *Heuchera* 'Palace Purple.' The gray-green color of *Nepeta siberica* complements a slightly grayish gravel.

Or you could create striking contrasts between the paving material and the foliage and flowers of plants near it. Gray-leaved plants such as snow-in-summer (*Cerastium tomentosum*), many dianthus, *Artemesia* 'Powys Castle,' edelweiss (*Leontopodium alpinum*) or *Santolina chamaecyparissus* would contrast nicely with dark red brick.

If you have existing paving that looks expansive and featureless, consider taking up sections or even breaking sections of the paving with a hammer and chisel to open up planting holes. Excavate the gap with a trowel and then fill with soil appropriate to the plant you want to set in. For example, many alpines will appreciate gravelly soil, even scree, that is well drained. *Dianthus deltoides* and *Papaver alpinum* both tolerate very dry, gravelly soil whereas *Arenaria montana,* a sandwort, will need soil that is well drained but moist.

Plants can also be set into steps to soften their hard edges and link them with surrounding plantings. Rosemary Verey notes in her book, *The Art of Planting:* "Ivy in variety and variegated lamium have been planted [in my garden] between the steps, and other plants are allowed to self-seed, changing a formal stairway into a relaxed, luxuriant set of steps. The only maintenance needed is to clip the plants back occasionally—especially the lamium—to keep the treads reasonably clear." Once you get plants established in a pathway, the amount of weeding is reduced because the perennial invariably fills the gaps, thus preventing weed seeds from taking hold.

FACING PAGE: In the Prozzo garden, designed by Gordon Hayward.

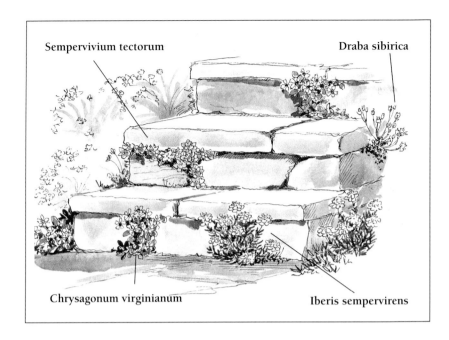

Sempervivium tectorum

Draba sibirica

Chrysagonum virginianum

Iberis sempervirens

ESTABLISHING PLANTS IN GAPS

Plants other than alpines do flourish in a richer soil, however. Patrick Chassé fills what he calls 'green joints' with equal parts sand and topsoil to which some compost has been added so that the soil will drain well yet have organic content sufficient to sustain growth.

Take seedlings from your beds and transplant them into the sandy loam in the gaps. Place an openwork wooden bushel basket over the seedlings or set up stones or concrete blocks on the steps and place boards on them to shade the newly transplanted seedlings for a few days. This shade will also keep the rocks cool and thus hold more moisture in the soil.

Use pine needles as a mulch to keep the sun's rays off the stones, and to hold moisture in the soil around the young seedlings or transplants until they become established after two or three weeks.

MOSS IN THE GAPS

Moss is an especially good plant for gaps between stones in a shady path. Timothy Atkinson of the Carolina Biological Supply Company is an expert on mosses. He finds that collected moss sections survive transplanting best if taken up when wet with rain. He stores moss patches in the shade, and keeps them moist until he is ready to plant them.

Prepare a site by uprooting all existing plants and watering the soil until it muddies. Spray the underside of the moss patch (also called sod) with water before gently pressing it into the new site. Moss can be stretched slightly to fit the space, but if gaps remain, fill them in with soil a week later.

No winter mulch is necessary. A solution of dried skim milk or buttermilk (1 part milk to 7 parts water) applied twice a day for 2 weeks in the spring restores winter damaged moss and helps acidify the soil. NEVER lime the area. Manure tea makes a good, all-purpose fertilizer. To make it, steep a burlap or cheesecloth bag of one bushel of fresh or dried manure in a barrel of water for 3 weeks; the resulting liquid should be the color of weak tea.

This can be applied in the spring and early summer, at intervals of a few weeks.

Be forewarned: gardens and ground covers of moss are not care-free. They must be hand-weeded, and they need careful attention to watering. If grown in a high-traffic area, moss wears down and must be replaced periodically.

Propagating moss is a little tricky. Prepare a shallow flat by lining the bottom with either very fine screening or slitted newspaper. Pour in an inch of a growing mix of equal parts fine sand and ground peat moss or sawdust. Level the mix and cover it with dampened cheesecloth. Crumble pieces of dried moss and sprinkle them evenly over the cheesecloth. Cover that layer with a second piece of cheesecloth that is cut slightly larger than the flat, and tuck in the edges. Water the flat by sprinkling gently but thoroughly. Keep this "seeded" flat shaded and moist for 6 to 8 weeks. When the moss grows through both layers of cheesecloth, it is ready to be lifted out carefully and planted where needed. The cloth rots away in time.

RECOMMENDED PLANTS

Following is a list of plants that can be used in or along pathways. I have divided the material into two major categories. First, I look at sun-loving plants: those that can be stepped on and not be harmed; those that will release their fragrance when stepped on; finally, low, ground huggers that are good for setting in the risers of steps or at the edges of pathways, where they will not be stepped on. Second, I look at shade plants: first at those that will tolerate being stepped on and so can be planted right in the walkway; next at low ground-hugging plants that do not like to be stepped on and so belong tucked into gaps in the risers of steps or along the edges of walkways.

Much of the information in the following list comes from the most up-to-date U.S.D.A. Plant Hardiness Map as reflected in Jacqueline Heriteau's 1990 *The National Arboretum Book of Outstanding Garden Plants* and is marked USDA*. If the specific plant cited is not included in Heriteau's book, the zone information will be marked USDA. The reason for making this distinction is that the pre-1990 USDA recommendations are based on very old data. The previous USDA map, revised in 1965, was based on average minimum winter temperatures from 1899 to 1938 with adjustments for 34 states based on information from 1931 to 1952. Since then, massive changes have taken place across the nation, which the 1990 map has taken into consideration.

For gardeners in the West—that is, from Montana south to New Mexico and west to the Pacific—more detailed zone information will be cited from *The Sunset Western Garden Book* (see bibliography), which divides that part of the country into 24 zones; that zone information will be labeled WEST.

Be aware that zone classification relies on general information that can never take into account the specific microclimates of your garden. For example, dense evergreens at the bottom of a slope through which a narrow path passes can trap cold air, dropping the temperature considerably, whereas a south-facing stone walkway with several bulky stone steps can collect heat during a sunny day and raise the nighttime temperature along the walk several degrees as the stones release the stored heat. You need to look at zone information as a broad stroke, and make your detailed decisions regarding planting according to local information from fellow gardeners, nursery people and your own experience.

FULL SUN
Plants that will take a lot of abuse:

- *Acaena buchananii:* 2" mat-forming hardy perennial with small grayish green foliage that thrives in well-drained sunny sites, though it will burn in hot sun. (See next entry for zone information)

    A. microphylla: 2" prostrate mat of yellow-bronze foliage; large red burrs follow inconspicuous flowers; USDA 6–7; WEST 4–9, 14–24.

- *Alchemilla mollis* (lady's mantle): gray-green hexagonal leaves with chartreuse flowers in summer; sow seeds directly in gaps; USDA 4–7.

    A. alpina (dwarf lady's mantle): 4"–6" alpine form with greenish-yellow flowers in late spring; USDA 3–4.

- *Arabis* spp. and cultivars (rock cress): appreciates well-drained soil in partial shade; USDA 4–7; WEST all zones.

- *Arenaria montana* (sandwort): 4"–6" mat-forming plant blooming white from late spring into early summer; will tolerate foot traffic, though it does need reliably moist soil in full sun; USDA 4; WEST 2–9, 14–24.

- *Campanula rotundifolia* (harebell): 6"–10"; leaves green; broad bell-shaped bright blue flowers July and August; self-sows in favorable sites; USDA* 3–9; WEST 1–9, 14–24.

- *Cerastium tomentosum* (snow-in-summer): gray-leaved, white flowers in early summer; requires good drainage; USDA 2–7; WEST all zones.

- *Erigeron speciosus* var. *macranthus* (Aspen daisy): small, daisy-like flowers; excellent for crevices between paving stones and in steps; native to Rocky Mountain area; USDA 2–8; WEST all zones

- *Gypsophila repens* (baby's breath): 6"–9" high trailing stems with clusters of small white or pink flowers in summer; USDA* 2–3; WEST 1–11, 14–16, 18–21.

- *Hippocrepis comosa* (horseshoe vetch): forms 3"-high mats with sweet pea-like golden yellow flowers in spring; tolerates drought and poor soil; good to hold soil around steps; WEST 8–24.

- *Mazus reptans* (mazus): to 1" creeping mats with lavender flowers in May–June; very vigorous with 1" leaves; takes light foot traffic; USDA to zone 3; WEST 1–7 (freezes to ground in winter, 14–24, evergreen).

- *Phlox subulata* (moss phlox): stiff, needle-like evergreen leaves on creeping stems; forms 6" mats with flowers ranging from white, pink, rose to lavender blue in early summer; USDA* 2–3; WEST 1–17.

- *Phyla nodiflora* (lippia): flat, ground-hugging mat; a lawn substitute with gray-green leaves; lilac-rose flowers spring to fall; good in desert areas; WEST 8–24.

- *Sagina subulata* (pearlwort or Irish moss): a dense, mat-forming perennial that forms 5" flowering stems (Cultivar 'Aurea' —called Scotch moss has yellow-green leaves); both need good soil, drainage and ample water; USDA 4; WEST 1–11, 14–24.

- *Saponaria ocymoides* (Rock soapwort): a 3"–6" spreading perennial with bright pink flowers in summer; it can be walked on primarily because it

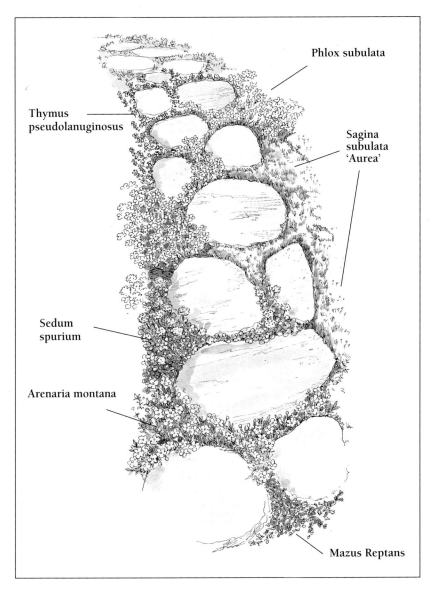

Phlox subulata

Thymus
pseudolanuginosus

Sagina
subulata
'Aurea'

Sedum
spurium

Arenaria montana

Mazus Reptans

spreads rapidly and setting it between paving stones and walking on it will serve to contain this vigorous plant; USDA 2–7; WEST all zones.

- *Sedum* dwarf types: these low, drought-tolerant plants won't withstand tromping, but along the edges of a path in full sun plants such as *Sedum acre* var. *aureum,* with its yellow flowers and carpet-like foliage will satisfy; USDA 3–8; WEST all zones.
- *Thymus pseudolanuginosus* (wooly thyme): 2" silver gray mats; lavender flowers in May – June; USDA 4–9; WEST all zones.

   T. praecox 'Albus': Emerald green mats with white flowers in May–June; USDA 4–9; WEST all zones.
- *Vinca minor* 'Miss Jekyll'—white flowers and "Bowles'—blue flowers (periwinkle or myrtle): these cultivars, particularly 'Jekyll,' are tolerant of full sun though they do like rich soil; tough and drought tolerant; USDA 4–9; WEST all zones but in 1–3, 7, 10–13 they will grow best in shade.
- *Zoysia tenuifolia:* creeping fine-textured mounding grass/ground cover that creates a mossy, Japanese effect; likes sun but tolerates some filtered shade; WEST 8, 9, 12–24.

Fragrant plants for the pathway:

- *Chamaemelum nobile* (chamomile): forms 3"–6" mats of lacy leaves; yellow flowers in late summer; fragrance of apples when crushed; WEST all zones.
- *Dianthus gratianopolitanus* 'Old Spice' (Cheddar pink): double-fringed salmon pink, very fragrant; great in steps out of harm's way of one's feet; *D. g.* 'Snowbank': highly perfumed, shaggy, double-white; USDA* 3–9; WEST all zones.
- *Geranium macrorrhizum* 'Ingwerson's Variety' (cranesbill): highly scented leaves that form a 10"–12" mounded perennial with pink flowers in late spring; USDA 3–8; WEST all zones.
- *Malcomia maritima* (Virginia stock): 6"–9" annual; seeds will give rise to plants with mixed colors: lilac, pink, red, white; sweetly scented; sow seeds directly into gaps between stones in paving and mulch with pine needles until they get established.
- *Mentha requienii* (Corsican or creeping mint): creeping or mat-forming ½" mat to create a mossy effect; tiny light purple flowers and round, bright green, tiny leaves; needs partial shade and a rich evenly moist soil; minty, sage-like fragrance when walked on; WEST 5–9, 12–24.
- *Thymus citriodorus* (lemon thyme): lemon scented; variegated gold and green leaf; lavender flowers in late spring; 'Aureus,' gold variegated leaves; 'Doone Valley,' golden highlights on foliage; USDA 3–9.

  T. herba-barona (caraway thyme): 4"–5" wiry, prostrate stems form dark green mats with rose-pink blooms in May–June; caraway fragrance when stepped on; USDA 4–9; WEST all zones.

  T. serpyllum (mother of thyme): 2"–6" high; dark-green aromatic leaves form dense green mats with cerise flowers; USDA 4–9; WEST all zones.

Low plants that can't take a lot of abuse (good for setting in the risers of steps, or at the edges of steps or pathways). Alpines and thousands of other rock garden plants are suitable for such a setting. Consider androsaces, saxifrages, arabis, *Dianthus alpinus*, *Campanula portenschlagiana*, armerias, arenarias, *Raoulia lutescens*, *Sedum spathulifolium* 'Capa Blanca' and other low sedums. Any catalogue of alpines or rock garden plants will stir your thoughts. And here are some specific recommendations:

- *Achillea tomentosa* 'Aurea' (wooly yarrow): lacy, ground-hugging gray-green foliage with yellow flower heads on 8" stems in May–June; USDA* 2–9; WEST all zones.

  A. t. 'King Edward VIII': pale yellow flowers on 10" stems in May–June with lacy green foliage.
- *Aethionema warleyense* (stone cress): 3"–8" low, bushy plant topped with clusters of rose-pink flowers; light soil, excellent drainage in full sun; foliage bluish-gray; USDA to zone 4; WEST 1–9, 14–21.
- *Antennaria dioica rosea* (pussytoes): flat gray mat with pink pussytoe-like flowers in May; requires excellent drainage; USDA 3–8.
- *Arctostaphylos uva-ursi* (bearberry): a woody, prostrate ground cover with small shiny bright green leaves that turn red in winter; a North American native; likes sandy soil; USDA* 2–8; WEST 1–9, 14–21.

- *Armeria maritima* (thrift): narrow stiff leaves in compact tufts; white, pink or rose globe-shaped flowers on 8"–10" stalks over much of the season; USDA 4–8; WEST all zones.
- *Aubretia deltoides* 'Red Carpet': 3"–4", spreading, with gray-green leaves; flourishes in well-drained limey soil in full sun; blooms deep red in spring; cut back after flowers have faded to keep it neat; USDA 4–8; WEST 1–9, 14–21.
- *Chrysogonum virginianum* (golden star): 5" carpet of yellow on green all summer; likes soil surface damp; USDA* 5–9.
- *Draba sibirica*: prostrate foliage, yellow flowers in April and again in October; USDA 4.
- *Iberis sempervirens* (evergreen candytuft): about 10" high, narrow-leaved evergreen; dense white blooms in mid-spring; USDA* 4–8; WEST all zones.
- *Oxalis adenophylla*: 4" high tufts of crinkly, gray-green leaflets with lilac pink flowers on 4"–6" stalks in late spring; good drainage in full sun; USDA to zone 5; WEST 4–8, 12–24.

    O. hirta: drought tolerant; in late fall bright rose pink flowers over clover-like leaves; plant bulbs in fall; WEST 8–9, 14–24.
- *Sempervivium tectorum* (hens and chickens): rosettes of succulent leaves 4"–6" across; very few ungainly flowers on 4"–8" stems; USDA 3–8; WEST all zones.

FULL OR PARTIAL SHADE
Plants that will take a lot of abuse:
- *Ajuga reptans* (bugleweed): there are many cultivars, all low to the ground with 4"–6" flower stems that bloom in May in blue, white or pink; leaves can be shiny dark green, bronze, crinkly, variegated white and green or variegated white, pink and purple; USDA 3–9; WEST all zones.
- *Alchemilla mollis* (lady's mantle): 1'–2' high plants that will tolerate a great deal of shade; see description on page 214.
- *Cornus canadensis*—recently renamed *Chamaepericlymenum canadensis* (bunchberry): 6" hardy carpetlike perennial that enjoys moist, peaty woodland soil; tiny clusters of white blooms in May and June followed by red berries. In autumn, leaves become burgundy red. Will tolerate dry shade as well; native to northern California to Alaska and eastward; USDA 2; WEST 1–7.
- *Cotula squalida* (New Zealand brass buttons): evergreen leaves are soft fern-like bronze green 2"–3" high; flowers like tiny brass buttons; will tolerate sun as well as medium shade; WEST 4–9, 14–24.
- *Dichondra micrantha* (dichondra): a ground-hugging plant (and lawn substitute) with leaves shaped like miniature water lily pads; will tolerate sun as well; sow seed in April or May around stepping-stones; WEST 8, 9, 12–24.
- *Gaultheria procumbens* (wintergreen): a native groundcover, to 6"; creeping stems with shiny leaves with tiny white flowers in summer followed by scarlet berries; USDA* 4; WEST 2–7, 14–17.
- *Mitchella repens* (Partridgeberry): native, to 3"; very small, rounded evergreen leaves, light pink flowers and red berries in fall; USDA to zone 3.

- *Mazus reptans* (mazus): see description on page 214.
- *Phlox stolonifera* 'Bruce's White' or 'Blue Ridge':
- *Polytrichum commune* (common haircap moss): a moss found world-wide; excellent for gathering around stepping-stones in woodland settings; tolerant of a wide range of light and moisture conditions; the toughest, most versatile of the mosses; zone hardiness not established; if it's native in your part of the world, use it.
- *Saxifraga stolonifera* (*S. sarmentosa*) (strawberry geranium): creeping plant that makes runners like strawberries; roundish, white-veined leaves 4" across; white flowers; moist soil essential; WEST 1–9, 14–24.
- *Tiarella cordifolia* (foamflower): 6" high; white flowers that bloom in spring over heart-shaped leaves along creeping stems; a New England native; USDA 3–8.
- *Vinca minor* 'Bowles' (periwinkle or myrtle): see listings on page 215.

Plants that won't take much abuse (good for setting in the risers of steps or at the edges of steps or paths):
- *Asarum europaeum* (European ginger): 3"–4" ground cover with glossy, heart-shaped, evergreen leaves; *A. canadense* is more heat-tolerant but lacks shiny leaves (USDA 8); *A. hartwegii* is Sierra wild ginger, an Oregon and California native; USDA* 4–8.
- *Astilbe hybrids*: 'Inshirach Pink': 10" pale pink spikes over dark bronze-green foliage in July–August; USDA 4–8; 'Sprite': 12" pale pink spikes over dark lacy foliage; USDA* 4–8; WEST 2–7, 14–17 (short lived in 8, 9, 18–24).
- *Bellis perennis* 'Pomponette' (English daisy): rosettes of dark green leaves 1"–2" long; mixed pink, rose, white or red daisy flowers in spring and early summer to 6"; USDA to zone 3; WEST all zones.
- *Chrysogonum virginianum* (golden star): long, triangular-toothed leaves; bright yellow, daisy-like, long-blooming flowers; to 6"; USDA* 5–9.
- Hostas: there are many varieties and cultivars, but if you choose any, choose the smallest, so they snug into the risers in steps or along the edges of shady paths made of stepping-stones. 'Wogon Gold' is a dwarf hosta that brings a golden light to the shady woodland. 'Saishu Jima' is another very small hosta with dark green, lance-shaped leaves and violet flowers in August–September; don't plant where deer are a problem; USDA 3–9; WEST 1–10, 12–21.
- *Soleirolia soleirolii* (baby's tears or angel's tears): a tiny-leaved carpeting plant 1"–3" high for around stepping-stones, for example; leaves and stems easily injured but quickly rejuvenates itself; WEST 8–24.
- *Viola cornuta* (violets): tufted plants 6"–8" high with oval leaves; well-drained, cool conditions will give rise to the range of flowers available in this common plant; USDA 6–9; WEST all zones.

    V. labradorica (species of violet): hardy perennials with purple-tinted mats of foliage and mauve flowers in spring; slightly moist conditions, though it will tolerate dry conditions; USDA 3–9. 🪷

Appendix A: Sources

GARDEN STRUCTURES AND GATES

The things the paths lead to or through.

The Bow House
P.O. Box 900
Bolton, MA 01740
(508) 779-6464
Fax: (508) 779-2272
A creative woodworking business manufacturing a variety of architecturally and aesthetically pleasing summer houses, pool houses, cabanas and gazebos in kit form. They also manufacture bridges for pathways, arbors, and a Chinese-inspired, serpentine fence that can follow a curved path. Materials used are southern yellow pine, redwood for structural members, white pine for trim and red or white cedar for clapboard and shingles.

Dalton Pavilions
7260 - 68 Oakley Street
Philadelphia, PA 19111
(215) 342-9804
A fourth generation of woodworkers constructing western red cedar gazebos since 1954.

The Garden Concepts Collection
4646 Poplar Avenue
Suite 202
Memphis, TN 38124-1233
(901) 756-1649
Fax (901) 755-4564
Gazebos, pergolas, arbors, gates, planters, painted wood furniture, trelliswork; they use iroko (an African teak substitute) and Honduran mahogany; will custom-build according to your specifications.

The Garden Gate
P.O. Box 1117
Cedar Ridge, CA 95924
(916) 272-8109
Fax (916) 346-6756
John Gunderson's new business offers handcrafted redwood and poplar garden gates including a sunrise design, heart and tree motifs and latticing.

Gazebos by Evans
2867 Calle Esteban
San Clemente, CA 92672
(714) 361-5096

Gloucester Street Gate Company
P.O. Box 281
Salisbury, MD 21801
(301) 546-4384
Stephen Slaughter offers six traditional designs in painted white oak and cypress; designs can be made to custom sizes.

Herndon and Merry, Inc.
519 West Thompson Lane
Nashville, TN 37211
(615) 254-8771
Fax (615) 254-6471
Custom-made iron gates.

Historical Fence and Ironworks
P.O. Box 141459
Cincinnati, OH 45250-1459
(513) 244-1442
Manufacturer of quality handcrafted ironwork fencing and gates, including driveway gates.

Ivywood Gazebo
3rd Floor
P.O. Box 9
Fairview Village, PA 19409
(215) 584-9699
Fax (215) 631-0846
Fine wooden gazebos, arbors and bird-feeders built from western red cedar or pressure-treated southern pine.

Machine Designs, Inc.
652 Glenbrook Road
Stamford, CT 06906
Landscape buildings, pergolas, trelliswork.

New England Tools Co., Ltd.
P.O. Box 30
Chester, NY 10918
(914) 782-5332
Fine metalsmiths who create garden gates for estates or intimate settings; historical reproductions; custom work.

Seahorse Trading
Berryville, VA 22611
(Write for nearest distributor)
Victorian wirework garden structures.

The Timeless Garden
P.O. Box 5406
Arlington, VA 22205
(703) 536-8958
Beautifully handcrafted, authentically re-produced, historic garden gates.

Vixen Hill Gazebos
Main Street
Elverson, PA 19520
Gazebos, with a video showing gazebo assembly, for $10.

BENCHES AND FURNITURE

Places to sit along the way; means to drawing people into the garden.

Adirondack Designs
Cypress Street Center
350 Cypress Street
Fort Bragg, CA 95437
(707) 964-4940
George Griffith's company employs disabled adults to make high-quality Adirondack-style furniture of second growth Mendocino County redwood.

Alpine Millworks Co.
70 S. Allison Street
Lakewood, CO 80226
(303) 238-4894
British-style furniture in teak and mahogany and Adirondack-style furniture also available in redwood.

Amish Country Collection
R.D. 5 Sunset Valley
Newcastle, PA 16105
Wood reproduction garden furniture.

Barnsley House Garden Furniture,
Barnsley House,
Cirencester,
Glos., GL7 5EE
UK
Teak garden furniture from Charles Verey, Rosemary Verey's son.

Bergdorf Goodman
754 Fifth Avenue
New York, NY 10019
(212) 753-7300
Antique garden furniture.

British-American Marketing
Welshpool Road
Lionville, PA 19353
(800) 344-0259
Teak benches, tables, planters and lampposts.

Brown Jordan
9860 Gidley Street
P.O. Box 5688
El Monte, CA 91734
(818) 443-8971
Fine furniture of aluminum framing with vinyl straps.

Cassidy Brothers Forge
Route 1
Rowley, MA 01969
Hand-forged ironwork: gates and custom orders.

The Cedar Shop
Brimley, MI 49715
(906) 248-3392
Steve Lepine supplies Shutt Manufacturing with benches, gingerbread roofed settees and gazebo kits of red cedar, and is designing his own furniture and gazebos of locally harvested and milled white cedar from Michigan's Upper Peninsula.

Christopher Design
1901 South Great S.W. Parkway
Suite 214
Grand Prairie, TX 75051
Bent willow furniture of fine design made by the most recent generation of craftspeople in this family.

Johns H. Congdon Furniture
RFD #1 Box 1765
North Fayston, VT 05660
(802) 485-8927
Garden furniture of the highest quality, offered with or without hand-carved floral design motifs. Custom hand-carved wooden furniture.

Country Casual
17317 Germantown Road
Germantown, MD 20874
(800) 872-8352
(301) 540-0040
Designers and direct importers of solid teak garden furniture made in five of England's finest joineries and custom workshops. Designs include modular architectural trellis of solid iroko wood. All freight costs paid within continental U.S.; orders are shipped within four working days.

Garden Concepts
P.O. Box 241233
Memphis, TN 38124-1233
(901) 756-1649
A very broad collection of superior wooden chairs, benches, tables, arches, entrance ways, gates and planter boxes in mahogany, teak, cypress, poplar or maple, painted or unpainted, in such designs as Newport, Biedermeier, Lutyens, Holwell, Oakley, Pedimental, Chinese Chippendale. Contact Memphis office for your nearest distributor.

Garden Source Furnishings
200 Bennett Street NW
Atlanta, GA 30309
(404) 351-6446
Suzanne Currey offers Southern-flavored garden furniture including Appalachian willow twig furniture, Tennessee porch rockers of ash or sassafras, rustic cedar "lodge" chairs and tables and the Winterthur collection of graceful, wrought-iron furniture. Catalogue, $3.00.

Grant's
One Wilmington Road
Lake Placid, NY 12946
(518) 523-3400
Rustic Adirondack furniture.

Grosfillex
Muhlenberg Industrial Mall
4201 Pottsville Pike
Reading, PA 19605
(215) 921-9151
Synthetic-resin furniture and umbrellas.

Horticultural Design Products
Lenora Square, Suite 201
1000 Lenora Street
Seattle, WA 98121
(206) 292-8155
Furniture, stone containers.

Irving and Jones
Village Center
Colebrook, CT 06021
(203) 379-9219
Wrought-iron furniture reproducing classic Regency period designs. Galvanizing and painting prevent rust, so can be left in the garden year-round. The pieces in white, black or woodlands green are hand-crafted and produced to last for generations.

Kingsley - Bate Ltd.
P.O. Box 6797
Arlington, VA 22206
(703) 931-9200
Fax (703) 931-6124
Carved benches and seats made of Honduran mahogany from "carefully controlled government plantations and Javanese teak with ensured replanting policies." Their Smartwood Certification from The Rainforest Alliance ensures that all wood in their products comes from renewable sources.

Lloyd-Flanders
3010 Tenth Street
P. O. Box 500
Menominee, MI 49858
(800) 526-9894
Victorian - Romantic styles are designed to resemble Lloyd Loom wicker furniture of the early 1900s. All-weather wicker is processed to eliminate pores so it won't become brittle and dry out. It is dipped in latex and topped with a baked-on polyester finish. The wicker is contoured to an aluminum frame and is appropriate for indoor or outdoor use.

Lyon-Shaw
P.O. Box 2069
Salisbury, NC 28145
(704) 636-8270
Wrought-iron and contemporary furniture

Moultrie Manufacturing Co.
P.O. Drawer 1179
Route 5, Quitman Highway
Moultrie, GA 31768
Wrought-iron furniture, urns, fountains, plaques.

Newport Woodworks
767 East Main Road
Middletown, RI 02840
(401) 849-6850
Wooden furniture.

Smith and Hawken
25 Corte Madera
Mill Valley, CA 94941
(415) 383-2000
Teak furniture from renewable resources.

Summit Furniture, Inc.
P.O. Box S
Carmel, CA 93921
(408) 394-4401
Fax (408) 394-5242
Award-winning plantation-grown teak furniture from designer Kipp Stewart; contact a designer or the Carmel Office for the name of a showroom in your area.

Wood Classics
Osprey Lane
Gardiner, NY 12525
(914) 255-7871
Fax (914) 255-7881
Eric and Barbara Goodman's two generation, family-owned company manufactures handcrafted teak and Honduran mahogany benches, chairs and tables, including a carved art collection designed by Hudson River Valley artist Ben Bishop; free catalogue.

Woodbrook Furniture Manufacturers
P.O. Box 175
Trussville, AL 35173
(800) 828-3607
Distinctive wooden garden furniture.

Worthington Resort Furniture
P.O. Box 53101
Atlanta, GA 30355
(404) 872-1608
Elegant teak and painted cypress furniture inspired by the world's great resorts; cast natural stone or terra-cotta colored planters.

Adam York
Unique Merchandise Mart - Building 6
Hanover, PA 17333
Outdoor furnishings, birdhouses.

GARDEN ORNAMENTS, STATUARY, PLANTERS

For points of interest that will draw people into the garden: at the base of steps; next to gates or entrances; on terraces or patios; at junctions where paths cross; to terminate a view down a straight path.

Abbey Garden Sundials
Indian Hill Road
P.O. Box 102
Pakenham, Ontario
Canada KOA 2X0
(613) 256-3973
Cast bronze sundials designed in Wales by expert craftsmen with or without quotations or commemorative messages or dates.

American Sundials, Inc.
300 Main Street
Point Arena, CA 95468
(707) 884-3082
Solid brass sundials.

Architectural Antiques, Ltd.
410 St. Pierre
Montreal, Quebec
Canada H24 2MZ
Salvaged columns, balustrades, fountains, etc.

Boston Turning Works
42 Plympton Street
Boston, MA 02118
(617) 482-9085
Peter Maguire makes finials, columns, column bases and caps, porch posts, balusters and newel posts.

Cape Cod Cupola
78 State Road
Route 6
North Dartmouth, MA 02747
Copper, aluminum and cast metal weather vanes, sundials, lettering and, of course, cupolas.

Joan Cook
P.O. Box 21628
Fort Lauderdale, FL 38335
Planters, outdoor furniture.

Country Floors, Inc.
300 East 61st Street
New York, NY 10021
Imports unglazed terra-cotta paving tiles suitable for outdoor use.

East/West Gardens
1259 El Camino Real, Suite 196
Menlo Park, CA 94025
(415) 326-6997
Metal garden sculptures from the Orient.

Florentine Craftsmen
46-24 28th Street
Long Island City, NY 11101
(718) 937-7632
(800) 876-3567
Cast aluminum, cast stone, wrought-iron, hand-carved limestone furniture. Bronze sundials, lead and cast iron animals, figures, birdbaths, urns. Wrought-iron wall fountains, many cast aluminum and lead free-standing fountains, all with recirculating pumps and plumbing.

Garden Iron
166 North Clifton Avenue
Louisville, KY 40206
Steel topiary forms in three stock shapes: flame, cone, sphere; will custom make.

Garden Source
200 Bennett Street, NW
Atlanta, GA 30309
(404) 351-6446
Whimsical Tennessee rustic painted bird-houses with names like Potato Barn, Country Store, Gas Station, Fish Camp and Aunt Edna's, or twig birdhouses; $3.00 catalogue includes furnishings.

Haddonstone, Ltd.
Seahorse Trading Co., Inc. (Importers)
P.O. Box 677
Berryville, VA 22611
Cast stoneware urns, planters and balustrades from England.

Hen-Feathers
10 Balligomingo Road
Gulph Mills, PA 19428
(215) 828-1721
Fax (215) 828-8617
Classical garden sculptures, planters and fountains.

Hughes and Wentworth
Main Street
P.O. Box 35
Francestown, NH 03043
(603) 547-3633
Jenny Hughes and Craig Wentworth create elegant wooden birdhouses and feeders.

International Terra Cotta Inc.
690 N. Robertson Blvd.
Los Angeles, CA 90069
Imported Italian handmade terra-cotta pots, sandstone and bronze statuary, urns, fountains; will custom fabricate.

Irreplaceable Artifacts
14 Second Avenue
New York NY 10003
Antique ornaments from demolished buildings.

Lazy Hill Farm Designs
Lazy Hill Road
Colerain, NC 27924
(919) 356-2828
Handcrafted birdhouses of cypress with rounded miniature cedar shingles. Betty Baker's designs range from bluebird houses to an eight-compartment minia-turized English dovecote for songbirds as well as a birdfeeder and a shelter and grotto for figurines.

Kenneth Lynch and Sons, Inc.
Box 488
Wilton, CT 06897
(203) 762-8363
Fax (203) 762-2999
Fifty-year-old company created by Ken-neth Lynch, a gifted ironworker, who, with four helpers, spent four years repair-ing the Statue of Liberty in the twenties. Now son Timothy runs the company, which offers a vast range of sundials and spheres, weather vanes, benches, foun-tains and fountain nozzles, pools, Japan-ese stone lanterns.

New England Garden Ornaments
38 Brookfield Road
North Brookfield, MA 01535
(508) 867-4474
Humphrey Sutton's firm is the U.S. source for Chilstone Garden Ornaments, made in Kent, England, plus English trel-liswork, cast-iron garden edging and lead ornaments.

Provendor
Tiverton Four Corners
3883 Main Road
Tiverton, RI 02878
Garden ornaments, terra-cotta pots.

Robinson Iron
P.O. Box 1119
Robinson Road
Alexander City, AL 35010
(205) 329-8486
(800) 824-2157
Cast-iron fountains, statuary, urns and vases, furniture, and posts and finials available in many finishes. They recycle local scrap and salvaged iron as well as the sand used for molds. Call for a cata-logue ($5.00) or the nearest representative.

Christine Sibley
15 Waddell Street, NE
Atlanta, GA 30307
(404) 688-3329
Fax (404) 688-0665
Sibley has cast reproductions of her highly original and romantic sculptures, including wall pieces, planters, birdbaths, coping stones and borders, pavers, tiles and curbing. Each piece is handcrafted in fiberglass or reinforced concrete in four pigments with four other color washes available. Send for catalogue that in-cludes a list of sales representatives.

Southern Statuary and Stone
3401 Fifth Avenue
South Birmingham, AL 35222
Garden sculpture.

Urban Archaeology
137 Spring Street
New York, NY 10012
(212) 431-6969
Artifacts from demolished buildings, new cast iron from Robinson Iron, urns, fences.

Wind and Weather
P.O. Box 2320
Mendocino, CA 95460
Weather instruments, weather vanes and sundials.

Windrow Forge
Stevens Road
Lebanon, NH 03766
Ray Sobel is an artist-blacksmith who does custom blacksmithing of highly re-fined weather vanes, signs and garden sculptures. All his work is commissioned, unique and thus, as the English say, "one off."

Zona
97 Greene Street
New York, NY 10012
(212) 925-6750
Garden furniture, ornaments, garden tools, terra-cotta pots.

LIGHTING

To draw people into and through the garden at night by lighting the way.

BEGA / FS
Forms and Surfaces
Box 50442
Santa Barbara, CA 93150
(805) 565-1575
Low-voltage garden lighting that is ele-gant, energy efficient. 12-volt floodlights, spotlights, pathway and accent lighting, much of which was designed by Ron Rezek, one of Southern California's fore-most lighting designers. Free catalogue and pricing are obtained through their network; contact Santa Barbara office.

Classic and Country Crafts
5100 - 1B Clayton Road, Suite 291
Concord, CA 94521
(415) 672-4337
Ted Siekierski first designed Carmel Lily copper and bronze landscape light for his own garden. It comes in several styles and uses low-voltage (12v) design for safety and economy.

Doner Design, Inc.
2175 Beaver Valley Pike
New Providence, PA 17560
(717) 786-8891
Five handcrafted copper landscape lights in two styles, traditional and mushroom.

Genie House
P.O. Box 456
Charles Street
Medford, NJ 08055

Greenlee Landscape Lighting
1220 Champion Circle, Suite 116
Carrollton, TX 75006
(214) 466-1133
Functional, simple designs for spotlighting and moonlight effects; fixtures accept incandescent or mercury vapor lamps.

Hanover Lantern
470 High Street
Hanover, PA 17331
(717) 632-6464
(800) 233-7196
Fax (717) 632-5039
Terralights are functional, decorative, even fanciful lighting systems made of cast and painted aluminum for quality and long life. All terralights can be converted from 120 volts to 12 volts for safety, ease of installation and economy.

Kim Lighting, Inc.
16555 East Gale Avenue
P.O. Box 1275
City of Industry, CA 91749
A comprehensive list of outdoor fixtures of copper and spun aluminum for concealed and accent lights or spotlighting. Bulbs limited to 150 watts.

Lighting Services
Tom Longhurst
7130 Thompson Road
Lantana, FL 33467
(407) 966-2440
Fax (407) 966-2343
Longhurst worked with Willem Wirtz and Cy Roossine, preeminent garden lighting designers on the East Coast. Roossine designed this fixture, clearly the finest, most durable on the market. Heavy-duty cast aluminum fixture that will accept an aluminum shield, and "egg crate" louvre to shield the bulb from sight in exposed places as well as bulbs from 10 to 250 watts. Heat-treated lens, spring-lock hinge (not set-screw) for easy bulb changing. In oceanside gardens for 20 years with no problems yet; guaranteed unconditionally for three years. Longhurst designs and installs garden lighting.

Liteform Designs
P.O. Box 3316
Portland, OR 97208
(503) 257-8464 in Oregon
(800) 458-2505
Outdoor lighting products in various styles: contemporary wood made of California redwood; post-modern metal; natural earthen ceramic; aluminum.

Nightscaping by Loran, Inc.
1705 East Colton Avenue
Redlands, CA 92373
(714) 794-2121
Fax (714) 794-7292
Low, 12-volt outdoor lighting fixtures of all kinds, painted black.

Popovitch Associates, Inc.
346 Ashland Avenue
Pittsburgh, PA 15228
(412) 344-6097

FINE TOOLS
Hand tools to construct and maintain your paths.

P.J. Carroll and Co.
Customer Service Center
2515 E. 43rd Street
P.O. Box 23667
Chattanooga, TN 37422-9910
A source for Wilkinson Sword garden tools including the hard-to-find long-handled, vertical action edging shears for maintaining the edges of lawn paths.

Clapper's
1125 Washington Street
West Newton, MA 02165
(617) 244-7909
Fine tools from around the world.

deVan Koek
Dutch Trader
3100 Industrial Terrace
Austin, TX 78759
(800) 992-1220
Superior Dutch tools, including the only turfing iron (a tool for taking up lawn) available—as far as I know—in the United States.

Ecosentials
69 Elliot Street
Brattleboro, VT 05301
(802) 257-9377
Christine Serrentino carries Livos nontoxic wood preservatives and stains made in West Germany; water-based and oil-based preservatives and paints from plant oils and natural resins for people who are sensitive to harsh chemicals. Livos, the Celtic word for light, life and sheen, was founded 15 years ago. (A West Coast dealer for this product is Plant Chemistry, 1365 Rufina Circle, Santa Fe, NM 87501 (505) 438-3448.)

The Gardener's Eye
P.O. Box 22382
Denver, CO 80222
Thoughtfully chosen, environmentally sound gardening products including fine hand tools.

Green Mountain Glove Company, Inc.
P.O. Box 25
Randolph, VT 05060
(802) 728-9160
*Goatskin gloves—the best type when
working with stone, brick, concrete or
rough wood.*

Kinsman Co.
River Road
Point Pleasant, PA 18950
(800) 733-5613
(215) 297-5613 in Pennsylvania
Fax (215) 297-0210
*Graham and Michele Kinsman offer a
fine selection of plant supports, English
watering cans, forged cultivating tools,
arches and arbors and German birdhouses; free 72-page catalogue.*

Langenbach
P.O. Box 453
Blairstown, NJ 07825
(201) 362-5886
Fax (201) 362-5115
*Fine tools from around the world: hand
tools by Yankee Craftsmen are perfect for
weeding and cultivating between stones
and pavers; lawn and edging shears by
Rolcut; Jenks and Cattell, Ltd. stainless
steel tools; a fine assortment of long-handled hand tools; wheelbarrows.*

A.M. Leonard, Inc.
6665 Spiker Road
P.O. Box 816
Piqua, OH 45356
(800) 543-8955
Fax (513) 773-8640
Wide range of tools for professionals.

Walt Nicke Co.
36 McLeod Lane
P.O. Box 433
Topsfield, MA 01983
(508) 887-3388
*A small company with a 30-year tradi-
tion of selling fine gardening tools, many
from England and Europe, and a thoughtful, black and white, no-nonsense free
catalogue called "Garden Talk."*

Ringer Corp.
9959 Valley View Road
Eden Prairie, MN 55344
*Natural gardening catalogue along with
excellent hand tools.*

Smith and Hawken
25 Corte Madera
Mill Valley, CA 94941
(415) 383-2000
*Tools, garden clothing; a business that re-
sponds to your letters and special re-
quests, to the environment, to the changing needs of environmentally conscious
gardeners.*

Appendix B: Indigenous Materials

The best materials for the surface of your paths may well come from nearby.

NORTHEAST

Stone:

- Marble (crushed or sawn flagging; white or streaked with gray) from Proctor, Vermont
- Pennsylvania or New York bluestone— gray or blue-gray, cut or random
- Goshen schist or Conway schist from near Goshen, Massachusetts; easily split for stepping-stones or stone carpet
- Delaware River stone—gray, smooth sedimentary river rock
- Old Spruce Mountain quartzite from Connecticut—a gray quartzite with sparkly flecks of mica and a light copper "wash" on the surface
- Silver Lakes Connecticut quartzite— a very hard shiny dark gray surface with tiny black flecks

Hard Loose Materials:

- Oyster shells on the eastern shore of Maryland
- Red granite screenings (a gravel) from Pennsylvania
- Pink crushed aggregate from Concord, Massachusetts
- Pink crushed granite from Maine
- Crushed gray granite in varying sizes and grades from New Hampshire
- Peastone (aka grit)—⅜-inch stone in mixed colors

Soft Loose Materials:

- Native mosses
- White pine or spruce needles

SOUTHEAST

Stone:

- North Georgia shale (aka Cherokee)
- Georgia sandstone
- Crab Orchard, Tennessee sandstone—dark or light gray and buff
- Granite from Stone Mountain, Georgia—cut or crushed
- Red river stones from Georgia
- Tennessee and Georgia fieldstone— sandstones
- Shell cap boulders, the top layer of the bedrock under the central spine of Florida
- Multi-colored beach pebbles— whitish-yellow to white

Hard Loose Materials:

- Marl—broken or crushed Florida bedrock stone
- Crushed seashells from Boca Grande, Florida

Soft Loose Materials:

- Processed melaleuca tree bark mulch from southern Florida
- Cypress bark graded from fine (A) to very rough (C)
- Cedar bark
- Pine needles from longleaf pine (*Pinus palustris*) or slash pine (*Pinus elliottii*)

MIDWEST

Stone:

- Limestone from Bloomington, Indiana—a light gray, almost white (aka Indiana buff or Sherwood cut stone)
- Dolomitic limestone from quarries in Lannon, Wisconsin near Milwaukee—light gray to buff, orange, brown, gray or blue

MOUNTAINS

Stone:

- Colorado pink or reddish sandstone
- Idaho quartzite—bright gray or gray and gold; glitters because of the quartzite in it; very hard
- Utah sandstone in browns, tans, creams (random or cut)

SOUTHWEST

Stone:

- Arizona sandstone (aka flagstone) in pinks, reds, browns with names such as John Brown, Dark Rose, Buckskin—cut or random edged
- Arizona river rock, smooth and rounded, in sizes ranging from ⅜ inch to 12 inches, in reds, browns, buffs, beige
- Texas Laredo blend—a light gray, shiny, very hard quartzite

Hard Loose Materials:

- Arizona decomposed granite gravels in reds, amber, golds, buffs that come with names like Mission Red, Yavapai Silver, Madison Gold

WEST COAST

Hard Loose Materials:

- Pea gravels, rounded, in grays, reds, beige and browns
- Decomposed gravels in grays, ginger and blonde

- Crushed rocks in light-coffee, grays, blue-greens, gray-greens and green serpentine
- Crushed volcanic stone in dark red and black from the southern Cascade Mountains and California
- Crushed rocks in reds, purples, yellows, greens and jet black from Southern California
- California smooth river stones in grays and browns, some with brick color within rock

Soft Loose Materials:
- Redwood bark mulch from ½ to ¾ inches
- Redwood sawdust mulch

Appendix C: Associations, Manufacturers and Suppliers

Arc Garden Products,
ARC Conbloc,
Westington Quarry,
Chipping Campden,
Glos., GL55 6EG, UK
Tel: 0386-840226
An excellent range of bricks, concrete brick paving systems, Yorkdale pavers, reconstituted stone paving slabs, aggregate, stone chippings, all in many colors.

Ashfield Flat Stone Company
Hawley Road
Ashfield, MA 01330
(413) 628-4773
Contact Jerry and Johanna Pratt.

Bergen Bluestone
404 State Highway
Paramus, NJ
(201) 261-1903
A broad selection of stones for walkways.

Bowmanite Corporation
81 Encina Avenue
Palo Alto, CA 94301
This company casts concrete in place that is then colored, imprinted and textured to simulate far more expensive paving materials such as cobblestone, brick, flagstone or tiles.

Bradstone,
S.O.T.U.C.O.,
76800 St. Etienne du Rouvray, France
Tel: 35.66.04.44
A wide range of paving materials in various colors, materials and shapes.

Brick Institute of America
11490 Commerce Park Drive
Reston, VA 22091
(703) 620-0010
Write for technical information and publications. One on exterior paving, which costs $1.00, is especially useful. They also answer mailed questions regarding paving with brick. They will provide information regarding the dealers nearest you who offer a wide range of bricks.

Cal-Ga-Crete Industries, Inc.
803 Miraflores
San Pedro, CA 91734
This company makes high-density tiles and pavers for outdoor use in a wide variety of patterns and colors.

Connecticut Stone Supplies
311 Post Road
Orange, CT 06477
(203) 795-9767
Suppliers of many types of paving materials.

Halquist Stone
23564 West Lisbon Road
Sussex, WI 53089
(800) 255-8811
Fax (414) 246-7148
A family-owned and operated supplier of stones, countrywide, since 1929. They quarry Wisconsin limestone from Lannon, near Milwaukee, but also ship paving stone from across America to local distributors nationwide. Contact the Wisconsin office for your nearest supplier.

Hilltop Slate Company
Middle Granville, NY 12849
Quarries and manufactures paving stones in a number of colors.

Goshen Stone Company
(Mr. George Judd)
Goshen, MA 01032
(413) 268-7590

Lehigh Portland Cement Company
718 Hamilton Mall
Allentown, PA 18105
(215) 776-2600
Masonry cements in white and colors.

National Concrete Masonry
Association
2302 Horse Pen Road
P.O. Box 781
Herndon, VA 22070-9480
(703) 435-4900
Fax (703) 435-9480
Contact this association for sources of concrete pavers that might not be readily available locally. They will send you the name of the nearest dealer with a range of different colors and shapes of concrete pavers.

National Lawn Institute
Box 108
Pleasant Hill, TN 38578
(615) 277-3722
(Mr. and Mrs. Elliot Roberts)
Information, in part from the USDA Turfgrass Evaluation Program, for home owners, on mowing, watering, lawn renovation and seed cultivars suitable for different areas of the country.

Rolling Rock Stone Company
R.D. #4
Boyertown, PA 19512
(215) 987-6226
Supplier of crushed gravels and flagstones of varying colors and textures for stone carpets or stepping-stones.

Stabilizer
4832 East Indian School
Phoenix, AZ 85018
(800) 336-2468
Phone for the nearest distributor of this patented, organic soil stabilizer. This is an organic glue that will enable you to bind fine naturally occuring gravels and sandy soils to the point at which they become hard paths. See page 209 for more details.

Terra Designs, Inc.
211 Jockey Hollow Road
Bernardsville, NJ 07924
Produces handmade and hand-painted paving tiles in early American and pre-Columbian designs. Custom work.

Gary Warner (Goshen Stone)
P.O. Box 332
Goshen,. MA 01032-0332
(413) 584-3654

Appendix D: Annotated List of Public Gardens Worldwide

AMERICA

Northeast

- The Asticou Azalea Garden, Northeast Harbor, Maine. Narrow gravel paths set in lawn, with good transitions to other materials such as lawn, cut stone, stepping-stones and stone steps.

- The Japanese Garden at The Museum of Fine Arts, Boston, Massachusetts. Fine embedded concrete path to garden entrance; cut stone paths into the garden; inaccessible stepping-stone path through the garden.

- The John P. Humes Japanese Stroll Garden in Locust Valley, New York. Call (516) 676-4486 for opening times. A fine example of the role of paths in a Japanese garden as created by a Japanese landscape designer for Ambassador Humes and his wife in the early 1960s.

- Dumbarton Oaks, Washington, D.C. Beatrix Farrand garden; a variety of superb examples of paths and paving materials.

- Longwood Gardens, Kennett Square, Pennsylvania. An extensive path system, and one spectacular, small path through the Silver Garden, designed by Isabelle Greene, a California landscape architect.

- The Russell Page path around the Pepsico Headquarters, Purchase, NY. A gravel path through the expansive lawns and arboretum that provides a setting for a collection of large sculptures by internationally known modern sculptors.

Southeast

- The Four Arts Garden in Palm Beach, Florida. Brick, cut stone, stepping-stone and natural, old coquina stone paths through many fine established gardens.

- In Palm Beach, near The Breakers Hotel, the gardens behind the church Bethesda-by-the-Sea. Cut-stone paths through fine memorial gardens.

- Vizcaya Gardens, in Coral Gables, Florida. Willem Wirtz, noted landscape garden designer and garden lighter notes, "Save the airfare to Italy and go see Vizcaya."

- Charleston, South Carolina, and Colonial Williamsburg for superior use of brick.

Southwest

- The Desert Botanical Garden, Phoenix, Arizona. Landscape architect Steve Martino is developing gravel paths through part of this superior Southwestern public garden.

West Coast:

- The Bloedel Reserve, Bainbridge Island, off Seattle, Washington. Recently opened property of the Bloedel family who have, over the last 30 years, created a tranquil series of Japanese and natural gardens throughout which a variety of paths offers intimate views into moss-covered woods, Japanese-inspired gardens or out into Puget Sound.

- Strybing Arboretum and Botanical Gardens in San Francisco. Gravel paths through the native plant collection.

- University of California Botanical Garden in Berkeley, California. Gravel paths through the native plants garden, designed by Steve Lutsko.

- The Portland (Oregon) Japanese Garden, which shows many elements of Japanese path making.

- Lakewold, a Thomas Church garden recently opened in Tacoma, Washington. Brick and lawn paths.

CHINA

- Suzhou is the Kyoto of China; that is, the place where the most public gardens are gathered in one place. David Engel, an expert on Chinese gardens, suggests the following gardens in Suzhou, all of which provide excellent models of Chinese garden paths. These were private gardens of wealthy families, but are now open to the public:

Liu Yuan
Zhou Zheng Yuan
Xi Yuan
Yi Yuan
Cang Lang Ting
Wang Shi Yuan
Shi Zi Lin
Cang Lang Ting
Shi Zi Lin

ENGLAND

- Sissinghurst, Vita Sackville-West and Harold Nicolson's garden in Kent. A wide variety of paths: lawn, cut stone, brick and fieldstone combined, roofing tiles on edge through one of the preeminent gardens of the world.

- Barnsley House near Cirencester in Gloucestershire. Rosemary Verey's garden: On either side of the laburnum walk (with its path of pebbles embedded in concrete) are a lawn path and a brick path; brick and concrete pavers outline a matrix of paths through the potagerie inspired by medieval garden design.

- Hidcote Manor Garden near Chipping Campden in Gloucestershire. Lawrence Johnston's garden, one of the gardens described in Chapter 1 of this book. Paths of lawn, cut stone, stepping-stones, gravel, brick and fieldstone that lead you through 10 acres of gardens and garden rooms.

- Stourhead in Wiltshire. A garden path that follows the story of Aeneas.

FRANCE

- Parc Floral des Moutiers, Bois des Moutiers, 76119 Varengeville-Sur-Mer in Normandy. Private gardens around the only Edwin Lutyens house in France. Gardens around the house and through the woodland are now open to the public. Excellent use of cut stone, brick and crushed flint paths. Call 35.85.10.02 for opening times.

- Princess Greta Sturdza's garden Le Vasterival, 76119 Sainte-Marguerite-Sur-Mer in Normandy. Lawn paths give shape to countless planting beds; this superior garden of several acres convinced the Royal Horticultural Society to award Princess Sturdza the 1989 RHS Veitch Memorial Gold Medal for her "outstanding contribution to the art and science of horticulture." Phone 35.85.12.05 to make arrangements for a tour guided by Princess Sturdza.

- Manoir d'Eyrignac, 24590 Salignac, near Sarlat in the Dordogne Valley. A seventeenth-century formal garden recently, and impeccably, restored. Fine use of gravel paths, lawn and cut stone give strong formal lines to the garden. Call 53.28.83.42 in Salignac or 47.66.51.21 in Paris to make arrangements.

ITALY

- Villa Lante, in Umbria, outside Rome. A Renaissance garden with many paths specific to the Italian Renaissance garden style.

- Farnese, near Villa Lante: gravel paths, lawn, water courses down steps.

- La Pietra, outside Florence.

- Collazzi Villa, outside Florence.

JAPAN

The following gardens have a variety of paths through them that show how the Japanese use cut stone, gravel, large and small fieldstones and many other elements of path materials and design. Kyoto is the center of the great gardens of Japan.

Tokyo

- Meiji Shrine: was an Imperial garden that is now open to the public
- Rikugien: an old villa, now a public park.

Kyoto

- Daitoku-ji: a large Buddhist temple complex north of Kyoto; some of the sub-temples are open all year.
- Fushimi Inari: a Shinto shrine in the southeast part of the city.
- Hakusasonso: once a private garden now open to the public; a walled garden in the city.
- Katsura Rikyu Imperial Villa - based on a tea garden, one of the best.
- Shugakuin Rikyu - An Imperial Villa in Kyoto.
- Murin-an: once a private garden now open to the public, built in early 1900s.
- Zuiho-In: a sub-temple.

SPAIN

- The Alhambra in Granada. A garden begun in 1238; paths and paving materials in a garden that incorporates all the elements of Moorish design (also see the paths through the gardens of the nearby Generalife).

Appendix E: Bibliography

Alexander, Christopher, et. al. *A Pattern Language.* New York: Oxford University Press, 1977.

Armitage, Allen M. *Herbaceous Perennial Plants: A Treatise on Their Identification, Culture and Garden Attributes.* Athens, Georgia: Varsity Press, 1989.

Balston, Michael. *The Well-Furnished Garden.* New York: Simon and Schuster, 1986.

Berrall, Julia. *The Garden – An Illustrated History.* New York: Viking, 1966.

Beston, Henry. *Herbs and the Earth.* Boston: David Godine, 1990 (reissue of 1935 text).

Brookes, John. *The Garden Book.* New York: Crown, 1984.

Brookes, John. *The Small Garden.* London: Reader's Digest, 1978.

Bye, A.E. *Art Into Landscape: Landscape Into Art.* Mesa, AZ: PDA Publishers, 1988.

Cheng, Ji. *The Craft of Gardens.* New Haven: Yale University Press, 1988.

Church, Thomas. *Your Private World: A Study of Intimate Gardens.* San Francisco: Chronicle Books, 1969.

Davidson, A.K. *The Art of Zen Gardens.* Los Angeles: Jeremy Tarcher, Inc., 1983.

Douglas, William Lake, et. al. *Garden Design, History, Principles, Elements, Practice.* New York: Simon and Schuster, 1984.

Druse, Ken. *The Natural Garden.* New York: Clarkson N. Potter, Inc., 1989.

Eaton, Leonard K. *Landscape Artist in America: The Life and Work of Jens Jensen.* Chicago: University of Chicago Press, 1964.

Eberline, Harold D. and Cortlandt, Hubbard. *The Practical Book of Garden Structure and Design.* New York: Lippincott, 1937.

Eckbo, Garrett. *Home Landscape.* New York: McGraw Hill, 1956.

Fell, Derek. *Garden Accents*. New York: Henry Holt and Co., 1987.

Forestier, J.C.N. *Gardens: A Notebook of Plans and Sketches*. (translated by H.M. Fox) New York: Scribner's, 1928.

Frieze, Charlotte M. *Social Gardens: Outdoor Spaces for Living and Entertaining*. New York: Stewart, Tabori and Chang, 1988.

Garland, Madge. *The Small Garden in the City*. New York: George Braziller, 1973.

Hand, Harland. "The Concrete Garden," in *Pacific Horticulture,* January, 1976.

Heriteau, Jacqueline, et. al. *The National Arboretum Book of Outstanding Garden Plants*. New York: Simon and Schuster, 1990.

Hibi, Sadao. *Japanese Detail: Architecture*. San Francisco: Chronicle Books, 1989.

Hyams, Edward. *A History of Gardens and Gardening*. New York: Praeger, 1971.

Itoh, Teiji. *Space and Illusion in the Japanese Garden*. New York: Weatherhill/Tankosha, 1985.

Jekyll, Gertrude. *Garden Ornaments*. New York: Scribner's, 1918.

Jerome, John. *Stone Work: Reflections on Serious Play and Other Aspects of Country Life*. New York: Viking, 1989.

Keswick, Maggie. *The Chinese Garden*. New York: Rizzoli, 1978.

King, Peter, et. al. *Gardening with Style: A Private View of the World's Most Innovative Gardens*. London: Bloomsbury, 1988.

Lawrence, Michael. *Backyard Brickwork: How to Build Walls, Paths, Patios and Barbecues*. Pownal, VT: Storey Publishing, 1989.

McHoy, Peter. *Outdoor Floors: The Design and Maintenance of Lawns, Patios and Ground Covers*. New York: Harper and Row, 1989.

Midgley, Kenneth. *Garden Design*. London: Pelham Books, 1984.

Moore, Charles W., et. al. *The Poetics of Gardens*. Cambridge, MA: MIT Press, 1988.

Nuese, Josephine. *The Country Garden*. New York: Scribner's, 1970.

Page, Russell. *The Education of a Gardener*. New York: Vintage Books, 1983.

Paterson, Allen. *Plants for Shade and Woodland*. Markham, Ontario: Fitzhenry and Whiteside, Ltd., 1987.

Perenyi, Eleanor. *Green Thoughts*. New York: Random House, 1981.

Pollan, Michael. *Second Nature: A Gardener's Education*. New York: Atlantic Monthly Press, 1991.

Prieto-Moreno, Francisco. *Los Jardines de Granada*. Madrid: Demyi, 1952.

Roper, Lanning. *Successful Town Gardening*. London: Country Life, Ltd., 1957.

Rutherford, Don, et al, editors. *The Sunset Garden and Patio Building Book*. Menlo Park: Lane Publishing Co., 1983.

Schenk, George. *The Complete Shade Gardener*. Boston: Houghton Mifflin, 1984.

Seike, Kiyoshi, et. al. *A Japanese Touch for Your Garden*. New York: Kodansha International, 1989.

Slawson, David A. *Secret Teachings in the Art of Japanese Gardens*. New York: Kodansha International, 1987.

Steele, Fletcher. *Design in the Little Garden*. Boston: Atlantic Monthly Press, 1924.

Strong, Roy. *Creating Small Gardens*. New York: Villard Books, 1987.

Strong, Roy. *A Small Garden Designer's Handbook*. Boston: Little, Brown and Company, 1987.

Tanner, Ogden. *Gardening America: Regional and Historical Influences in the Contemporary Garden*. New York: Viking, 1990.

Taylor, Patrick. *The Garden Path*. New York: Simon and Schuster, 1991.

Van Valkenburgh, Michael, et. al. *Built Landscapes: Gardens in the Northeast*. Exhibition Catalogue, Brattleboro Museum and Art Center, Brattleboro, VT, 1984.

Verey, Rosemary, ed. *The American Man's Garden*. Boston: Bulfinch Press, 1990.

Wilkinson, Elizabeth and Henderson, Marjorie, eds. *The House of Boughs: A Sourcebook of Garden Designs, Structures, and Suppliers*. New York: Viking, 1985.

Wilkinson, Gerald. *Woodland Walks in Britain*. New York: Holt Rinehart and Winston, 1985.

Williamson, Joseph F. et. al. *The Sunset Western Garden Book*. Menlo Park: Lane Publishing Co., 1988.

Wilson, Helen Van Pelt. *Helen Van Pelt Wilson's Own Garden and Landscape Book*. New York: Weathervane Books, 1973.

Photography Credits

Richard W. Brown: Figure 3.2, 3.3, 3.7, 4.10, 4.11, 5.6, 5.7, 6.8, 6.11, 7.4, 9.1, 9.2, 9.5, 10.4, 10.6

Patrick Chassé: Figure I.1, 2.13

Gordon Hayward: Figure 1.12, 1.14, 1.16, Part I Opener, 2.1, 2.4, 2.5, 2.8, 3.6, 4.5, 4.9, 5.5, 5.9, 6.1, 6.6, 7.1, 8.5, 9.8

Saxon Holt: Figure 2.2, 2.11, 3.4, 3.5, 3.9, 4.6, 4.8, 5.1, 6.2, 6.3, 6.4, 7.6, 7.9, 8.3, 8.6, 8.7, 8.8, 9.3, 9.4, 9.6, 9.7, 9.11, Part III Opener

Sandra Ivany: Figure 1.1, 1.2

Peter C. Jones: Figure 7.2, 7.5, 7.7

Jerry Pavia: Figure 3.1, 9.9

Joanne Pavia: 4.13

Jonathan Plant: Figure 1.3, 1.4

Jane Reed: Figure 1.10, 1.11, 1.13, 1.15

David Schilling: Part I Opener, Figure 1.5, 1.6, 1.7, 1.8, 1.9, 4.4, 6.10

Michael Selig: Figure 2.3, 2.6, 5.3, 8.1, 10.1, 10.3

Erica Shank: Figure 3.11

Alan Ward: Figure 2.7, 4.2, 4.3

Martin Webster: Figure 5.8, 8.4, author photo

Cynthia Woodyard: Figure 2.9, 2.10, 2.12, 3.8, 3.10, 4.1, 4.7, 4.12, 5.2, 5.4, 6.5, 6.7, 6.9, 7.3, 7.8, 8.2, 9.10, 10.2, 10.5

INDEX

About the Author

GORDON HAYWARD had an early introduction to gardening as a child, helping in his family's orchard in Connecticut. He has been a professional garden designer and writer since 1979. Hayward has created and restored many gardens throughout the Northeast. He also spent a year restoring an estate garden in England, and has led three garden tours to Great Britain. He is a regular contributor to *Horticulture* and has also written for *Harrowsmith Country Life*, *Fine Gardening*, *The American Horticulturalist*, and *Country Journal*. He is the author of *Designing Your Own Landscape*.

His own garden surrounds a 200-year-old farmhouse in Westminster West near Putney, Vermont, where he lives with his wife Mary and son Nate.